ADDITIONAL PRAISE FOR *DISARMED*

"A detailed personal account of a young soldier's journey through life, with gripping, gritty details of soldiering and firsthand combat experience—including being wounded in action and the hideous aftermath and struggle of recovery—all of it packed with witty writing that makes it entertaining to read. Ultimately, Izzy Ezagui has shown the world that despite being a one-armed man, or a person with any other disability, for that matter, you can still be a deadly soldier for your country."

—Keith R. Nolan, deaf former US Army ROTC cadet

"This story of an American Jew who lost an arm fighting for Israel is a Jewish story, an American story, and a human story about young people in battle. A fascinating account."

—Benjamin Ginsberg, author of *The Worth of War*

DISARMED

DISARMED

UNCONVENTIONAL LESSONS from the world's only ONE-ARMED SPECIAL FORCES sharpshooter

IZZY EZAGUI

 Prometheus Books

59 John Glenn Drive
Amherst, New York 14228

Published 2018 by Prometheus Books

Cover design by Nicole Sommer-Lecht
Cover design © Prometheus Books

Inquiries should be addressed to
Prometheus Books
59 John Glenn Drive
Amherst, New York 14228
VOICE: 716–691–0133 • FAX: 716–691–0137
WWW.PROMETHEUSBOOKS.COM

22 21 20 19 18   5 4 3 2 1

Library of Congress Cataloging-in-Publication Data Pending

Printed in the United States of America

CONTENTS

Chapter 1

A HALF-HEARTED WAVE

A s a kid, I consumed comics like crack. Saw every superhero movie on opening night. And, like every kid, I aspired to heroism but found my cape always came up short. I mean, how can we mere mortals ever reach the same heights as, say, a Kryptonian with the power of flight? An alien who'd rocket past the stratosphere if he accidently stretched his arms too high while yawning?

But I, like all of us, have at least one thing in common with the heroes we revere in our culture. There's always a villain intent on mucking up the works—you know, just to keep life interesting, just to keep my show's ratings from plummeting. Superman's got his Lex Luthor, his Doomsday. Spider-Man's got Doc Ock, and Green Goblin. Batman has the Joker—that master of chaos—among his Rolodex of rogues.

By the time I turned twenty-one, my supervillain—let's call him Phantom Fuckface (Phantom, for short)—had come into his own. Like all villains, pain had nursed him; trauma had trained and warped him into something ugly. Now he stalked me, obsessed over me, invented novel ways to inflict all manner of discomforts. It seemed his only purpose in life was to destroy me. And how could I stop him? He appeared far more formidable and more enduring. He was such a fuckface.

He'd first revealed himself to me in the desert, in the form of a premonition. It was the night before my injury. He was already stalking his quarry from afar. As soon as he pounced, it seemed like he'd hound me forever, a twisted twin born of that blast. Unless I could somehow satisfy his hunger, his thirst. So first I had to figure out exactly what he wanted from me. And what do all supervillains want? They want what you've got. To possess your power, your resilience, your spirit.

But I didn't feel particularly powerful or brimming with spirit. Sure, I'd experienced stuff, put myself in harm's way at nineteen— and not just for the adrenaline rush. I really believed in something, so much so that I was willing to risk my life for it. Of course, when people say that, they're not really thinking anything bad could ever happen to *them*. That's the sort of tragedy that occurs to *other* people, and you send a card.

So, sure, I'd survived something at nineteen that most people don't get to experience in a lifetime. I didn't exactly ask for it, but what are you going to do? I was that guy who lost his arm in a mortar attack. I have no idea who I would have been if that had never happened.

Why was Phantom torturing me?

There were times, whole days, whole weeks, sometimes, when Phantom allowed me to focus on nothing other than his own pressing needs, his own desperate appetite. He was nothing if not a glutton. Of course—without my suffering, the ghost of my past would shrivel and die. That's how phantom pain works. The second you stop feeling it, it's gone. Kind of like an orgasm.

So Phantom constantly vied for attention with a persistence I couldn't help but admire. Over time, I began to feel that if I were to slay him somehow, maybe I'd be lonely. After all, without a thriving criminal syndicate, the need for the superhero vanishes, and he might as well become a used Toyota salesman.

DIPPING A TOE

August 2009. The gleaming glass-office complexes give way to stately palms on Ayalon 20—Herzliya's main highway—and we can start to smell the shore, all salt and seaweed. Kobi and I in my silver Toyota RAV4, speeding with the windows open, Phantom in the back seat, kicking back in the breeze to some Black Eyed Peas. "Boom Boom Pow!"

How long has it been since I've gone to the beach? A year? But I've seen plenty of sand, lots of dirt in the meantime. The kind on the Gaza border that sucks at your boots.

Anyway, that was the border where this Fuckface was born. Maybe, I relent, my friend Kobi had it right. Maybe his prescription of a relaxing "day at the beach" will work just as well as the morphine I've recently kicked. I'm tired of drugs, tired of doctors, hospitals, therapy. I'm tired of the omnipresent specter that remained after I gave up a chunk of myself in a tent by that fence—I'm exhausted by Phantom's constant throb—"Boom Boom Pow!"

I hate that Kobi knows me better than myself. It's always easy to see what the other guy needs to do to get happy, rich, beloved by the ladies—it's much harder to see that stuff on your own.

How long has it been since I haven't felt sorry for myself, saw the sun without cringing? The sun that just then creeps out from under high summer clouds. Can I allow myself to enjoy this day at the beach the way I used to, growing up in a suburb of Miami? Or will Phantom darken my sun forever?

Don't forget, with the light comes the rockets.

Yeah, thanks, Phantom. I haven't forgotten.

Our tires chew over gravel as we park. Only after opening the car door do I notice my naked feet. I forgot to wear my flip-flops. First, I traded my favorites for a pair of clunky red boots when I arrived in Israel two years ago after deciding to join the Israel Defense Forces (IDF) to take a stand against those who threatened peace, stability, and democracy. I really was that idealistic. At the time, though, I didn't know it was unrealistic to expect I could make a difference. To expect I could never be the guy who gets blown up, the extra in the action flick who tumbles backward exaggeratedly in slow motion, dumb expression on his face. Yeah, that moron was me.

Now even those boots are gone. I don't have anything here I used to consider essential. Not even my dominant arm.

Sand blown up from the beach has swallowed a swath of pavement in the parking lot, and my heels chafe against the roughness. How long ago did my blisters from those boots abate? Now the unguarded sun has baked the beaten path and threatens to resurrect them. Sometimes walking in this country feels like a trek through the underworld—not the cool kind, filled with lycans and vampires. I've long since stopped searching for shade. *Thank Hamas*, I think, *for making my feet and the rest of me tougher*. My pain threshold has—ironically—skyrocketed since my injury seven months ago. Of course, Phantom's no slouch in the agony department: He was forged in torment.

We trudge through deep dunes of sand on a path that soon hugs the waterline. My balance is getting better. A few months ago, at the beginning of my recovery, I'd have been anxious traversing this uneven ground.

Amplified by a megaphone, a lifeguard's voice crackles and drones from a whitewashed tower, reaching the far-flung corners of his domain. "Warning. The tide today is extremely dangerous." He delivers this news in the nonchalant way an LA waiter might drone back your tapas order. "Do not swim too far out. You will not make it back to shore."

His precautions bring a forgotten fear back to my attention. I turn to Kobi, walking behind me, and raise my eyebrow. "Dude, it's just the undertow," he says. "Sometimes it's strong. But don't freak out. We won't go far."

Just like Phantom: Find a way to ignore the lifeguard and he'll go away. Right?

As if to disagree, he repeats his blithe caution.

Don't swim out too far? As if I have the stones to do that. Even without the succubus of an undertow, I'd be freaked out. Just something about the water now. The *Jaws*-like scene from the first time I tried to swim in the rehab pool comes flooding back. The grimy H_2O, laced with the odor of heavy BO, biting like a great white. Cooped up in bed for weeks, watching a troop of one-legged soldiers wheel themselves up and down the halls of Sheba Hospital in Tel HaShomer, I was so eager to relive the joys of swimming that I cannonballed into the center of the pool. Big mistake. The rehab nurse eyed me knowingly, fingering an unlit cigarette.

I swam in circles for an eternity, trying to find a ledge or handhold. I was a de-winged fly spiraling in a bowl of broth. Would this be my life from now on? Damn. Phantom executed a perfect reverse-inward two-and-a-half with a twist in pike position off the ten-meter platform.

Repressing a shudder, I remind myself I've practiced swimming a lot since then. I've gotten stronger, more resilient. I've learned to compensate for my missing arm, learned to travel in a more-or-less straight line.

But there's no pool deck to save me out there. No hero to jump in and pull me to shore. Well, there is that lifeguard, but he sounds inattentive up in his grand ol' tower. A tower that's looking far away already. He's probably watching porn on his iPhone.

Standing at the water's edge, curling my toes snugly in the sand, I can't see or sense any obvious danger. It's all so calm.

That's how they get you—

This time it's not Phantom, but my father's voice in my head. He ought to know. Always, *always*, just when he thought he had things under control—*WHAM!* Right in the shorts.

The waves barely brush over my ankles. That's the thing about an undertow—just because you can't see the damn thing doesn't mean it won't bite you in the butt—or bite off your arm. Mine begins to tingle.

Kobi and I take the plunge. Neither of us ventures very far, though. We swim out just enough for the cooling waters to reach Kobi's chest—and right above my navel. The average Israeli is half a foot shorter than I am, and not just because I'm taller than six feet. I bend my knees and allow a calm to rush over my body, my head, to envelop me. The sun, still beating on my back, the contrast of hot and cold, reminds me of a past life. Of leaping into the pool at the Bay Club for maximum splash, my sister whining to my mother about the tsunami that followed. My mom liked to watch us from beneath the tint of her stylish aqua sunglasses, one eye open as she soaked in the sun. With my head underwater, I couldn't hear the lifeguard whistle, the other kids howling, or the Backstreet Boys over the PA. The whole world was mine alone, and it whispered, *All is well.*

Now I drop my head below the water again. Same ocean as Miami, thousands of miles away, many years. A different life. How long has it been since I felt such serenity?

I stand again, shaking my head. In front of me, Kobi splashes around. "Awesome," he bellows—"no jellyfish!"

No stingers. They usually littered the coast, bobbing in all tides in the shallows, sniffing out a juicy leg for brunch. "Nice," I say, but then I remember the lifeguard's blasé alert, and I suspect they've all been sucked out to sea. As I concentrate, I realize I can feel the current pulling ripples of sand over feet I have to will to stay planted. "I hate to say it, you curly-haired douche," I laugh. "But you're right. I needed this."

"Of course I'm right." He grins back. "You should've listened to Doc Kobi the first eight hundred times I told you the beach is the best Israeli medicine."

It's true. The ocean's pulse eases my frayed nerves, unknots muscles I didn't know I had. If the traumatic injury doesn't kill you, the rehab will. That's probably why I skipped most of it.

As I float here, time freezes for a while. Waves lap the shore behind us, marking many minutes. I feel almost . . . normal. Almost whole.

How long has someone been screaming?

SIDESTROKE

My eyes shoot open. A glance at Kobi finds his gaze directed past me, back to the shore.

"*Tatzil otah!*" a girl cries out from the beach. "Save her!" She's frantically pointing toward me and Kobi. *Who? Us?* We lift our three hands, palms up, in confusion. She's running back and forth on shore now. "Please save my friend!"

"Oh, *behind* us!" Kobi shouts. Out to sea.

We turn toward the horizon. I stand taller to better survey the surface, which suddenly seems rougher, less inviting. Where is this person? *Time's wasting.* "There!" Kobi points. "Oh, God." We spotted her at the same time.

Yes, *there.* Way out. She's flailing, fighting the ocean's grip. She's losing her strength. Has to be. I know that feeling well, and it translates perfectly across the distance.

What happens next is not a choice. It rarely is. You'd think that what happens after you hear a cry for help reveals who and what you already are. It's not like that.

The whole idea behind the military training I just underwent is to short-circuit higher-level thinking. Not that the army doesn't want you to use your brain—it does—just not so much of it that you freeze. In the military, you have to make split-second decisions that aren't really decisions at all, but more like instant adaptive reactions. It has to be this way, because lives are often on the line. You hear about such things all the time. As I write this, some American Marines on vacation in France jumped into action to subdue a heavily armed terrorist on a train. They saved dozens of lives.

There were those "Let's Roll" guys on United Flight 93. All those soldiers and first responders who poured into lower Manhattan on 9/11 simply because they couldn't stand to be anywhere else but in the action, "the suck." It's a bit of a paradox, I guess. They train *out of you* too much thinking, and train *into you* just enough thinking so you don't have to calculate too much when that would stop you from acting. Without such training, cops and firefighters, paramedics and surgeons, and especially soldiers, would cease to be able to perform under the stressful circumstances that define those jobs.

So I find myself not exactly flinging all caution to the shore, not abandoning all I've carried with me to the beach—just not considering any of it. Not considering any of the self-doubt occasioned by my new "mutation," as I call my injury, perhaps in homage to the *X-Men*. In this moment, I'm not thinking of myself as less than, as weaker than, as imperfect, or "disabled." If I actually stop to think, I probably would think only, "Ahhh! *Ahhhhh!*"

I've *never* been a badass. The kind of guy I imagine the likes of Chris Kyle (*American Sniper*), Marcus Luttrell (*Lone Survivor*), and Pat Tillman (*Where Men Win Glory*) were. Even when I still had both my arms. Those humans, for a time, achieved superhuman status. I'm just a nerd from Miami. And now I'm a one-armed nerd. Sure, I'm a combat veteran—but I'm the kind of guy who'd still rather read a good book about extraordinary heroism than suffer the drawbacks of being an actual hero. Bad knees, astronomical insurance premiums, hot girlfriends who stand on the balcony in their lacy undies, waiting for you to swing by on webs for a kiss. Screw that noise.

I'm just talking about calling on a combination of training, instinct, and adrenaline, to respond to a call out of necessity. The key is the response. I learned that lesson one morning seven months ago, January 8, 2009. The day I looked down to see my arm dangling by a thread of my sleeve, and learned the number one attribute necessary to survive is just to keep moving, keep going forward. Even if you have to crawl to the call, then you just crawl. Don't stay frozen. I might have forgotten that lesson for a time. Phantom didn't help my recall any.

But now a drowning girl is calling. So out from my shallow abyss I surge, and, kicking off the ocean floor, I hurl myself toward deeper water, the dark I've been dreading for more than half a year. I swim out toward the call. It might not be elegant. But focused on that call, I find no imbalance. No asymmetry. No swimming in circles. No pain, either. When you're motivated by your mission, Phantoms fade. You've wrestled away their powers.

Still, I struggle to keep my trajectory true. Within a few more strokes, I feel myself—this body—propelled like those jellyfish out to sea, some combination of the girl's desperation and the ocean current tugging me out farther. The undercurrent is potent, a subsea windstorm that carries me like a bundle of twigs through a gushing sewer. Me. Kobi. The girl. I hear Kobi's hands slapping the surface behind me. I know he's there. Just like Amir was, like Jonny, and Lieutenant Fuks, and Oren before him. More on that posse later.

Swept along, but still so far from her. Her head dips under, her mouth gasps for the surface in a last-ditch effort to score oxygen.

Too late. Another failure. Another loss. Can I handle that? How much can one nerd take in a year? I know that if I arrive at the spot to find the girl gone, I'll be sure to read the headline: "American IDF Volunteer Who Lost Arm in Mortar Attack Dies at Beach." Funny way to go, after all I've been through. Real funny. I can see my mother dying of laughter.

Sure enough, with only three meters or so between us, the girl sinks from view. "Where'd she go?" Kobi shouts. We're both out of breath. And far from shore.

"I don't know. Kobi, check that spot! I'm looking over here."

"We've gotta go under!"

He's right. Diving below, I find no girl—no girl's body—and come up twice before spotting the hair. Long brown hair undulating like waterweeds. The head attached to that hair has decided, *Nope. No more. I'm done.* But help is just a breath away. So often the case, I've found.

I consider Captain Rosner. How we set off to retrieve his body that day in Gaza, to bring him back home. Except it was different for him. He knew. Like all of us, he knew going in. Early that day, under the rising sun, Rosner understood those fading breaths would be his last. He knew—he'd seen men die—the medics couldn't seal his gaping neck. He knew he'd not survive the hour. And yet, despite the torture of drowning—on land—he fought on. He continued rasping out orders so his men might live through the onslaught of enemy RPGs. Yeah, *that's* courageous. Different from dying alone in the ocean for a stupid decision.

Or failing to rescue someone dying alone in the ocean. No, Rosner really was Superman, soaring outside the atmosphere of Earth. The living embodiment of the superheroes I worshipped as a boy.

Yeah, but somebody's gotta be the ninety-eight-pound weakling. Somebody's gotta get sand kicked in their face.

UP, UP, AND OY VEY

The girl.

Her hair, fast flying toward the bottom, reveals her path of descent like a tracer bullet's red glow scarring the air behind.

Thrashing blindly, I follow the trail of hair to her neck and shoulders, and find her arm. I tug. *Come on. I've got you. Come on.* But the undertow wants her, too. It pulls even harder. A tug of war now against the girl's weight, her will to sink and end the struggle. Her own briny Phantom. I yank harder. I won't let him have her. I have to pull her up, which will require both holding her and somehow swimming. I'll have to use my legs, those that have marched hundreds of miles under a punishing rucksack. Those legs that helped me jump over a seven-foot wall to prove myself worthy of combat status, that propelled me up that rope. Those that helped me stumble and crawl away from the explosion.

So I kick. Never harder. I kick while pulling. Then her face, strewn with hair, all that brown hair, breaches the surface, and mine does, too, coughing up seawater. She gasps, slurping air. Eyes wide.

She's been sapped of all the energy she needs to stay afloat. Complete dead weight. "It's a pack," I tell myself. "It's just the pack you carry in training, the pack you take in the field every time. You can handle that weight."

Lightweight.

Holding us up there, resisting the current, not getting sucked farther out to sea—that is hard. The currents and eddies and waves feel like a mob of liquid zombies, rigid and cold with rigor mortis, snatching at us, hauling us down, trying to consume us. An irresistible meal we might make for the wading dead. If I had a dime for every zombie comic, movie, and graphic novel I've ever read, I could buy this beach (and fire that lazy lifeguard, fire him right out of a carnival cannon). There are lots of ways to evade a zombie. The best way? Run.

The legs, remember. It's all about the legs now. I kick with everything I've got.

The cavernous ocean seems to convulse with a laugh, flexing its gills. It wants this girl. But so do I. She's mine.

Not so fast.

DISARMED

Mine and Kobi's. He's finally with us. He's holding her, too, kicking, too, and trying hard to stay afloat. Three arms are far better than one. That must be an expression, right?

Kobi and I catch each other's wild eyes. "Oh, man," he says, gasping. "Oh man, oh man." He takes some of her weight just when I've given up hope. "So much for a relaxing day at the beach."

"Screw you, Kobi," I say, choking on my own words.

The tide continues to rip us away from shore. Now, instead of one victim, three struggle to stay afloat. We're too far out now to hear the girl's friend, too far from shore to see over the waves. The waves. So small on the beach as I stood and wondered, and now they're surging. They crash on our heads. Is this really it? After everything I've been through? Where the hell is that lifeguard?

Yep. We're on our own. If I survive this and can manage to close my fingers after this brutal swim, I vow to punch that lifeguard in the throat. It'll be worth breaking my final fist.

HEAD ABOVE WATER

No. You don't just die. My mother is not coming here to claim her waterlogged son. In a desperate last effort to survive, I plummet my legs downward. I keep thrusting them down, keep at it, going deep underwater to find some answer, to find something. I'm not sure what I'm looking for.

But I find it. There. I find sand. The current is dragging us parallel to the shore now. As my head goes under the surface, my outstretched toes dig into the ocean floor. I still cling to the girl's arm above me, a vise-grip, and extend her up—I shove her—as far up as I can. Her mouth must be sitting just above the surface again. And I can feel her straining upward, reaching, her and Kobi. They're both heaving, vacuuming air. She wants to live. She *can* live, for now.

"So, OK," I think, finally able to ponder, to plot a potential escape. "We're anchored in place here, and two of us, at least, are breathing up there. Good start, a fine start." I consider that line from the first *Superman* movie: "You've got me? Who's got you!?"

Old plan: Keep moving. New plan: Hold your breath.

I've always had a talent for this feat, ever since the long weekends, hundreds of them, back home in that pool a world away. At age eleven, I even won a volleyball, betting against my neighbor, a fat, bald Israeli guy, that I could hold my breath underwater for two full minutes. A volleyball? What the hell kind of a weird bet is that? I lived in the pool back then. The ocean, too. In Miami, I learned to test those waters, to test my breath for as long as I could. It was a game.

This is not. This is no fun at all. Exertion and fear have robbed me of air. "Oxygen stores are depleted," I think, calling on the scraps at the bottom of my will.

Without oxygen, the human body can only survive—

That's enough out of you, PF!

To be fair, though, he has as much at stake as I do. *So what do we do?* I wait a beat. Ten seconds. Fifteen. Twenty. Decision time, Izzy. Let's go. I reckon this all with a growing despair. They say drowning, when you're finally drowning, is supposed to be peaceful. So why is my whole chest heaving? I know if I let go, then my friends won't fare any better. If I let go, they're dead.

Yep.

For the second time in less than a minute, something emerges from the depths for our aid. Some mighty force, summoned by God only knows. The tide begins to recede, fast, almost as if we've passed some test. Almost like those parting Red Sea waters I learned about in Hebrew school. Somehow the waters lower, though barely enough for my chin to breach the surface, my Adam's apple tickled by the slosh. And with that neck outstretched, I swig in a delicious mouthful of air, just as the next breaker smashes over our heads. *Deus ex machina* at its salty finest.

"All right. You've got what you need, Izzy." The new burst of O$_2$ has given me the strength, the resolve. I have just enough in reserve to kick off the sand and—with my friends above—to creep to shore. It's three feet forward, one foot back. All the way under, then up just enough. And the closer we get to the shoreline, the friends, the crawl, become less and less of a toil. "I've twice survived now," I think. And this time, I'm coming out in the same number of pieces, with a *heavier* load to bear, not less.

Finally, Kobi and I stagger out of the waves. We hold up the girl between us. A sopping ragdoll, she collapses on the sand into the embrace of her friend. I hit the deck, heaving, all acid and salt. The indignity of being down on all threes. This body. This one. If it could do all that—maybe it can do anything.

And it's alone. For the first time in nearly eight months. It seems that Phantom has left me, maybe swept out to sea, jetsam on his way into a clutch of hungry jellyfish.

And just where on God's sandy Earth has the lifeguard been this whole time? Taking a piss? Chatting up a girl? By now, I'm really hoping he'll die of mono. I'm willing to contract it myself so I can pass it to him.

HAND IN MARRIAGE

With both knees and one palm planted in sand, I force my eyes open, look over at the girl. Straining to assess the damage my rough grip must've caused her, I discover an interesting thing. I feel my cheeks flushing—she's no girl. Not a young girl, but a woman. A young woman cradled in another young woman's arms. A stunning woman. And I don't breathe again. Can't.

It's oxygen deprivation. It's another near-death experience. No, whatever the reason, my mind races knots and knots ahead. This is exactly what happens in romantic movies—in chick flicks, in Lifetime TV movies. And, let's face it, this is how Superman lands Lois Lane, how Spidey webs Mary Jane.

This is how they *always* get the girl. My heart is battering its cage, only half because of the rescue. The other half is . . . no—not *love* per se. That would be cheesy. But with surety, deep knowledge of what's to come. "Amputee Saves Woman from Death. Woman to Be One-Armed Savior's Bride." Yes. A much better headline now. My mother will prefer to come to this beach for a fall wedding.

"OK, Izzy?" Kobi wheezes from somewhere above and behind me. How is it he's still standing?

I nod robotically, but keep my focus on the woman, on breathing and dreaming, on what will be. I think of our vows—"I'll hold you up, always"—but before I can memorize any more, she stands up on her own. She comes toward me on fawn-like legs. Her eyes, a seafoam green. They meet mine.

This is it.

She wipes her delicate lips with the back of her hand. She says, "Thank you." Then, with an arm on her friend's shoulder, she turns away. Limps out of my life. I remain on my hand and knees. I shake for a while as the adrenaline subsides. I'm out to sea again.

With Kobi's help, I get up for the silent trip back to Shoham. The sky seemed to darken, though I see on the dashboard clock that it's only four. Halfway back, I close my eyelids to see if I can feel it. Him. I open my eyes on the yellow line. We're flying home. All three of us. Phantom never really left.

The moment I recognize him here with us, rockin' out to "I Gotta Feeling," I feel the pulsing pain in the place where my arm used to live. What's a guy have to do to feel good about himself? To feel like he knows what the hell he's doing with his life? To feel like he's going places? What's a guy have to do to slay his Phantom?

"Kobi," I murmur. "What would you say if I told you I was going back to combat?"

He stares ahead for a minute, absorbing that insanity. Then he smiles. "I'd say that's looking at the glass half full, Izzy."

"The ocean, Kobi. The ocean half full."

chapter 2

(ONE-) ARMED AND DANGEROUS

"The arm."

"What?"

"My arm." Can't they understand me?

One of the eighteen-year-old girls on the ambulance crew—a pretty girl with curls—looks over at one of the other eighteen-year-old girls, who smiles. There are three (the other's a redhead with bright-blue eyes). Or maybe my vision's screwy and I'm seeing triple. "What's he saying?"

"Not sure. He seems pretty doped up."

"Don't . . . forget . . . my arm." I say through clenched teeth. I consider unstrapping from the gurney to go hunt it down myself.

"He wants *this*," says Amir, my squad mate, appearing outside the back of the rig. He shares an uncanny resemblance with Sgt. Zim from the movie *Starship Troopers*: big nose, square jaw, deep-sunken eyes. Amir produces my left arm, cradling it like a puppy. The last time I saw it, it was soaring up into the sky. Seeing the thing again now reminds me just how deep in the doghouse I really am. At least I can't see more than one Amir.

"Oh . . ." says Blue, the third girl on the crew.

Amir passes the appendage as though handing over a roasted marshmallow on a stick. She tucks it beside me, under the strap of stretcher. So this is what it takes to hold hands with a girl? My damn arm is doing better unattached to my personality.

They communicate my vitals. No sign of fuss about the whole

I'm-handling-your-severed-limb thing. These teenaged medics are the real deal. Behind Blue is one of those tear-off, page-a-day calendars, compliments of Big Pharma. I mark the date: January 8, 2009. There's a tiny drop of something—blood?—on the bottom left corner of the page. It fades in and out of focus. Please don't vomit in front of the girls, Izzy. Not easy with this alien warmth pressing against my ribs.

Amir jumps in the back doors and looks me over, chewing his lips. "You're gonna pull through, Izzy. I'm telling you."

A promise from Amir is no small thing. He's a damn Spartan warrior. I close my eyes a moment, and my whole world spins. I open them on Amir. He narrows his eyes, and leans down to listen to whatever words of wisdom I'm about to utter. These could be my last, the much-anticipated meaning of life.

Wait for it.

"Listen. I have, like . . . two packs of Mike and Ikes in my rucksack."

"Izzy, I—*What?*"

"That's Grade-A American candy. If I don't make it, promise you'll go to town on them."

"OK, Willy Wonka," Blue cuts in, folding up her blood-pressure cuff. "We're ready to roll."

Smiles jumps out the back doors. She must be sitting up front with the driver. Curls straps into the jump seat to my side, obscuring the calendar. But Amir won't let go of my arm, the one still attached to my personality. He wants to say something. I can see it on his face.

Wait for it.

"I don't really care for Mike and Ikes. Any Starburst floating around your pack?"

Blue peels him away and shoves him out the back. He jumps down, turns around, and the ambulance starts to pull away. The back doors are still flung open.

The last thing I see is Amir staring straight at me through the doors bouncing open and shut. He's yelling something, but I can't hear him over the engine. He cups his hands around his mouth and shouts each word slowly, so I can understand: *"You're . . . not . . . a . . . pus-sy!"*

Those are the kindest words Amir has ever aimed in my direction.

I am not a pussy.

A CALL TO ARMS

"Pussy!" Amir spits. Three months earlier, and I'm strapped to a stretcher during a forced march.

He bears the brunt of my weight, scowling at me the whole way back to base. "You better thank your friends for carrying you. You goddamn better."

Amir isn't pissed *at* me. Lifting a nerdy American private like me is child's play for the natural-born warrior. Amir's angry *for* me—on my behalf. He knows only "pussies" volunteer to ride the stretcher in this exercise.

He's right. I'm the one who wanted this. I wanted to leave the suburbs of Miami, my Xbox and comics, my pool and my bookcase full of fantasy to join an army half a world away. But I didn't fly all the way to Israel to *play* soldier, for *real* soldiers to carry me.

HANDLING BUSINESS

Just a few months later, and I'm no longer playing victim. Now I'm doing the heavy lifting. This is "the shit" I heard so much about. And just in time for Hanukkah. I never expected it to be fun, exactly—but I didn't expect *this*, either; I didn't sign on for quite this level of suckage. *Did I just lose my damn arm?*

DEADLIFT

December 27, 2008–January 8, 2009. They keep repeating this is *not* a war. This is barely a call to arms. The brass, the politicians, the commanders—they practically shout it at us: NOT A WAR!

"What's that, sir? Your sister's not a whore? I can barely hear you with these rockets exploding above my helmet!"

This is what they call a minor military "operation," a series of surgical strikes aimed at Hamas in Gaza. Maybe an "operation." But without anesthesia. And not always perfectly surgical. The Israeli military has designated this campaign Operation Cast Lead. None of us boots-on-the-ground knows what the hell that means. The rest of the planet is calling it "The Gaza War." The Arabs are calling it "The Gaza Massacre." To us in the field, it doesn't really matter what you call it. Nobody but the vultures, already circling, will call these next twenty-two days a good time.

Especially the thirteenth day. Lucky thirteen. Just before dawn on January 8th, my platoon is on an all-night stakeout on the fence. We rookies have yet to tramp a foot outside of Israel. We're right on the line, though. We don't know it yet, but over the border in Gaza, the flying fragments of an RPG have just ended Captain Rosner, one of our battalion's veteran officers.

He's already dead. I'm on the "safe" side of the fence, thinking about my buddies, Mike and Ike, chilling in my pack, and Captain Rosner's already dead.

ARMED TO THE TEETH

While Rosner's unit is a few clicks away at the tip of the assault force, taking heavy fire from a platoon of well-entrenched enemies— "Dirties"—our skeleton crew of fifteen spends the night fighting fatigue, trying to stay warm, trading candy, only the bitter wind for company. Our detachment spends ten hours on high alert, sighting every mule, dog, and rat. All those innocent, four-legged dudes escape our fire.

We lie stock-still on an incline of frozen soil. What are we waiting for? For the ground to cave in around us? For Hamas to break the surface of their tunnels and crawl out like the undead from their graves?

Actually, yes.

That kind of nonsense has happened before. We have it on good authority (Israeli intelligence) that it's going to happen again, exactly here. We're right on top of a known Hamas "breach point." They could be under us right now, creeping with their AK-47s. There's other intelligence, too: Hamas leadership has ordered drivers to ram explosive-packed cars into the border fence. We're told they plan to send two-man crews to follow on dirt bikes into Israel. To inflict havoc upon the nearby Ein HaShlosha kibbutz—the communal settlement adjacent to our base—and slaughter as many civilians as possible with 39mm bullets before we can hunt them down.

How do they convince their people to die so willingly for their cause? To mow down women and children? "They dope them up with a cocktail of wicked drugs," says Kobi. Whereas we're shivering and exhausted, they will feel invincible.

So far, nothing has come of it. Nothing but blue lips, stiff joints, and the shivers. Belly-down in the dirt, we feel only the distant reverberations of the "operation" (This is NOT a goddamn WAR!) coming from just beyond the fence. We don't know yet what's happening to Rosner's unit.

Now our lieutenant, Fuks—his *real* name—has relayed the order from whoever that our platoon is to pull a 180. We're heading back to base. So we stand, stretch our muscles, and direct our frozen posteriors so they face the Gaza border. It's time to march even farther away from the conflict.

DISARMED

The formation begins fanning out as a pocket of icy air rattles the electronic fence between the two turbulent territories. Wearied and frozen as I am, I can't help but feeling as though I'm running away from the war. Aren't the enemies of freedom dug in the *other* way? Of course, in heading deeper into Israel, I'm just following orders. But marching *this* way, in battle formation, yet away from the frontline, toward my own ranks . . . It's as though we're going to war with ourselves. But isn't that where we fight all our real battles, all our significant wars? I don't know. Maybe I'm too exhausted to think straight. All I know is, before I came here, I didn't feel certain who I was or where I was going. The good thing about the army, I guess, is that they tell you exactly who you are, and exactly where to go. There's a comfort in that.

A gust rustles an ocean of crops on the Israeli side of the perimeter, deeper into which we advance. I can't decipher what grows here. At this stage of growth, the plants don't reveal the fruit of their labor. I feel like that, too. I don't know who I'll be. I spent so much of my young life as a couch potato, a fiction reader, and a passive witness to life. Is it possible I'll bloom into something more colorful, perhaps even deadlier? A cherry? Cherry is the name and symbol of Israel's elite undercover unit, Duvdevan, the spearhead of counterterrorism in the region. I'd give my right arm to be a Cherry.

Why do I keep looking back across the border? What's to see inside Gaza? Nothing but blacked-out windows, like sunken, gouged eye sockets.

The wind soon dies down enough for me to hear our boots slogging through the mud. I have a habit of looking down at my feet when I walk. Or watching the soles of the soldiers marching in front of me. Helps pass the time. Works as a hypnotic. I'm engaged in that as usual, limping on my bad ankle—remnants of a months-old injury, about which the less considered right now, the better—when the stench of tobacco hits me. Smoking is a big "hell no" in the field.

That kind of cherry—the one on a lit cigarette—produces a target for a sniper working at night.

Cigarettes aren't my poison. Not my temptation. What I crave as we forge ahead is a phone call home. Rules govern those, too. No talk of locations, actions, maneuvers. Blah-blah-blah, I know. I just want an update. How's Dad doing lately? Is prison taking its toll on him? Is my sister recording *Smallville* and *Entourage*? Mom, please help the war effort, send more Mike and Ikes.

Our formation has become unkempt. The wind keeps at our back, harassing us as we plod away from Gaza. Even when it's cold, we don't wear jackets. This is to avoid overheating when we're drawn into a firefight. Behind me, a gunner's untucked shirt flaps rapidly in protest. A couple of paces farther back, our medic, Chen, grapples with the cold by stringing together tirades of creative curse words: "*Kus emek . . .*"

The shirt-flapping, boot-thumping rhythm accompanied by Chen's swearing creates a hybrid rap: "*Kus-mahrt-ahbuk, Kus-mahrt-ahbuk . . .*" Not that I enjoy thinking of the anatomical anomalies of my comrades' mothers. I just find the rhythm of the language strangely pleasing. Out here, you take what you can get.

This pleasure is short-lived. A blast of biting air strikes me butt-on, warps my grin into a cringe. My asshole shrinks into oblivion. Every soldier looks as though he's giving birth to quadruplets.

I'm about to invent a few curses of my own when my gaze hits Amir, my counterpart at the head of our small formation's "backward wedge." As expected, Amir, our light machine gunner, evinces zero reaction to the freezing gale. Amir is what we in the military call a goddamn ninja. The guy's always in beast mode. It's not that he's insensitive or taking things casually. On the contrary, he's a model soldier, always focused, ever attentive.

On the march, Amir never stares down at his boots, rather, at the task ahead. And his eyes never betray the burden of his pack, even though he lugs the same load we all do—minus the Mike and Ikes. With his chin he motions from Lieutenant Fuks, who shadows us about ten meters behind, to the center of the wedge. He's reminding me what we're here for: Amir and I are tasked with securing Fuks so he can focus on command. He's a hulking guy, our lieutenant, 6´3″ and 230 lbs., with a big, balding head, and huge paws. That last part is consistent with his first name, Kfir, which means "lion cub" in Hebrew.

So Amir's silent message to me is *Keep it together, dude*. Or, more likely: *Stop being a pussy*.

As if to punctuate that reminder, my ankle throbs. I still haven't dealt with my leg. I know I'll have to eventually. Here's all I know right now: It would never occur to Amir to do such a thing to himself.

My string of verbal diarrhea stumbles to a halt. Amir and I might be counterparts in the field—the two soldiers responsible for returning fire at first enemy contact—but we are drastically different in almost every other way. It's not just that we're "cut from a different cloth." It's that someone sewed our fabrics in completely different factories. Amir is a bona fide badass—silent but deadly. Not to say he's anything like a fart. That association suits me far better. Like post-Chipotle gas released in a light Miami breeze, I tend to whine unpleasantly, and my surroundings waft me wherever they please. Right now they prefer to nudge me toward my distant cot. But Amir is more like an armored personnel carrier. Once his traction's dug into the dirt, nothing can knock him off that track, and he'll carry the whole unit with him.

ICY FINGERS UP AND DOWN MY SPINE

Slivers of chill slip down my collar despite how tightly it straddles my neck. Something about the wind feels malevolent. In this moment in the dark, in the boot-sucking mud, the pall grips my whole spine with a message more than meteorological. *This is no good, Izzy. Bad stuff goes down, my friend.* It doesn't feel like momentary paranoia. Bad things really do happen to people who wander this part of the world when the sun has yet to rise. If it's not some coked-up guerrilla chugging through a hole in the fence on a Vespa, strapped with C-4, it's something far more terrifying: the danger you *don't* see coming. I guess you could call this overwhelming dread I feel a premonition. A phantom menace.

In a few hours, during our brief time back at base, before our deployment into Gaza proper, I'll find myself scrambling toward the decrepit trailer bathroom to let slip the dogs of war (to drop a pre-battle deuce). I'll take my cell phone with me. Talking about the (*not-*) war will violate a couple regulations. Phone calls about troop movements in particular are strictly forbidden for obvious reasons, but I will feel compelled to call my friend Jonny. Not my family, after all, but my Canadian buddy, a fellow soldier I met while patrolling the bars of Jerusalem a few months before basic training. He was so laid-back that hanging out with him felt like popping a Percocet. Except while he helped me train, which included intense sprints up and down Jerusalem's hilly streets. And whenever he watched one of the war films he and his roommates kept playing on a continuous loop. It's hard be laid-back when *Platoon*'s on. Or *Full Metal Jacket*. I've already asked Jonny, in general, to console my parents should anything go wrong. Now I'm suffering a distinct foreboding about this mission, which will continue until I make that call. And I don't even believe in that kind of bunk. It's the sort of shtick they do in bad movies. Protagonist has a feeling "somethin' ain't right."

Meantime, the wind presses its way from the border into the Land of Milk and Contention. As do we. Despite my tender ankle, we're flooring it. Whenever Fuks is in command, nothing happens slowly, nothing lazily. Fuks is a bald and blue-eyed golem. In Hebrew, "Fuks" means "a stroke of good luck." But as a commander, if you get on his bad side, he really Fuks up your day.

DISARMED

The only soldiers who remain unfrozen are those crafty enough and with enough foresight to have packed their thick, olive-green sleeping bags for the stakeout. Bastards. Why didn't I think of that? Better yet, why can't I be more like Fuks? Like Amir? Anyone besides myself.

Just a pinkish inkling of sun on the horizon directly in front of us to the east. A mile of marching to go before we can sleep. I allow my M4 and its magnified scope to dangle freely by the strap around my neck. It, too, provides a gentle rhythm to accompany the painful walk.

The more my ankle hurts, the more it feels like a walk of shame. *Amir's* soooo *right about you, friend. You're a big sloppy puss.*

The sun shoots shards of orange out in front of us, and I await a hint of warmth. And wait. Nothing. Though by the constant clenching and releasing of my hands I experience a quantum of thawing. Amir motions with a nod to the upcoming sun. I nod back, huff. *Daylight—good.* I welcome the sun after so long and dark a night.

But with daylight comes rockets. Lots of rockets. Suddenly, I long for that now-fading darkness. This pretty much sums up the experience of being a non-Amir-esque soldier: Proceeding reluctantly from one lousy state to another, then suddenly pining for the prior state, which you cursed for the previous ten hours. Rockets versus frostbite, though? That's a no-brainer. But no ambassador from Hamas has crossed the border to conduct a survey inquiring of my opinion on such matters. Fingers crossed.

FINGER ON THE BUTTON

Wernher von Braun, the pioneer rocket researcher (who, not incidentally, began his career in Nazi Germany) was said to have quipped, "Once the rockets are up, who cares where they come down? That's not my department." If you move in Israeli circles, you'll understand when I say: Fuck that guy. For two months, beginning in November 2008, enterprising terrorists have been firing a constant barrage of deadly projectiles—sometimes precise instruments, and sometimes messy homemade contraptions—into populated areas of Israel. As a result, civilians in the south have spent a good part of every day trembling in their bomb shelters, trying to calm their children, attempting to explain to them the genesis of so much hate. But how do you explain?

The vast majority of Americans, myself included, have no idea. Imagine that instead of Jerusalem and Tel Aviv, it's Jersey City and Toledo staring down the daily business end of rockets, missiles, and mortars. Topeka. Akron. Albany. And we're not talking about an occasional scattershot offensive, either. Israel sustained 2,378 rocket attacks in the *first half* of 2008. Israel had finally had enough. So they called in the cavalry. Well, sort of. They called *us*.

Now we, too, have had enough.

Don't get me wrong. There's nothing particularly militaristic about me. If you met me randomly at a Starbucks, you'd assume I was a fairly mellow dude. I am. Almost everyone I know or have known in the IDF is, too. I very rarely see any of that John Wayne, gung-ho, let's-lock-and-load type of behavior that's stereotypical of soldiers elsewhere, at least in the movies. Not even Amir or Fuks behave that way. But for all my self-criticism, I do possess a preponderance of valuable training in the arena of euthanizing terrorists. *Phew! Phew!*

Why did I choose the Israeli military over the US armed forces? Because they're on the same frontline of the war against terror, but Israel's closer. Because Israel's people are in grave danger—today and every day—of losing their way of life, losing their very lives. We might have "lone wolves" in America, those few fanatics who seek to destroy us in novel permutations. But Israel must contend with huge swaths of its neighbors—as close as Hoboken is to New York—who want to obliterate it, men, women, and children alike. I made the decision to come here because I couldn't handle sitting on the side-lines. That's it. My entire rationale.

DISARMED

So here I am. Hour eleven. Barely on my feet. Base still ten minutes east. Yes, I'm afraid. And yes, part of me would love to be sitting in a café, eating biscotti and chatting up girls (as if that would ever happen), instead of traversing frozen fields, lugging a rifle and a heavy pack. But I have it in my head to send some villains to Valhalla.

You know how the expression goes: Man plans, and God . . . fucks his shit up with rockets. Surely that must be the expression.

WAITING FOR THE OTHER SHOE TO DROP

Late December 2008. Hurry up and wait. Our company of rookies arrives at the border by way of a green city bus at the start of Operation Cast Lead. "You guys aren't going in with the rest of the ground forces," Fuks informs us, and sixty helmeted foreheads dip to the ground in disappointment. He sounds bummed out, too.

Yes, no one wants to stick his neck out while rockets and bullets rain down—but neither does anyone want to sit around feeling useless and hamstrung while other guys get dirty. It's as devastating a blow as I've ever experienced thus far. "I signed up to make a difference, Amir. To fight."

"Chill out, bro," says Amir as he heaves his rucksack onto a cot a half hour later. "Don't go looking for trouble. If they hand you a dangerous job, do it, but don't *ask* for the beating."

"I know." He's right. There are no small parts, only small actors. Truck drivers need to motor field rations and water to the front; intelligence officers need to slouch behind their desks in Tel Aviv, feeding data to the commanders on the ground; politicians need to head off biased pressure from the United Nations with various lines of bull; and some unlucky schmuck has to dump chemicals into the latrines once a day, or else real war descends on camp. Or else "We're in the shit" takes on a literal meaning.

Amir puts his headband on. "Besides, it's not like we're just going to sit on our thumbs here. We're—"

"RED ALERT!" interrupts a robotic female voice (think of the climax of *Alien*). "RED ALERT!" The chilling siren that follows will become the background music of our lives for the next several weeks. And the explosions. Let's not forget the explosions.

TOES-UP

We've been at the forward base for two weeks. We're not inside Gaza, where the bulk of the fighting has been taking place, but we've faced our fair share of close scrapes already. We've spent every day since our arrival near the border, either patrolling it endlessly—or running like hell for the bomb shelter in our camp.

No one has scraped closer than a Jeep driver named Bogary, a perpetual *samal*—sergeant, with a penchant for peanut butter and double-dipping. Bogary is short, dark, and aloof. One day, he left the crowded bunker to check on a fellow driver during a Red Alert. You obviously *don't* leave the shelter, for any reason, during a Red Alert. "That's why they call it a goddamn *Red Alert*." This is Fuks scolding all of us, after the incident. Bogary was afraid his friend, some other even-lumpier sergeant, might have been asleep at the wheel—literally—and wanted to drag his lazy bum inside.

The moment Bogary slipped out between the concrete blocks that stood at the entrance, we took a hit. The thirty-odd soldiers crammed inside the shelter all tried to pile outside as a single, olive-green organism. We were going to collect Bogary, I guess. However many pieces of him we'd find. But Fuks single-handedly held back the tide until the explosion and aftershocks abated. He ordered us to stay inside the safe zone—now filled with the noxious fumes of burning gunpowder—and put himself at risk to go after Bogary. We'd have expected nothing less.

We heard later that Fuks found Bogary crouching outside the shelter door. His hands were covering his ears like a "hear-no-evil" monkey. He was shouting. The mortar had hit just seven feet away—we counted the steps. Bogary was lucky all he sacrificed was partial hearing, and only for a day or so. As if to punctuate the absurdity of the whole event, the other driver—the guy Bogary was trying to "rescue"—wasn't out there at all. He'd never stirred from his cot in an unprotected tent nearby. He'd slept through the entire ordeal. We found, in his tent, a military-grade helmet that shrapnel had split in two.

It must sound crazy to the vast majority of people, but there are those who prefer sleep above safety, hands down. Well, sleep is a kind of safety, isn't it? The bliss of ignorance. Even when the sirens are blasting and the sky's collapsing, these soldiers will not budge from bed. I envy them.

Living with the uninterrupted threat of dying in super-unpleasant ways—disemboweled by sizzling shrapnel, decapitated, suffocating under tons of sand in a collapsed tunnel—kind of makes my thumping ankle, annoying as that is, seem pretty paltry. Some soldiers, maybe the more pensive ones, or the ones more prone to philosophy, begin to grapple with the bigger questions. What little philosophy I've read refers to these as the "existential questions." Questions I suppose men and women have asked ever since either God, evolutionary adaptation, or some drunk wizard put us on Earth: Why is there pain? How fragile is our terrestrial tenure? Why do terrible things (e.g., beheading in front of a televised audience of millions) happen to good people? How do we know who the good people are? If all we do is trust our instincts, then half of us are apt to disagree with the other half, and then the killing begins. In the final analysis, what does it all mean? I have heard people wonder that, and sometimes people ask me what I think.

I don't think. Not about that kind of stuff. I think, "I should've brought a sleeping bag on that stakeout, man." Or, "I kinda wish green Mike and Ikes didn't exist, bro." The safest—and sanest—zone to occupy in a muddle is somewhere exactly between Nietzsche's atheist-free foxhole, and the guy who snores through Armageddon.

STAY ON YOUR TOES

I keep flexing my frozen fingers as we trudge toward base. I can smell myself even through the cold and my various layers. A shower would be nice. Important bits are starting to decay, or at least chafe.

We're so close to home. Funny how the word *home* is so elastic. I want nothing more right now, nothing more than a scratchy blanket and a creaky cot. My kingdom for a pillow.

Amir is indicating again with his chin behind us. When did it get so light? The soldiers back there, grimly slogging, with calcified expressions and filthy fatigues, look like I imagine battle-hardened veterans do. The kind who've taken part in a hundred maneuvers, who've been "in the shit," as the Americans used to say in Vietnam. But we're neither hardened nor veterans of real combat. Not even Fuks. This hike marks the return from our first real operation. I feel, if not *proud*, then maybe just a bit impressed by us. Got to be careful with that pride stuff.

But we've earned some badge of honor, haven't we? No, that feeling—even that tiny bit of self-congratulatory hubris—that's how life gets you, my father would warn. And my career in the military is about to fall pretty damn far. I might not have been personally responsible for any heroics on that border some hours before, but I could boast that at least I still had all my limbs intact. You tend to take this sort of thing for granted until the bloody evidence in front of you makes it clear the taking-things-for-granted phase of your life has passed.

There's base. The guard swings the gates open wordlessly. Once again, something just doesn't feel right. I can't put any of my ten fingers on it, but I know whatever I sensed stalking me earlier has breached the gates before us. It's CALLING. From INSIDE the camp. Some . . . phantom. It's with us even now.

I look furtively from side to side. I can see some of my fellow soldiers slowing down rather than speeding up. We're all but asleep on our feet. I think seriously about just stopping, curling up right here on the ground, just a dozen meters from the tent flap. Just for a few minutes of shut-eye. It would be worth it. But you don't fall down or suck your thumb when Fuks is coming up the rear, looking like he's got orders. So we all file through the front gate toward the parade ground, which is a fancy way of describing what is basically a bunch of whitewashed pebbles in the only space not crammed with tents and gear.

That's when we see it. Outside the Command Center. The old-timers, the tried-and-true warriors. All of them are weeping. "They got Rosner," Fuks says matter-of-factly. "The captain's dead."

LOOK MA, NO HANDS!

I've been lying to my mother. And this isn't a "who-had-their-little-grubby-hand-in-the-cookie-jar" level lie. This is the Big Kahuna. From the moment I kissed her good-bye, and every time we've spoken over the phone since I left home, I perpetuated this falsehood. At first, I didn't even want to reveal that I was near the front. I told her repeatedly that the army relegated my unit to washing dishes up north, by the border of Lebanon. "Yeah, it's real quiet up here. No worries. No, nowhere near Gaza. God, no. Gaza? Please, Mom."

I didn't say it glibly. I just didn't want her to worry. I justified my abject lying as my way of protecting her. Like a mother needs protection. She gives birth to you, she watches you grow. She lets you go. And you think *you* need to protect *her*. In *East of Eden*, Steinbeck writes that "perhaps it takes courage to raise children." *Perhaps*? I sold my mother far short, as so many young men do, often until they're parents themselves—or something happens and they get to see their mother's true colors.

I know she already has suspicions. A mother knows. Unavoidable circumstances have almost gotten me caught. Like that time a week ago when, as my mother and I were on the phone (she was insisting we go shopping for new jeans when I got home), a mortar fell close enough to shake the earth below my boots. "What—Izzy, what was that?"

"Nothing," I told her, trying to sound casual as I sprinted for the bomb shelter, my balls retracting up behind my pancreas. I could never tell her it was a mortar.

"Izzy."

"It's just artillery training somewhere near here. Happens all the time. Nothing to worry about, Ma. That's *our* side."

Don't worry.

But suddenly the worry comes knocking loud and clear. Captain Rosner's unit was ambushed in Gaza. Heavy machine-gun fire. Rocket-propelled grenades. Captain Rosner, deceased. Shrapnel from an RPG cut right through him, his radioman reported.

Captain Rosner, married only a few months earlier. Many of the officers and the enlisted men know his wife.

We *just* got back. Now we're going in. Gaza. Welcome to the Suck.

Fuks makes no bones about it. "Fucking mongrels . . ."

We who've just trekked all the way from the brink are going back—and over the line this time. We're going to do everything in our power to bring the captain home. We've all missed the last three meals, and yet I have to force myself to breathe slowly in order not to hurl. I'm regretting all that candy now. Good thing I skipped the green ones.

The whole thing instantly becomes extremely real. This is not a game of Warcraft or Halo. Rosner can't click "new game" and materialize with a dazzle of cool graphics and a jaunty keyboard refrain. Somebody we knew. And liked. And took for granted. Is now dead. Not going home. Someone whom other someones loved—just like all of us.

We're given just a few minutes. Not really enough time for sleep, and there's no room for illusions anymore.

Am I a good person? Am I somehow invincible, just because my intentions seem righteous? Because I'm a nice guy who helps old ladies cross the street?

Is this really *NOT* A WAR? Then why the hell are people dying on us? Should my mother be worried? Should I call her? Should I tell her the truth?

No—I have to call Jonny.

Thank God for Lieutenant Fuks. He addresses us all within minutes, finding us sullenly spread out in our tent. None of us will have any time to focus on those "existential quandaries" occasioned by war/"not war." Sleep-deprived, bedraggled, and now deeply shaken, our little detachment of greenhorns who have only peeped over that Rubicon are now going in deep. Fuks nods solemnly for a good thirty seconds, looking at each of us in turn. It's exactly what we need. And then he speaks.

GIVE THAT MAN A HAND

"We're it, guys. We're the only force available." His head reflects the dim fluorescent bulb swaying casually above. The light of truth. "It's gotta be us, and it should be us."

As far as I've ever been able to tell, Fuks is fearless. He's the kind of hulk you absolutely want next to you when the sky starts caving and shrapnel hails down. He isn't one to waste time crying. He doesn't even pause to let the news sink in. "Our mission is to reinforce the distressed unit—our guys are still out there—and to bring back Rosner's body, to bring him back home where he belongs. Prep your gear. We're out in twenty."

I fight a tide composed of rising bile. I see some of my friends (not Amir) doing the same. Sometimes you get what you wish for, I remember some famous author saying, so you must be careful what you wish for.

Once dismissed, I run for the latrine to unload my pre-battle nerves. And to call Jonny. Sitting there, I weigh the pros and cons of making the call. Despite the severe proscriptions against revealing movements, my need to talk overwhelms the requirement to keep my mouth shut. Jonny is a fellow foreign volunteer, though far more experienced than I am. The Canadian mentored me throughout my basic training, warned me what to expect, gave me endless tips and tidbits. I hesitate a moment, the phone cradled in both hands, thumbs hovering over the CALL button. I finally press it. Jonny answers right away. He's stationed at a border somewhere within the territories. "Dude, glad you called. But—where are you?"

"Yeah, sorry about the background noise. I'm surrounded by dudes taking dumps."

"Where?"

"Uh, the bathroom."

"Dude . . ."

"Some base near the big, bad border. Ein HaShlosha. But we're getting ready to go in. So, yeah. We're going in, Jonny. Look, if anything happens, please just—"

"What are you talking about?"

"I'm talking about Gaza. And I want you tell my family I—"

"Jeez. Izzy. You'll be back. You'll be fine . . ."

"Really? Because I'm guessing that's what one of our captains thought last night. *Anything* can happen, Jonny. Even though of course it's—"

"Right—*not a war*. Don't worry. I'll tell them."

Just then, I hear the voice of Fuks echoing deeply from a few stalls down. "Izzy," he says, "get off the damn phone."

Jonny hears. "Go. Call me when it's over."

Fuks and I flush simultaneously, and he stares me down as we exit the latrine. His cold blue eyes communicate he's none too pleased. But I don't appear to be in any trouble.

As I limp back to the tent, I feel steeled by Jonny's confidence. Between his optimistic voice resounding in one ear, and Fuks's steady and commanding one in the other, I'm almost looking forward to seeing a little action. *Almost*. And what a relief to know that Fuks is human. That he needs to drop the kids off at the pool once in a while, too.

Outside the Command Center—a ramshackle trailer crammed with aging communications gear—I spot two soldiers I've never seen before stacking white packets into the back of a Humvee: It takes me a second to figure out what they are. The eyes of one of the soldiers, a corporal, confirms it for me when they meet mine: Body bags. "They aren't meant for you, Izzy," I think. "Just keep on walking. Nobody else is dying here today."

In a deranged way, the only article of military gear more disconcerting than a body bag might be "bulletproof" armor. Obviously, you don't ever want to wind up zipped in a polyethylene bag. But once you're tucked in there, you're pretty much not worried about dodging bullets anymore. The bliss of the abyss. Whereas with the latter accessory, you're admitting to yourself and the enemy that you're a big, soft, 6´1˝ *target*. My heart hammers against the heavy ceramic armor as I don my vest, helmet, and pack. In a few minutes our small force is once again standing by the front gate. We're going to (*not-*) war at last. I have to take another dump.

Judging by the body language and the nervous chatter of the soldiers around me, our feelings about this upcoming mission run the gamut. Some, like Amir, seem entirely unconcerned, Fuks-like, no Fuks to give. And others appear to be pissing themselves, at least figuratively. My frame of mind, I find, rests somewhere semi-comfortably between.

Fuks strides up to the platoon with his usual unruffled swagger. "Too hot to go in," he tells us. "Take off your gear. Hit the racks. Await further instructions. You can bet I won't be shy. Oh, and no more goddamn phone calls." This, delivered directly at me.

I hear myself sigh as we slink back to our tents yet again. Tension pollutes the air like a stack of triggered smoke grenades. Nothing's worse than the wait.

Lior, "Rabbi," Second Platoon's unofficial spiritual leader, calls after those of us still in earshot. He follows us into the barracks, holding down his *yarmulke*. "Anyone want to put on *tefillin?*"

Surprisingly, everyone agrees, if only to keep busy. And maybe to hedge our bets.

"It couldn't hurt," he says, as if to convince the reluctant. *Tefillin* are the set of small black leather boxes containing scrolls of handwritten parchment inscribed with meaningful verses from the Torah. Observant Jews wear them—one on the forehead and one on the arm—with a leather strap entwined in a specific configuration, every weekday morning when they pray. Lior files through the ranks, helping each of us wrap the straps with the Holy Scripture tucked inside. First, the arm. "Arms before arms," I think to myself.

He speaks the words when some of us forget, and with the prayer concluded, I plop on my cot like a sack of Florida oranges. My God—I almost just went into Gaza with a rifle and a pounding heart, *without ever telling my own mother*. Without even considering the consequences of my "little white lie." I pull out my phone again, this time to look up the news. Sure enough, I see Roi Rosner's picture. The captain is smiling at seven million Israeli viewers, smiling from his nearby grave. Except he's not in his grave yet. He's still *there*, where the flies can pester him. We'll go get him. *We will* return him home. Will my mother recognize my unit's colors? See the insignia on his beret or shoulder? She's glued to the news back home, and pretty observant about that sort of thing: That's where I get it from. So . . . to tell or not to tell? I'll have to decide very soon, because I know in my bones they'll call us up, call us back, before we get time to sleep. Can I risk the wrath of Fuks? Dude Fuks you up.

I'm just so tired. As I switch my mind off, I notice the deep trenches the leather straps of the *tefillin* have dug into my arm—a familiar pattern of valleys and canyons, the straps being wound three times around the middle finger, then around the hand to form the shape of the Hebrew letter *shin* (ש).

I don't know it yet, but this will be the last morning I'll ever wrap the phylacteries—or anything—using my dominant arm. God and Hamas have other, rather pressing, plans for that appendage. How does that saying go again? Right: Man plans, and God . . . flings down flaming, metal deuces on him from the heavens. That must be an expression.

It's not because I fall asleep that I don't hear that mortar dropping directly on my tent. Qassam artillery, Katyusha rockets, BM-21 "Grad" missiles, and any number of homemade ballistic pipe bombs would all trigger the alarms. But the brass "forgot" to inform us that military-grade mortars wouldn't. Oops.

The sky falls.

The lady robot voice sleeps.

"The arm . . ."

"It's there," says Blue. "Right on the stretcher, right next to you."

Chapter 3

LIFE AND LIMB

There's a mole in our midst.

"Please. *Pleeeease* don't call her!" Standing over me, she crosses her arms on her ample bosom. "I'm seriously begging."

But there's no reasoning with Mrs. Gelb, my principal. There's no reasoning with any authority at any Orthodox middle school, anywhere. It's 1999. Outside, the South Florida sun is shining, and here I am, again, sitting in the stiff wooden chair of the principal's office, in the gloom cast by her filing cabinets full of demerits, records of misdeeds, and medieval torture devices, child-sized. "OK, how about I promise I'll never do it again. Never. Just please don't call Ma."

"No? Why not?" Such a serious stare.

Why not? Glassy-eyed, I gaze at my bright-red Air Jordans gliding beneath me like pendulums. Let me count the ways. Because I couldn't *help* myself, but I really *want* to help myself. Because I want the other kids, my teachers, even you, Mrs. Gelb, to like me. To smile when you see me. To tousle my hair like a normal kid you trust and respect. Because it feels like I'm on my Schwinn flying down a killer hill and my chain's snapped and my handlebars are wobbly. How do I stop my *self* when it's the bike I'm riding that's out of control?

Because I'm Fart Boy. At the Jewish Community Center's basketball camp last summer, back when I was still secular, all us kids were sitting together, bunched up, listening to Coach Sherman blather on about *de*-fense. I farted. I mean *audibly*. My butt released it with all the exhilaration of a pair of lungs attached to an adult male who just won the Lotto. I kept my eyes shut for a good ten seconds, sitting there cross-legged, with a hundred other boys and girls, hoping against all hope that it was just a bad dream, that no one had noticed my bum whooping for joy.

When I poked my head out of my shell, I saw the kids, and how they'd all escaped my orbit *en masse*. It was like Moses parting the Red Sea. I was alone in the center of a circle, untouchable, a three-foot perimeter between my closest counterpart and me. They called me Fart Boy. I mean *seconds* later. I had a feeling it would stick.

I had a couple of options. I could cry for mommy. Not cool. Defend myself? How could I? Everyone on the court that day would bring my fart home with them—it would continue to ring in their ears as they tossed in bed that night. On the spot, I decided on a third option: I *owned* it. "Yeah. I'm Fart Boy. I am 'The Boy of Many Farts.'" This miraculously defanged them. It "deflated" their taunts. Whatever they would throw my way, I owned it. No fun bullying the kid if he's practically stuffing himself in his own locker.

That day in camp, post fart, Coach Sherman arranged for water-sports in the big field outside. Slip 'N Slides covered everything, and I went tearing down the lawn in my bathing suit, announcing that, "*Yeeees*, I'm the kid who blew a crater through the ball court!"

Before long, kids were high-fiving me, cheering me on. "Go, Fart Boy, go!"

I learned a valuable lesson in self-defense that day, about the pre-emptive strike, even if that meant lauding my own leak.

But those were not Orthodox kids. I was starting to learn that my methods didn't work so well among Orthodox kids.

Of course, I can't tell Gelb any of this. She's actually smirking. She's looking as mean and pissed off as ever. She crosses her arms over her triangle boobs behind that ungodly, huge, wooden desk whose cheap laminate finish has all but peeled away. Like the souls of all past miscreants who've felt her wrath.

Maybe I should go for broke and spill the whole spiel. "The me inside me is not the me you see," or something along those lines. Is there any possible way to explain this? Would she—or anyone—believe me? She has picked up the receiver and tucked it ominously between her giraffe neck and sharp shoulder. She doesn't dial yet. There's still hope. Maybe I could turn out to be the hero of my own story, instead of always the bad guy, "my own worst enemy," as I have heard her and every one of my teachers say before, so many times I can see it coming. I try again, "All right, how about—?"

"*What*? Izzy—how about what? How about I let the inmates run the asylum? How about every eleven-year-old at my school just lives by his own rules? Let's act like zoo baboons! Let's not flush the toilets! Let's mouth off to everybody and their brother. Let's make a joke of everything—*ha ha*, I'm Jerry Seinfeld. Is *that* your proposal?"

How about it?

Beneath my Air Jordans, a sea of dull grey tiles seems to undulate like a pit of snakes. I try desperately not to sniffle, but the urge overcomes me. What is that *smell*? The nervous sweat of a hundred former victims, tearstained paneling, and fear? No. That's the smell of disappointment. It's not the office, but a noxious cloud that began condensing around me the moment they started trying to transform me into a proper little Jew.

"Look at me, Izzy."

We call it "the death stare." It comes with a slow-motion shaking of her helmet-haired head. It will wither the worst offender; even Grand Moff Tarkin would piss his starched pants in her presence, and Tarkin basically told Vader to go screw himself. I've seen kids almost pass out, throw up in their mouths, confess to crimes against humanity that happened well before they came out of the womb. Just being in that room. It's best not to look at the eyes, kids say. Look instead at the huge, angular mole Mrs. Gelb hosts at the corner of her thin upper lip. Whenever she speaks, it seems to dance a little hairy jig.

DISARMED

No escaping it. Trapped this way, a kid has no choice but to plead his case directly to the Mole: "I—I'm telling you. No more. I won't—God, please." Have I tried "please" already? How do I make it sound sincere? It *is* sincere. "How do I—?"

"Izzy, don't beg. It's unbecoming." She doesn't even need to search for the little card with my mother's number on it. She uses it so often, it's right at the top of the pile. Am I really that awful? So irredeemable? All this for some silly classroom *mishegoss*? Tapping my pencil on my desk?

Granted, Mrs. Kitch did ask me nineteen times to quit it. I was planning to before the twentieth. But under that kind of pressure and the extreme aridity of English class, the tapping just got worse. I can't stop the pencil. I can't stop the shaky leg. The bicycle's got its own mind. Defies my steering. The sphincter is independent of the brain. But if that Mole could enjoy an autonomous existence, then my yellow Faber-Castell No. 2, my tibia and femur, my bike, my anus, should all be in this hot seat.

And yet—here *I* am again.

What would my father say? "Be honest, Izzy." Oy, that's the worst. OK. So maybe it was more than the tapping. Maybe it was a little bit of that other thing. Maybe my feet came off the pedals a little and I didn't help matters.

Screwing up her lips, the Mole squints at the index card containing my mother's contact info—Digits of Doom. Soon, she'll probably know them by heart. To dial, she has to bend her spindly neck even farther to avoid losing the phone. A combined effort by both mole and shoulder hold up the clunky plastic receiver as she punches the numbers. Each faint beep and bloop brings my bike closer to the junkyard at that junction down below. Judgment Day. In a moment I can hear the punctuated cartoon squawk of feedback that is my anxious mother. No doubt she's standing at the kitchen counter, looking like the call really is about a loved one's horrible wreck. Mrs. Gelb looks up at me with an inscrutable expression as my mother says something, slowly and deliberately, on the other end. I've heard the other kids call the Mole a monster, likened to the devil of a religion not ours. I get that now.

This utterly sucks. Since I was nine or so, I've cultivated several successful tactics for weaseling my butt out of trouble, somehow righting the rampant bike at the last second. Clenching my cheeks. I'm actually a bit of an expert. To "be honest," I don't so much cower under threat of *punishment* as much as I despise disappointing my parents.

What was I thinking in Kitch's class? Why couldn't I think? Wasn't I just here in the Doom Room? All the sentences have blended. I've rarely made it through the week without a forced exile to face the Mole's summary judgment. And execution. It's as though all my teachers have simply abandoned the idea of disciplining me—they just dump me off in the Mole's lair and get on with their day.

I've seen on TV how they catch jets on aircraft carriers—with a bunch of hooks. Surely that kind of contraption could stop me?

It's not like I went looking for trouble today. But Trouble's like a big kid who breaks all the rules—who curses and guzzles schnapps and looks at dirty pictures even—and he always seems to lurk around each corner. He slinks around, waiting for me in the boys' room. He lingers in the study hall, ready to trip me with his ratty sneakers. What does he have against me? I've read about eccentric billionaires who hated school, who didn't make the cut, or who ditched altogether. Bill Gates dropped out of Harvard. Mark Zuckerberg, too. Steve Jobs abandoned his studies after only six months—he left skid marks. And the granddaddy of all dropouts? Abe Lincoln. Twelve years old. He did pretty well for himself, didn't he?

Yeah, all these guys were way too cool for school. They avoided Trouble by walking right out the door. School bored the bejesus out of them, and I get that. Did they follow rules? No, they followed their *impulses*. Ha. They were visionaries.

Yeah, but I'm just a silly kid who can't sit still.

Be honest, Izzy. You're kidding no one. Not the Mole. Not even yourself.

I want to do well—great—that's my shameful secret. I want to succeed. I want to feel good about solving problems, learning new words, writing essays that would wow my teachers; I want to get the pat on the back, the gold star.

I do not want to think of my mother biting her nails on the phone with the Mole. They'll never get me to brake my bike before it's too late. There's so little hope. What brake? I was *born* with a roving imagination. A wandering Jew of a mind. Not to mention the twin jackhammers that stand in for my knees. And there's that pencil tapping, too. No gold star for that. That's just annoying. But isn't all that in my damn DNA? At the same time they try to turn you into a good little robot, they shout from the rooftops, "Be Yourself!"

Honesty. OK, I can see how other kids, despite their complaints about education, even despite some obstacles bigger than too much nervous energy and lack of impulse control, kind of relish it. They actually like studying, listening to lectures. I envy them. Don't I? But I know that'll never be me.

The only place I ever seem to wind up is scraped up and confused in the principal's office. Where the Mole and I *kibitz*. "What's it going to be today, Izzy?" the secretary, Mrs. Fischer, asks drolly almost every day, before the first bell finishes ringing. I see more of these two ladies than I do my own mother.

"Rabbi kicked me out before class started," I'd mumble, collapsing into my assigned seat outside the Mole's lair.

"Too long in the bathroom."

"Eating Mike and Ikes during prayer. Slipped the green ones down Yossi's collar."

"'Fell out of my chair. Landed on Jacob's lunch bag. Pastrami everywhere."

"We're failing you," the Mole once said in a moment of empathy. At first I assumed she meant giving me an *F*. No. "*We're* failing you." She meant school, the whole educational system, the adult-run world. All of that was failing me. Wow. I stared at the tuft of hair next to her upper lip, and chewed my lower one. Finally, I found the courage to look up at her. "I guess we're sort of failing each other."

Now she hangs up, gently slides the phone away, puts the contact card back in the drawer, at the very top, for easy access. She takes a deep breath, and I see her rib cage expand. One kid claimed he once saw her smoking, and she kind of did smell a bit smoky. But that couldn't be. I'd zoned out halfway through her confab with my mother. And then I almost missed what she said. "Your mother's disappointed in you." There it was.

Of course she's disappointed. Who wouldn't be? How much better to be fuming, yelling, than silently disappointed? That's the worst. To embarrass Ma and Ta—the only fear that squelched the almost-insatiable fire under my bum. What worse thing could a kid do than bring shame upon his family?

The school is forty-five minutes from our house in Miami, the only institution that reached my mother's new standards of Orthodoxy. From now on, only the religious cream-of-the-crop for my sister, Jasmine, and me. So . . . forty-five minutes plus fifteen for my mother to get herself ready to meet the Mole on her home turf. That gives me an hour until the execution. Too much time to think. . . .

You know what this reminds me of? A couple of years back. You couldn't have been more than six or seven. Dad took Jasmine Rollerblading. Just left you, and took your sister. Is this ringing a bell? All he wanted was some quality father-daughter time. But when he came back, big smile on his face, what did you do? You punched him in the cojones. He doubled over. And when he came back up, what did you do? Did you apologize? No. You knuckled him in the nose. And then what did he do? Did he hit you back? Did he yell? No. He lay down on the couch, groaning, and Never. Said. A. Word.

DISARMED

That, *my friend, is the kind of son* you *are.*

If you want to punish a Jewish kid, you don't *have* to yell. All you have to do is leave him alone with his guilty thoughts for more than fifteen minutes. His mind will corrode. His body will crumble, limb by limb.

WAITING FOR THE OTHER SHOE TO DROP

Just wait.
  Wait.
  It's OK.
  You're OK.
  Why aren't I moving?
  This is not OK.
  Man, where am I, anyway?

I survey the space as the smoke starts to clear. My eyes are working, which is good. That means my brain's still in its cage. But I can't hear, except for some muffled shouting. *Is that me shouting? Damn. No. I'm OK.*

There's something else. A smell. It's bad. That smell is burning flesh, it has to be. And gunpowder. Light is shifting, and I can't tell if that's my eyes or the outside.

  What was I just doing? I was just on my cot, about to call—

Now shrieking, constant, a high-pitched whine. It's in my ears. My head. *Just wait. Watch. Some guys—why are they moving so slow? They don't see me. Why can't they . . . ?*

Flapping canvas. *Ah.* We're in the tent. The whole structure is swaying. Outside light. Some soldiers stumble toward it. Dust and debris trail them out. Like shadows.

Trailing them out . . . *You've got to get out. You've got to shift your ass now, Izzy.*

Does anybody see me here—I don't think I can move . . .

More light. Everything is tinted crimson, same shade as my old Air Jordans.

It's hard to lift my head, hard to recognize anything, to know what's going on. But it seems my left arm isn't where it ought to be. I stare a while, uncomprehending. People creep by me. I can see one soldier's mouth moving, but I don't hear a thing. My arm. It's . . . Well, there's my elbow. Exploded. Bits of white there, swimming in the red. Bone shards. I feel something soaking my uniform. *Well, that's it, Izzy.*

There's no way to survive this.

No—

I've got to focus. Nothing behind me but canvas. Right—all red. The cot—the one next to mine—Gone. Holy hell. The soldier who'd been on it—Alex—he's gone, too. Two-hundred-and-fifty pounds of him. Gone where, exactly?

Red's no good. The taste, no good—strong and soapy, bitter. *Is that . . . ?*

It's OK, Ma. No, it's maybe pretty bad. Ma? Where did you go?

Talk to her. Can you talk? Call for help. "Does anybody see me?"

SLIPPING THROUGH MY FINGERS

Can she see me? Are my cheeks blushed? My mother sits beside me in Mrs. Gelb's office. My head down and eyes up, I see her. Her eyes are crinkled, her lips etched with . . . What is it? It isn't anger. It isn't even disappointment anymore. This time it's—oh, man. It's *worry*. So much worse, Ma.

The Mole begins her diatribe. I can't focus, thinking about what my mother's thinking as she listens. "*Mrab mrab mrab* unacceptable behavior." She cocks her mole in my direction, not a trace of empathy on the rest of her face. I can't believe I'm here *again*. "*Mrab mrab*, the last time, *mrab*, before suspension."

Yeah, yeah. We know all this. Just get it over with so I can go home and wallow in my guilt, hopefully near the PlayStation.

"*Mrab mrab*, learn to cooperate. *Mrab*—bar of soap."

Same old—wait! What the—? Soap!?

My mother is dabbing her eyes with a tissue.

This is the moment of reckoning. It's one thing when they find you guilty. But then you have to stand and await the sentence—that's the crappy part. They could slap your wrist or send you to the chair. It wasn't just the pencil tapping, was it? The pencil tapping's old news. No, it was the nineteenth time Mrs. Kitch told me to stop: "Cease and desist, Izzy." I guess I might have . . . well, *mouthed off*, let's call it, just a little bit. By the look on my mother's face, the look of the Mole's mole, it was maybe a little *more* than a mere misdeed. I'm not getting out of this one so fast. I was expecting the misery of guilt and shame. I got that covered. But I didn't expect the soap. No one expects the soap.

Is she seriously suggesting we wash my mouth out with *Zest*? Really, Mrs. Gelb, 1904 called—they want their punishment back.

Here comes the soap. Here I am at the Mole's large oak table, gagging. Why does my mother have to watch this indignity, these suds? I'm the one who racked up on crimes. Gagging on the bitterness now. Gonna maybe die. Am I wearing clean undies?

"It's the *shame* you're choking on," the mole says with its little crooked mouth. "That's the whole idea." She says this as my mother helplessly watches, ropes of tears rappelling down her cheeks.

Ingenious penance.

A BLACK EYE

Post-frothing now, I'm in the front seat of the silver X5, and she's gripping the steering wheel of the BMW like the pilot of a nose-diving Cessna. We pass a playground. Kids—no *yarmulkes*, no strings attached—romping, stomping, shouting from the tops of their castles, not a care in the world. No guilt.

All these rules now. Boundaries of "appropriate behavior," laws of kosher action. It's not the old days anymore. Not like life at seven in that other world I came from. Ah, the life we left behind in a single minute.

Scene: Early on a Saturday, autumn 1995. Our modest two-bed-room apartment in Aventura, Florida. I'm crunching through some superb non-kosher cereal in front of the TV, courtesy of a commer-cial, reminiscing about a recent evening when I wiled away my time at Chuck E. Cheese's, drowning in arcade tokens. My parents call me and my five-year-old sister, Jasmine, to the black leather sofa. They have "exciting news," they say, but there's a certain nervous smell in the air around them, like vinegar. I'll take the bait, though. Is it Disney World? A puppy? They're buying stock in the Fun Zone and I can play for free, forever? "We're becoming practicing Jews!" My father is beaming from ear to ear. What the hell does that mean—*practicing*? Like football practice?

I ask, "Aren't we already good at being Jewish?" We've sat together for a meal each Friday night since as far back as I can remember, and these slow, deliberate dinners have been great. We spend time as a family, talking, joking, just being together. What could be more Jewish than that? We even attend synagogue once in a while—so what else do we have to do?

"This means we're becoming religious," my father says.

Oy Vey . . . I look over at Jasmine. She's got her toes wiggling in the carpet, no idea what's going on. But I know better. I know a few of those *"frum"* kids. A slew of rules they have to follow. A million potential pitfalls for my seven-year-old self. I'm dizzy with anxiety. It's like that time I spotted a cockroach underneath my desk at school and almost blacked out. I opted instead to climb atop my desk and scream like a little girl, but my *first* reaction was the dizziness.

"Does this mean synagogue every Saturday?"

That's just one of my questions: *"Yarmulke?"* "Black coat?" "Black hat?" God help us. But one paramount concern dwarfs all the others: "What about—? Will we—?"

"What is it?" my father asks.

"What about . . . *Scooby-Doo?*"

"Yeah," Jasmine chimes in, "*Scooby-Doo.*"

My parents look at each other, and my father is smiling. My mother is not. This matter is deadly serious. Jaz and I almost never agree on anything. But denying us prime cartoon time is on both our agendas. I've got her on my side. Cartoon Network is our *lifeblood* on Saturday mornings. We will absolutely die without cartoons. Even *prisoners* on death row get cartoons. I don't know if I can say this aloud, but I crave the vibrant colors that dance across the screen—I consider all those kooky characters my friends. I laugh at all the pratfalls like Bart and Lisa lose it watching *The Itchy & Scratchy Show. Tom and Jerry*, *The Flintstones, Looney Tunes* with its hapless Wile E. Coyote and his Acme bombs that always blow up in his face. And *Scooby-Doo*—Lord, what more religion does a kid need? If becoming religious means—

Uh-oh. You can forget Saturdays, Izzy. You'll be praying and eating gefilte fish from dawn to dusk. Yuck. What if—? Are they thinking of ditching the TV altogether? *Pinky and the Brain? Xena?* Not *Hercules!*

"Don't worry," my father assures us. "You'll still be able to watch some stuff."

My mother's frown might indicate otherwise. "Maybe you're a little too . . . *invested* in these silly programs," she says. Silly programs? We're talking about *Captain Planet* here. If God's holy day of rest and reflection doesn't invite Captain P's elements to combine, I'm outie. "This will be so good for us. As a family," my mother guarantees us with a smile born of such tremendous faith it nearly sways me. Nearly. The cockroach skitters off to some other desk and I can climb down and breathe again. She taps the knuckles of her slender fist against her heart. "It's going to be good for us—*in here.*"

"Good? This is gonna be great!" says my father, punctuating his claim by slapping his knees. "Right? Everyone? Great!"

HANDING IN MY CHIPS

January 8, 2009. OK, great. You're on your way at last. You're moving.

Well, I might be stumbling about like a zombie in his torn-up uniform, but at least I'm moving. Is there a difference between the walking dead and a dead man walking? I guess. The latter still has time—a few moments and a voice to say good-bye to mom.

Where'd I drop my phone? It was in my . . . *Don't look at that now—just look away. Look forward. Move toward the light.*

I push the tent flap aside. Light blinds me for a second. And there's the world in Technicolor focus. Crazy world out here. Time resumes to normal speed—no, top speed. Sirens blast, overwhelming the ringing in my ears. Soldiers and medics tear ass in every direction except toward our tattered tent.

"Izzy!" It's Kobi. A friend. No red on his uniform. Kobi's alive and he sees me. "Izzy!" he yells above the blare. "Come on, let's go." Kobi, my curly-haired friend, came back for me. Good friend. "Come *on*, Izzy! Shift your ass!"

I'm frozen, though. Only half out the tent. He sees, but he hasn't *really* seen. Sees only my head and left shoulder so far. The ruined rest of me is still cloaked behind the flap. I wish I could hide it from him, from the world—*Oh, God. My mother*—for just a few days—as if I'll last that long.

"Izzy," he shouts again, "*now!*" He has a weird expression on his face. I don't want to see his eyes. I feel like I'm naked behind a shower curtain and he's ordering me to get out with no towel. He wouldn't want to see this kind of naked. *Is there something to cover the source of—the place where my—where it should be?*

Go ahead and deal with it. *My left arm.*

"For Fuks's sake, Izzy." That's a little joke we have. What would the lieutenant do? Whatever it is, you do it for his sake, and you'll be OK. "They're still shelling! We gotta get the hell over to the shelter!"

Shelling? Right. Another mortar. A shockwave. Concussion. It comes in flashes. Nothing like when a Road Runner bomb goes off in Wile E. Coyote's face.

The mortar hits the ground on the other side of our ruined tent. The impact is ridiculous. The ground rumbles and what's left of my body shakes. It's like I'm a hamster in a shoebox—and some kid's rattling the box. Some asshole kid. Kobi ducks, recoils under a whirlwind of dirt and smoke and cinder and shrapnel. This is nothing like the movies. *Why am I barely registering the violence? Am I dead yet? Is it shock?* "Don't just stare at me like that. Move, goddammit! Izzy, I swear to God—" Kobi's eyes are absolutely frantic. *Have I ever seen anyone's eyes so wild?*

He's right. We can't stay here. We have to drag all six-plus feet of my busted-up self to the bunker. And surely I'm a few quarts down on my necessary quota of Red.

Coming out now. He's going to see. He's going to be the first one who sees.

Out—

This is him seeing. I watch him see the remains of . . . It's dangling by a thread of my fatigues. Still attached? No, not really. It's just sitting there inside my sopping sleeve like a—like a—

Oh, Kobi's eyes. He sees, all right. He really does. The eyes serve as proof. They're afraid, even worse than my mother's back when she drove her son home with the residue of *Ivory* suds in his mouth. Silent that whole drive home, gripping the wheel like a guide wire, agony in her eyes. Damn that Mole for making her watch that humiliation.

Don't say anything, Izzy. What are you going to say? *Stay quiet, and let him lead you toward the bunker. Help him drag what remains . . . You can do that.*

Kobi. Can you see? You've never been good at hiding the truth. Tell me, do you grasp how sincerely screwed I am? Be honest, now. I can already tell from your eyes.

HANDCUFFED

1995. I'm totally screwed. School already sucks. The second grade has not been such a swell time. Now my parents have reinvented all our lives, and (as the expression I once heard goes) *poop rolls downhill.* They're going to put me in a genuinely Jewish joint. I can see my mother at the kitchen table, reviewing forms and applications. From my perch in front of the TV, I can hear her making calls, asking pressing questions. Her upgraded standards will have to be met, or this whole enterprise is insincere.

There are two options under consideration, it seems, and both are a forty-five-minute drive from home. That's—*forever*. But nothing as trivial as geography will ever stop my mother from meeting a goal. She's willing to spend three hours on the road each day, shuttling me and Jaz to and from our new Orthodox school. She does not consider this a sacrifice, I hear her tell my father late at night when they don't know I'm awake. Just the opposite, she says.

"This is going to happen," I whisper down to Jaz, who is on the bottom of our bunk bed. "You know her. She'll do whatever she has to for our 'best interest.'"

"Are you best interested in going to Jew school?" she asks.

Ha. "That's not what it—look, our 'best interest' means whatever they say goes, and we just have to do it. And that means there's no way we're getting out of this."

"Oh. OK." She smiles. Innocent kid. What do five-year-olds know? She turns over and hugs Teddy—that's her teddy's name. I roll over and stare at the ceiling fan. Jasmine will adjust. She's about twice as smart as her older brother. She'd adjust to life on a Mars colony if she could bring Teddy and maybe a Fisher-Price dollhouse. But I'm completely screwed.

Sure enough, before we ever really understand all the implications of what's about to happen—the extreme revolution of our young lives—our mother drops us off at our new school. The boys and girls are separated, of course, so I'll never see my sister in this building again.

But I find myself thrust onto a planet of little *tzadiks*, mini rabbis-to-be, classmates with whom I have absolutely nothing in common. Scooby-*Who*? As far as they're concerned, the last and only Abraham who led his people out of a mess was not named "Lincoln." There's no way of relating to my fellow students. I'm an alien landed on a bizarre and occasionally hostile Planet of the Hebrews. How can I survive this mystifying landscape?

If it's adapt or die—I'm already dead, ready to be buried.

In addition, I find it's nearly impossible to maintain the few friendships I've accumulated during my previous, albeit short, "social life"—kids back home who I assume think of me as one of them—not one of "them." How am I supposed to go over to friends' houses when I can't even think of getting in a car come sunset Friday? When I'm not supposed to partake of those hot dogs with melted cheese? Why would any kid want to come over my place if we can't work together to ensure that Sonic and Tails kick Dr. "Eggman" Robotnik squarely in the butt? What else is there? What's the point of waking up in the morning?

I saw a movie once, one I probably shouldn't have seen. A war movie. Some brave American pilot is forced to eject and para-drop into a demilitarized zone. It's a fierce winter. Dark. He's shivering. He gets separated from his gear. He's got just a few hours to save himself. It's like that. But it's worse—and this is what twists my intestines every morning. Because this enemy—the "Super-Jews"—are proving they can be every bit as cruel as the enemy officers in that movie. There's a line in the children's book, *The Velveteen Rabbit*: "The wild rabbits have very sharp eyes." This was never truer than among these kids. As soon as they spot my differences, my vulnerable stuffing, they zero in for the kill. The magical tactic that surfaced on the ball court has no bounce with these players. I could own a moniker like "Fart Boy" all I wanted—they'd find more biting ways to mark my difference.

I soon become the constant butt of their jokes. Here I am, forced to be among them, yet they still think of me as a Muggle, non-"chosen." No matter where I turn, I'm bound to take a bullet to the frozen ass-cheek, and limp through the rest of the day. Even the teachers get my number pretty quickly. Enough wise cracks, and when you actually do know the answer, the teacher says, "Put that hand down, Izzy. We heard enough from you today."

Take PE, for example. Every so often, our athletic director, Mr. Martinez, leads a few classes through the gates within the prison-like walls of our school, across the street to Flamingo Park, which seems a world away. And like a prisoner on lockdown, this "rec time," no matter how fleeting, is the highlight of my week. Dead grass? Diseased, one-legged pigeons? A breeze that reeks of tobacco and stale vomit? Yes, please. The smells of chalk, dusty prayer books, and twenty boys who have barely figured out deodorant, are enough for me to beg for clemency. Or see me hanging from the rafters of my cell by June.

One bright Sunday, my ragtag team of classmates performs a

bona fide miracle, beating an older grade in a tight game of touch football. It's a hard-won victory. We fight for every inch of patchy, dry lawn against our meatier counterparts. So this triumph is so sweet, so rare, it's cause for serious fanfare. My heart leaps into my throat like a squirrel up a drainpipe. We're a real *team*, and with teamwork we beat those bigger, "better" guys.

After the final play, while everyone on our team is cheering and high-fiving each other, and perilously taunting our momentarily shocked opponents, I approach our quarterback. His name is Dov. Which means "bear" in Hebrew. He's short and stubby, but also agile and talented at every sport I've ever seen him play. His two front teeth recall Bugs Bunny. Adrenaline's still racing through my veins. "Hey, man," I say, smiling, lifting my hand for some reciprocated slapping. "You were awesome. That last throw—"

"Forget it," he says, and instead of high-fiving me, he spits between his two front wood-chippers onto the turf by my Air Jordans. So my hand is frozen in air as he stares me down.

Pull your hand back, for God's sake, Izzy. Why won't it move? I've stopped all breath. Two great blocks and one touchdown, and I *still* haven't won their approval?

But wait. Maybe he misunderstood me? Maybe Dov's thinking of someone else, maybe mad at someone else for something. "You think I'd *touch* the likes of you?" he says, looking me right in the eyes still. "You're *nothing*. Izzy Something? No—he's nothing. You get it?"

Does a Dov shit in the woods?

In *Charlotte's Web*, one of Jaz's books, some asshole animal tells Wilbur he's "less than nothing," and Wilbur reasons that there can't be anything that's less than nothing: "Nothing is absolutely the limit of nothingness. It's the lowest you can go. . . If there were something that was less than nothing, then nothing would not be nothing, it would be something."

There *is* something less than nothing, if only in a feeling that overcomes you in the darkness of a stare, in sight of that saliva glistening on the turf. That feeling you get in the un-slapped hand.

Nobody else hears Dov, no one sees me planted on the grass as he darts off with the winning ball into a sea of acolytes and accolades. All around me, everyone else is jubilantly fist-bumping, whooping it up. Even Martinez blows his whistle to commemorate the coup. *Just move, Izzy. Damn it, walk off.* But I'm still standing there dumbfounded, stung, like he kicked me in the gonads. That would have hurt less.

What would my father say? "This kind of challenge forges character." Really? This kind of thing feels like crud. It's several seconds before I can muster just a little bit of something. I finally retract my hand. It's a while before I can figure out what to do with it.

PUT DOWN THAT HAND

January 8, 2009. What are they going to do with my mangled forearm? The brain says flex, make a fist, raise it up. But it's unresponsive. Wasn't programmed with Wi-Fi. It's dead. A horror-movie prop. I can't stop staring at it now as Kobi drags me along. It's just so unbelievable. I can run, a little. More of a stumble.

Wait. Shouldn't I be in horrible pain? Did I forget to hurt? Shouldn't I be screaming, maybe? Yeah. I already am. Roaring. Huh. Just noticed that. It's involuntary. A howl born below. From the pit where fear festers, expecting some chance to reveal itself to the world, like a caged demon waiting for you to open up wide.

It's all the times I *wished* I could scream, all that waiting in the Mole's office, every time Dov and the rest of them dissed me.

It's my father—what they did to him. All the grown-up Dovs of the world. How they fucked him. How they arrested him at the airport, shackled him, threw my father in a cell. In jail. How so many of the people he tried to help along the way turned their backs on him, trying to make a dollar.

It's that time when I was eighteen, drunk, lurching through the streets of Jerusalem at four in the morning, and got ambushed by a bunch of kids. How they promptly beat the crap out of me. It's how I sat there on a curb, suddenly sober, bleeding from my right eye, my mouth. How they laughed and enjoyed their lame handshakes as I whimpered by their feet. A fellow Jew.

It's the evictions, how my parents had to pack our most essential stuff—"We can't take your books to Israel, Izzy, sorry . . ."—and vacate us by morning. How they tried to make it into a game so my sisters, now three, wouldn't figure out the truth.

It's bashing down the walls of the decrepit apartment in the Wolfson Towers with a sledgehammer every night before the start of basic training, eyes stinging with detritus and paint, just to create a livable space for my parents and siblings. How responsible I had to be. How grateful I was each time Jonny showed up to help.

This is absolutely not my voice, and that's . . . liberating. Izzy simply isn't home anymore. You can leave a message, but he might not get back to you—not ever. Whatever this is, it will be heard. The sound of a nightmare that's crept into the light of day.

It's all my childhood phantoms back for a visit. It's the gremlins again, at Jordan's house. A sort-of-friend of mine. 1997. My mom and her workout partner go to Gold's Gym and leave me with Jordan at his house. Jordan's two years older, so I try to stay out of the way of whatever he and his buddies get up to. They want to watch *Gremlins*. Will the little pussy boy wet his pants? No way. But the images gnaw at my bones. I'm afraid the moment the cassette clicks in the VCR. Oh, I'm in it now. It's the way they *ignore* the old man's *warning* and allow water to meet the mogwai. How all hell breaks loose. On screen. In my intestines. They're laughing, Jordan and his friends. And it's all I can do to *not* mess my pants.

It's how that hell follows me home. How it's coiled, biding its time in the pipes under our drains, getting wet. Waiting. How, for a month, I can't sit on the toilet without staring wide-eyed into the bowl, holding my little nut sack in trembling hands. How if I look away, even for a moment, I *know* gremlin claws are going to yank me by my nuggets, right down into the sewers, where the alligators live. How I don't shower for weeks. How my mom bursts into the bathroom one day because she can't understand why I've been smelling so bad lately, and finds me pressed against the wall opposite the tub, fully dressed, eyes wide, just watching the water run, just waiting for the claws. How she has to make me leave the door open afterward. For months. Those talons.

Nooo, I'm no pussy . . .

It's how a few years earlier, after I beg Dad to take me to my first Batman movie, the Penguin's cackle invites a million more nightmares. It's Chucky, Spawn, and that horrible freak from *Jeepers Creepers*—how that thing removes the back of Darry's head. And takes his eyes.

It's the punishment I get after the Mole rats me out to Mom. How she convinced her that I had "too many distractions." How they take my Warcraft III online expansion set, my books, my Game-Cube, and throw it all into U-Haul boxes and stack them in the garage. My whole life. How I come home a few days later and see all the boxes are gone. "Goodwill," my mother says. She's making my favorite, spinach tortillas, and instead of eating, I run upstairs, lock my door, and block it with a dresser. Flop on the bed and scream into the pillow. How I pee in the plastic bucket every good Jew is supposed to use to wash their hands and pray first thing in the morning. How I piss on that. How I fling that piss out the window, miss a day of school, won't leave my room, not for any damn thing. How thirty-six hours later, all my stuff is back. No explanation. The Goodwill logo still gets me sick.

Like the Sbarro sign.

It's the look of that rock tumbling after it crushed my left foot. Twice.

Don't you know who you are, Izzy? Why you're here? You're a soldier. Is it OK with you that someone else *is screaming in you now? From you. Using your lungs? Is it all right to just allow this creature to occupy your body, unhinge your jaw, and just bellow? Giving stuff up is not supposed to be easy—nor painless. Didn't you learn anything from your father?*

The only thing they can't take from you, Izzy, is what you've already given.

What you did with that rock . . .

Not now.

Kobi, beside you, is flinching. The sound coming out of you, the scream would break glass if the mortars had left any windows on base intact. *Get it together. Take charge of this, Izzy.* It's not a sopping monster that got you. Not a gang of street thugs. It's not a clutch of cops surrounding you at JFK. You're not your father. You'll never be that great. Wouldn't have been, even if you had lived to see twenty-one.

It's closing your eyes and praying—truly praying—that no one heard you let one rip. How when you open them, a hundred kids have fanned out, how a gulf has opened between you and every other human being in the world.

It isn't like that here. You have friends who look out for you. You're not on that gym floor anymore. These streams of liquid dripping down your side aren't from those waterslides outside the JCC.

Yes. It's all clicking into place. The border of Gaza. We're moving. The battlefield. An encampment of Israeli soldiers. A hard target for a mortar attack. Kobi shouting something over the clamor. Kobi nodding, making sure you understand whatever he's saying. You don't understand. Not the words, at least—but you get the idea. You are more than something to Kobi. You're some*one* worth saving. Your friend is letting go of you now, falling backward, sprinting, stumbling up ahead over his own boots and legs, kicking up a storm of gravel and pebbles in his wake. Kobi's going back for someone else. This is a rescue operation. And others need to be rescued. You're not alone.

You don't need to be some kind of seer to see how this will end. There's not too much to figure out. They've disarmed you. Forcing yourself to look down at this reality again, you realize your scrutiny has stilled the screaming. For a moment, standing outside the flap of the tent, you hear nothing.

So now you die.

Shouldn't there be lights, a tunnel, epiphanies, your grandparents and Uncle Julio on a welcome wagon? No, Izzy, you're not having an out-of-body experience here. You are altogether back in your body. Your spoiled sack of flesh. No tunnel of light. That's obviously not what happens. You just bleed out, pretty quick, and then, as the Frost poem "Out, Out—" you read in sixth grade goes, "Little—less—nothing!" And that's it then. Well, fine.

You start out with nothing, and to nothing you return.

But wait. That can't be true. I started out with a mother. *Ma. Sorry. It's OK. A thing worth fighting for, Ma. A just cause. Just . . .* I'm going to fall now, I can feel my knees crumpling. For once, I am not consumed by shame and regret. Just another few seconds now. I feel warmth envelop me like an olive-green sleeping bag. *No suffering, Ma. It's all good, I promise.*

"Izzy! Izzy! Can you hear me? You gotta come with me."

Fuks. Lumbering giant, crystalline eyes. *OK, Fuks. Coming. Just about to die first.*

"Izzy," he says again forcefully, grabbing my good elbow and insisting I meet his gaze. "Man, it's really time to go."

We're walking. For Fuks's sake. All the red on my uniform's starting to chill. What happened to that warmth? "I need to call my mother. Where's my phone?"

DISARMED

"Izzy, just walk. Just keep up with me. You're not calling anyone, not right now."

"My phone," I say again.

He stops for a short second. I stop. "NOW," he enunciates. "Just walk. We're going to the bomb shelter. It's not your phone we need to find."

That's right.

The shelter. The shelter's as good a place to call it quits as any other. Through the gaping entrance I see strewn all over the floor gloves and shredded uniforms, bandages covered in the red, little bits of concrete shaken loose by the blast. More drifting down. I don't go inside. Not yet.

Fuks has left me alone a moment to tend to another one of our wounded.

CANVAS FOR ONE-ARMED MAN

Is this really happening to you right now? You're outside the shelter's entrance. You're all alone. Keep moving. Go inside. No, you should raise both your arms the way a human raises arms. Yes, like that, from the shoulders. Do it with supporting muscle, bone, and tendon. But why perform this action? Some symbol of triumph?

Before you can figure that out, your right arm goes up. But the weight of the remainder of your left arm leaves it swinging, spraying red. Your uniform sleeve surrenders to the burden, the threads of cloth beginning to shred apart. You can tell that no longer does the worn, olive-green material fasten an arm to its man. Yet you try again to swing your left arm up, and off it goes. Your hand, wrist, and forearm has taken flight. It's soaring skyward with all the confidence of Superman's fist, attached to its Kryptonian wrist. It's almost amusing, watching it go. Almost "ha-ha" hilarious. You can't help grinning stupidly now. Is that drool down your chin? So be it. At long last, some part of you has found the guts to aim for the sun, to reach for greatness, a goal beyond your grasp. Everything's going to be OK. The rest of this body will follow. The only place to go from here is up.

For a split second, gravity slumbers, and you can sense it, how your feet are milliseconds from leaving their prison ground, how your whole body's about to take flight. But then the arm stops reaching. It's like one of those blooper reels of impotent rockets—failure to launch. You watch the thing begin its descent. But the sun in your eyes has blinded you, blocks you from seeing where that piece of your puzzle lands. Maybe, just maybe, you heard the soft thump of its landing.

You grow woozy. This has turned out to be a terrible idea. Life is flinging out of the wound in impossible arcs now, painting the side of a tent, the gravel, in Red Modern Art, drowning weeds and clods of dirt and rubble for meters all around you, and still soaring up into the steel sky. But the sky says *no thanks*, wants no part in this nonsense. The sky discarded your arm, and now it rejects all the Red from inside you, sends it raining back down like some Biblical plague. There's a circle of it and you're swaying alone in the center, untouchable, an endless perimeter between your closest counterpart and you.

So tired. Barely standing. Just want to rest, just a few minutes.

Damn it.

Damn it all.

Chapter 4

ARM'S LENGTH

January 8, 2009. Fuks returns, sees all the blood around, and yanks me past the threshold of the shelter. Doesn't seem to notice my arm's taken wing. Within the debris-strewn structure is Amir. I can tell he's just come inside, too, with another wounded soldier. Both he and Fuks have been out there in harm's way, collecting the men of the Second Platoon. Now Amir is standing on a concrete block, trying to get reception on the radio. Fuks is growling orders. During training, I got used to seeing Fuks smile, his eyes dancing as he did paperwork, his phone playing muffled pop songs from inside his shirt pocket. I'm used to commanders calmly, almost mechanically, giving orders. But right here, Fuks is an unblinking machine who doesn't seem to run out of battery. He's wearing a face I don't recognize.

Amir drops the radio, comes over as soon as he sees me. "Why are you moving like my grandma?" he says, spitting detritus.

I look down at my wound. He does, too, and his mouth opens again despite the ambient dust. I see Amir charging outside. I just know he's going to search for the rest of me, even if that means losing part of him.

The entire bunker's smaller than a two-car garage, and packed with thirty soldiers or more, some injured. Help those guys. A sea of olive green parts to let me through. They all see. It's still total disarray out there, but in the bunker now all is still. All is quiet on this front. "For God's sake, help him down!" someone shouts; "Here! Over here!" another soldier yells, and instantly, commotion re-erupts. Much scurrying, a kind of controlled, chaotic collaboration ensues, a form of swarm intelligence. Fellow soldiers go after my blood-soaked uniform. Bare hands tear through the rugged canvas. I'm on my back now. Fuks must have lost his knife in the melee. He's on his knees, digging his face right into the thread above my wound like some vampire—what's he doing? He starts shredding thick fabric with his teeth and then his hands. I remember. During training, they taught us to strip an injured soldier of all his clothing, to search for occult damage. You never know what else is under the uniform. When he lifts his head, his cheek is covered in the Red. My eyes drift as he roughly sponges his forehead with his sleeve, spreading the Red further.

I look past him. The floor of the shelter really is a sight. I see a spool of gauze roll by, a capsized boot, a bloody belt. My mother would have a panic attack if she came home to such a clutter.

Under any other circumstances, she'd be ordering her little soldier to sweep the floor clean.

A GRAND, SWEEPING GESTURE

Any given Tuesday, 1992. I'm helping my mother sweep the floor while my father's at work. It's raining outside. The floor in our Brooklyn apartment is hardwood. My father built this whole apartment building with his bare hands. Amazing. I picture him laying every one of the exposed bricks and concrete blocks the way I do with Lego pieces.

This morning before he left, I heard him tell my mother I was "sharp." What's that?

Now she smiles at me from the stove, where's she's making lentil soup for lunch. She says, "Such a big boy!" I am. Four, actually. I see myself in the reflection of the stove window beside her—still surprising to see my hair cut so short in the Upsherinish *ceremony. My father told me getting my hair cut wouldn't hurt, and it didn't.*

My mother turns back to her cooking.

The broom's so heavy. It's easier to pick up the stuff with my hands. The next time she turns toward me, she sees my squirrel cheeks. She rushes over and pulls me hard. I have to spit out the stuff—a dead potato chip, a watch battery, and two matching screws from who knows what. "Izzy— that's bad. You can hurt yourself," she scolds. "You have to be careful, OK?"

I can shelter my mother in 2009. No bomb will drop on her Jerusalem home, the same way no bomb could drop on me. This lie—that's the perfect shelter. I need my phone right now so I can lie to my mother, to tell her nothing bad has happened. Some kids are sharp, it's true, and some soldiers. But I'm the kid who sucks on screws. And stale chips. And mortar shells.

I came here to be—what? A hero? What's a hero anyway? The one who suffers the blow on behalf of his brethren, or the medic who scrambles from the wounded to the dead, and back again? Is he a hero under the tombstone or still only charging overland toward danger? Can you, so young, even remotely consider yourself brave, devoted, willing to give up everything for your beliefs, when there are so many men among the reservists who risk leaving their children fatherless? How do they endure that possibility? How does Chen the medic deal with all the Red, all the screaming? He's only twenty, like me, drafted a month after I volunteered. Chen, the medic who tends to curse at the wind and the sand, now tries to tie a tourniquet above the space once occupied by my left elbow. "It's too slick," he says. "*Kus emek!* It won't hold."

The steady outpouring of Red keeps the area too slippery for any bandage to stay in place. With help, Chen tries again. Another medic attempts to stanch the bleeding with a second tourniquet, higher up. More crying out. "Gonna dope him," someone says, and then that someone stabs a morphine pen through my thigh flesh and an all-over warmth washes through me. A breath. In and out. How long have I been holding my breath? Now here's a third medic. He sees, quickly, serenely, then leans down and tickles my bare chest with something cold. With difficulty, I raise up just enough to see he's written out the time with a Sharpie: *13:10.*

Time of death?

Makes sense. The world slows again. How long can 13:10 last? "My phone." But no one listens. Maybe I'm mumbling. "My phone. Please." But no one's dashing out toward the tent to retrieve my old Sony Ericsson while mortars are still pummeling the base. "You don't need your phone," Chen whispers. He's staring straight ahead at nothing. At the concrete wall of the bunker. At Gaza, two kilometers beyond it.

I see colors. And I'm floating, the way your body stays bobbing in the salty Dead Sea. Dark purple, green, a sunset lavender. Now I'm sinking, slowly drifting down under the concrete foundation, through the soil, down, down into black.

My phone.

Love you, Ma.

I'm calling to say I . . .

HANDS OFF THE MERCH

January 8, 2009. "What am I doing here!?" I don't mean in the ambulance—I know why I'm in the ambulance. I mean what the hell am I doing in *Israel?* "I'm fucking American!"

The two female medics—Blue and Curls—flicker in and out of focus above me. They glance at each other, and although I can't get a bead on their faces, I can tell by their body language that they're confused. *Did I say that out loud? Did I slur? Do they even speak English?* Yes—they've been talking to me the whole time, I remember now. What have they been saying?

I hear my bones crunching. No. It takes me a moment to recognize that it's the sound of the water bottle I've been clutching in my right hand, crushing with every flex and contraction. Thank God I didn't accept Blue's offer to hold my hand for the ride. I would've broken her fingers. "So, where are you from?" Curls asks, a blatant attempt to keep me talking. *Didn't I just yell that?* Curls is different from the other one somehow. They're in their late teens, but something about this one seems more . . . mature. Her voice comes without any panic or pressure. I listen to her easy talking. She tells me matter-of-factly everything she's doing. I feel her practiced movements on me. This is not her first time knee-deep inside someone else.

Curls keeps up an easy banter with Blue. To me they're all about encouraging, explaining. It doesn't matter what they're saying—it's the *shape* and tone of their words, how they surround me. They build a wall around me, a force field. Like all those I watched go up in the dozens of sci-fi films my father took me to (then promptly starting snoring); I had to keep elbowing his copious belly. *Shields up.* Armor against the hysteria sneaking through the cracks. My sight and hearing are fading in and out, but still, the words of Curls soothe me. I watch them roll off her tongue, hear them uttered in perfect, unaccented English.

When I close my eyes I can tell I'm smiling, slightly.

Meds.

And blood loss.

I remember now that one of them asked me if I've gotten morphine. I have, in the bunker, but I must have said no when she asked. I'm back in Miami. Lying by the pool, the sound of a volleyball taking a beating in the distance. My body's still dripping from my last cannonball.

Dripping. I open my eyes. That's my Red pattering on the deck. "Give him a bump," Curls tells Blue. "OK, little prick."

Well, excuse me! It's cold without clothes on and . . .

Mmm. The pain's still there, but way down, way under all the morphine, deep, deep, deep. Something inside me scrambles to get out from under, like a hermit crab below meters of sand. "Hang in there, Izzy," says Curls, and for just a moment I can feel her hand pressed on my chest, her fingers lightly spreading underneath my time of death.

I can't even tell if my eyes are open. A vague image dawns through the dark, of a half-naked soldier smeared in Red, sprawled on a gurney in his underwear. Over this soldier, a poised young medic with red hair and bright-blue eyes. In the jump seat, another medic, curly hair, taps a syringe. The soldier's on a slight angle across his stretcher, writhing a little, and shaking his head from side to side, slowly.

How am I seeing all this from the ceiling?

Blue leans over the soldier. I want to see the girl's face. I float down toward the pair. Open my eyes. Now I'm looking up. I try to fix my eyes on hers. I can't. I try to bring her other features into focus. It's no use—it's all a blur, as though space itself is rushing around us so fast it's smearing. As in, "Punch it, Chewie!" Light speed.

"It's OK," says Curls. "That's the morphine talking. We've got you."

At which Blue leans down again, leans over me, to get something, fix something, move something. Her shoulder, her clavicle, her neck so close, and there, I can focus. There's a pendant there, stuck to her skin with sweat, in the hollow of her collarbone. What is it? I can't make it out. A thin, gold chain bunched up there. A hazel tan that's stretched across that elegant bone I see inside the half-open lapel of her olive-green fatigues. A fleck, two flecks, a spatter of blood on the collar—more modern art. A little something of me I've left with her, too.

There's a bright light over Blue's head, and the light, dappling through her hair, lands on my face. I feel her hand slide underneath me. She has to move me just a bit, to shift my frame on the gurney. For a second or two, I realize, I'm literally *in her arms*. How many like me have died this way? And this is what I say. I say, "What's your name? Do you know how beautiful you are? You don't belong here. Not like this, not with a nerd from Florida dying in your grasp. You and your friends should be flirting with jocks, sprawled out on the grass at Bar-Ilan University, sun streaming, nose-deep in trig or history or Amos Oz."

But God knows what it sounds like. Not human speech.

"It's OK," she says. She thinks I'm moaning. I *am*.

I can't make out her face because of the eclipse. But now I think maybe I see her lips arching upward, unexpectedly. From where I lie, her smile's upside down. "Well?" she urges. "You never told me where. San Francisco? New Jersey?"

I'm preparing to respond. I will concentrate completely on the words, the syllables—*My. Am. Ee.*—and we'll be talking. But suddenly I feel the gurney shift an inch or two up toward the cabin, then the ambulance stops short. Blue and Curls hop out. When the back doors open the whole bay fills with the unmistakable *whomp-whomp* of rotors. "Your ride's here," Curls says, and I want to smile. I want to thank her.

They pop some unseen lock somewhere and slide me out.

I feel a hand lift off my chest. *Good-bye, Curls. Good-bye, Blue.*

A hot blast of air punches me, sucks whatever breath I have left from my lungs, and gets my heart galloping again. The chopper crew clambers hastily around me. The two crews commiserate. Blue gives the guys my vitals. I remember then I'm still grasping the water bottle in my right hand, but the moment I recognize its heft there, I feel it roll out and onto the ground.

Nothing soft about the touch of the chopper crew. But no less reassuring. Two fierce-looking operatives wearing thin, black combat vests carry my stretcher to an idling Blackhawk. They shove me inside. It's gutted in there, clear of seats and all other unnecessary impediments to airlifting wounded soldiers. I count three of my platoon mates, variously laid out across the deck inside. If I look as bad as they do, I'm screwed.

First, Roj'e—our platoon's light machine gunner—is gashed across both his knees. One arm is better than two legs, right? Or . . . ? Roj'e likes to kick the ball around. I hope those days aren't over now.

Then I see Elgozi, another private, his head resting in Roj'e's lap. It's hard to turn my face far enough to get a good look at him. But I catch a glimpse of a stomach wound. He's barely breathing. In contrast to Roj'e, whose rib cage is rising and falling dramatically, his mouth twitching beneath a dusty five o'clock shadow. I wish I could grow a beard. On Elgozi's face I can see nothing of his usual buoyant personality. "Stay with me, Elgozi, you're gonna be fine," I hear Roj'e shouting down at him over the wash of the propellers. Isn't he going to be fine? The wound doesn't look deadly—it's maybe the size of a quarter. So why did the medics Sharpie the words "critically wounded" on Elgozi's chest? I look down at my own chest, where I'm shocked to find the words "moderately wounded." Is it better to be comforted, or to be told the truth?

The whine of the props or the engine or something pitches higher—we're about to take off. I see another one of my squad mates, Lior—"Rabbi"—slumped in another corner, his femur shattered. His eyes are shut tight but his lips are moving just perceptibly. He's either praying, hiding from the pain, or both. It hasn't struck me yet to pray.

We lift off so quickly my stomach remains grounded with the water bottle. I've seen these guys work before. The elite Unit 669, heliborne rescue and evacuation squad of the IDF. They sometimes have to slash through enemy lines to get to their patients, *plus* they're primo combat medics. You couldn't possibly be in better hands.

Hands . . .

I start to shiver. Shock and wind and loss of blood—it all leads to the cliché dying man's lament from every war movie ever made: "So . . . *cooold.*" And the spasms occasioned by the faintest pang beneath my shoulder. "You get morphine?" shouts the guy standing sentry above me.

"No," I tell him, and within moments another dose of warm relief dives into me, all the way through me. But this high is interrupted very soon by more incessant shivering. My whole body quakes. "*F-f-freezing!*" My teeth are clacking into each other, audible even over the din of the flight. "*Kar li*," I sputter. In one swoop, the flight medic covers my feet with a blanket—a tender mercy.

We bank to the left. To my side, a member of the 669 squad hangs by the open door of the chopper as it whips over a blurred landscape, greens and browns, nothing but a strong grip on a ceiling strap separating him from a one-way trip to the ground.

At some indiscernible point, the unremitting beat of the rotors sinks into a soothing white noise. It gets inside you. You're gliding incredibly fast, but it feels so smooth, so controlled, like those water bugs in Miami, striding over the surface of puddles after an early evening rainstorm.

When did we land? It's a grassy clearing, and I can see the sign for Soroka Medical Center. So we're in Be'er Sheva. I still can't focus, though. In fact, it's getting harder with every minute.

You've lost a lot of blood, Izzy. You're cross-eyed from painkillers. You're in shock.

"You're gonna be OK, brother," says one of the heli-medics, shoving my stretcher off to the hospital staff, outside among the multitudes who welcome us.

"Reporters," Roj'e shouts to Elgozi as they pull him off right after me. "A mob of them, look, behind the chain-link fence."

"Oh, man," I'm thinking. "If my mother sees this on TV, she'll freaking kill me."

For the first time, I manage to sit up on the stretcher. With my five remaining fingers, I trace the length of my body, which seems never-ending, the wound a world away. Lashes of pain strike the back of my skull like whips, but I proceed to my target. It's unbelievable. Right there and no denying it, but unbelievable. I remember, for some reason, some words I had to look up online after having read them somewhere: *Cognitive dissonance.* This is it.

I pull the blanket up over my face, trying to ignore the gremlins clawing at my side, twanging through my whole body when they strike a nerve. I *try* to pull the blanket up over my face, but there's no overlooking the horror of reaching out with *two* hands for a blanket and coming up half short.

My arm is gone. It's still warm against my side, but really, it's just gone.

They roll my gurney across the clearing, nothing but blue sky above, a searing sun. Half an hour ago, I was about to rest my eyes, lie on a cot after that long morning slog, that endless night patrol. And now . . . This has got to be the mind's own force field, some adaptation or God-given gift (Lior would say): It's a good design that at a certain level, we can't quite wrap our heads around such a calamity, a loss.

A photographer standing by the sliding glass doors of the ER is trying to pull my blanket down. You've got to be kidding me.

Yes—he wants to snap the bloodiest shot of the devastation that used to be my arm. Wants a clear look at my tortured expression. I hold the blanket tightly with my right arm. I make a mental note to hate this vulture later, hate the vileness of his act. And to find him, if I ever recover, so I can beat him senseless with my severed appendage. And if I die, I'll stay in limbo so that I can haunt this bastard's nightmares.

The ER's air-conditioned, so my shivering increases. It's fluorescence, bustling, and a hospital smell like bacteria scented with Febreze. They wheel me past the door that says "Soiled Linens." Two lefts, a right, two sets of doors. They're whizzing me toward surgery. A plump female, an officer huffing alongside the gurney, asks, "Would you like to speak to your mother?"

"Yes!"

"I have her right here, patched through to my cell phone."

Now?

What do I say?

I remember my earlier conviction that I had moments left to live, my yearning to tell her right away I loved her, to tell her good-bye. Now, surging so strongly through me that it overcomes the abuse of morphine, I have the impulse to assure her I will be all right, I will survive. I just know it's true. I do.

WHITE KNUCKLES

January 8, 2009. A knock at the door. She sees them through the peephole. Three men in uniform. She collapses to the tile, sobbing, even though she knows there's been a mistake. Her son is safe, somewhere quiet, the border of Lebanon. They have him washing dishes. He's been complaining about soap-burn for days, washing and washing and doing nothing else. Nearly twenty minutes pass before she can force herself to open the door.

She just wants to tell them they've made a terrible mistake. Her son is alive.

They agree. "Yes ma'am, your son is alive."

She breathes again. Then the officers try to explain what happened. But they don't speak English. What little Hebrew she's learned evaporates in the panic, gets washed out by the cacophony of her three daughters wailing on the floor. An officer shows her a report on his clipboard. Hebrew gibberish to her. Then she spots the only two words written in English: "Moderate injury."

Oh, God.

It's OK.

He's alive.

One of the officers speaks her son's name and offers her his phone. She snatches it. He's alive and he can talk. *I overreacted*, she realizes. *He's barely injured—only moderately wounded. He's going to be fine.* "Izzy, my God," she sobs. "What happened!?"

She hears him, too, trying to catch his breath. As a child, he formed the bizarre habit of holding his breath. It began at the swimming pool. He spent much of his time at the Bay Club, underwater. He won contests for his underwater endurance. He still has white marks on his front teeth from swimming by the drain with his eyes closed, from bashing his mouth into the side of the pool, down at the bottom where he spent so much time. What was he holding his breath for? Waiting for what big thing to happen?

She'll know how bad it is as soon as he speaks. Only a mother could understand this.

"I'm all right, Ma."

"Are you really OK?"

"I got hit."

"Where? Are you—*tell me!*"

He doesn't respond.

"Tell me! God, please, just—"

"My arm."

Now she's holding her breath. "How bad?"

She has to plead with him until, for the first time in weeks, he tells her the truth: "Ma, I'm sorry. I lost it. It's gone."

She can't help it—she starts to scream once more, joins her daughters down on the floor, almost drops the phone.

He's silent on the other end. She can hear him breathing. How much effort it takes to fill his lungs. "Listen, Ma," he finally speaks. "Listen to my voice. I'm OK. You can hear I'm OK. Right?"

She's still sobbing. "Yes. You sound OK."

"Good, because I need you to relax. You have to be strong for the girls. For Ta. You guys have to be—" He's slurring now. "Ma. I'll see you when I get out."

Please, God, let that be true.

She wants to say something, anything. That she'll always stand in the way of those gremlins climbing up the drainpipes, no matter the form they take. She'll wrestle all his nightmares away, take them on. She won't try anymore to get him out of the house when he's been glued to the Xbox for two straight days. He can play until his thumbs bleed. He can play until he passes out. Will he ever be able to hold a game controller again?

She can hear people in the background now. She hears someone fumbling with the phone. She hears the click. "I love you," she says, knowing he doesn't hear her. Knowing he already knows.

She stands in the kitchen, still holding the phone. She watches the clock on the stove. She won't move until she knows he's under. So much time for the trip down the hall. Maybe an elevator? They transfer him to the operating table. The anesthesiologist arrives. "Here comes the medicine, *Turai*"—they call him "Private." "Cold in your nose for a second. Now count down slowly from a hundred."

He can do that.

So can she.

"Ninety-nine . . . ninety-eight . . . *nnnnn . . .*"

SMALL ARMS FIRE

March 2002. "Just breathe normal. Little pinch," says the nurse.

"*Now* what?" my mother asks over the phone. A not-unexpected sigh accompanies her inquiry, just deep enough for the 2,249 miles that separate us to lose all functional significance: I can hear all the fear, frustration, and love in that exhalation. I escaped the Mole's prison to attend Orthodox boarding school in Arizona six months ago, the culmination of our transformation into super-Jews, and not at all meant as a punishment. "Really, Izzy, what's it this time? Please tell me it's not serious."

"Define 'serious.'"

"Just tell me."

Tell her, Izzy. You're thirteen now—these things happen all the time to thirteen-year-olds. "I cut my arm."

"You're mumbling."

"I cut myself—my arm—playing football."

I'd caught a wicked touchdown pass, arm through the window. Only problem: the window was closed.

And now the nurse is wiping stinging stuff around the wound.

"Oh, Izzy—Again?"

"No, Ma. Not again. The last time it was a *contusion* and a *hairline fracture.* This one's a *laceration.* Just a cut."

The nurse smiles at my medical vocabulary.

"How, exactly, did you end up in the emergency room—again—over 'just a cut'?"

"Did you know Super Glue was discovered in 1942 in a search for materials to make clear plastic gun sights for World War II?"

"You're telling me this *why?*"

I explain that surgical glue will play a significant role in my treatment. I don't tell her what the nurse who called my mother kindly pointed out: "We don't use this kind of thing on mere paper cuts, young man."

The first year of the new millennium is turning into the Year of the Scars. Two neat scars on my left arm already since they installed me at the Yeshiva High School of Tucson, Arizona. Two trips to the emergency room. Two football injuries. Mr. Martinez would be proud.

No one believed that I fractured my arm the first time around. "You know, Izzy," Rabbi Z. lectured me in front of the entire class, "lying about a wound is a grave offense. One who isn't in need of a wheelchair shouldn't even sit as a joke." That was the Torah talking. "Besides, it calls down negative energy." That was the Arizona talking.

"But I'm not lying, Rabbi. I'm pretty sure my arm really is messed up." I tried to jiggle it, and winced. "Yeah. It's broken."

Rabbi Z. wouldn't budge on his assessment of my injury, not even a day later, when I returned from the hospital in a cast. That's how long it took—twenty-four hours—before someone believed me and took me for an X-ray. When the rabbi saw the cast, he just harrumphed. "More time for studying," he said. "Instead of football."

Fortunately, trip two didn't require any coaxing. My arm was vomiting blood from a mouth it wasn't meant to have.

"You need to be more careful, Izzy," my mother demands. "You have to—hold on." I can hear a voice in the background. "Your father wants to know if you scored a goal. What's that? Oh, pardon me—a *touchdown*."

"Yep—twenty yards." (*Suck it, Dov.*) "And I'll be more careful, Ma. I promise." Probably shouldn't tell her about the rattlesnake that greeted me in my room one morning last week. It's not for nothing the students all fought over getting the top bunks.

The nurse raises her eyebrow as only a mother could. It says, "You better keep that promise." I will. I don't promise anything to my mother that I don't intend to keep. She suffered enough drama during the past few years. It's absolutely imperative to ensure she's got nothing but smooth sailing from this point forward. No sudden shocks. No big losses. No more calls about family from hospitals.

So much worse than broken arms and gashes is having to sit by idly as your mother keeps hiking down endless corridors of hell. Helpless kid. Mother undeserving of such agony. And now so far away, incapable of keeping a direct eye on you.

"OK, say good-bye to Mom," says the nurse. "We've got to glue you back together. How did this happen again?"

Well, the short answer is *Brik*. Aaron Brik. My new best friend and former mortal foe. The architect of both the touchdown and the cut.

But I'm more inclined toward longer answers. And, lately, I've been asking myself this question a lot: *How did this happen?* How did I wind up in the desert? Playing football under the mountains? Horses neighing in the background? If you're looking to stay calm and cool while you're bleeding all over the only unstained white shirt you own, this kind of thought exercise works well. How far back can you go to trace the circumstances that led you to where you are right now? Thirteen years is a long time.

It works like this: If the parents of Reina Alegre Baruch—or, as Jaz and I knew her, Ma—hadn't fled from Cuba to *Estados Unidos* when the nefarious vibes of Communism became impossible to ignore, then I would not have sliced open my arm diving through a closed window for the most dramatic touchdown of my life.

If *their* parents, my great-grandparents, hadn't fled to Cuba via Turkey, and if *their* Sephardic parents—probably from Spain—hadn't had to flee . . . Well, you get the idea. The history of Judaism is festered with fleeing families. Just when we get comfortable somewhere, our "hosts" call an end to the party and we all have to bounce. This has been going on for more than five thousand years. I know, because now I actually pay attention in History class. It's why I get that Israel is so important. After five millennia, we finally got the keys back to our homeland. This is worth a few crabby neighbors who have the unfortunate tendency of lobbing everything from grenades to "Grad" missiles onto our front lawn.

Anyway, my maternal grandparents, Isidoro (for whom I'm named) and Susana Baruch, eventually settled in Southern California, leaving behind all of their worldly possessions, along with any vestiges of practicing Judaism. They'd never been particularly religious, but that has never stopped totalitarian regimes from slapping a yellow star on you and marching you off to the showers. It's not that they parted ways with God—I'm not sure they'd ever been acquainted—but Cuba had become yet another risky place for Jews. Castro had flipped the Welcome sign over, and that's all she wrote.

I never got to ask my maternal grandparents anything about their lives, because they both joined that Guy Upstairs when I was just a kid. But my mother told me some details. They wanted to avoid the terror of, once again, having to flush their soap down the toilet before Castro's henchmen bashed down the door to see if they were "wealthy" enough to afford clean dishes.

They thought it better to hide their history. Although the Holocaust hadn't touched my family directly, better to stay safe than find yourself suddenly sorry.

That decision landed my mother in public school in Los Angeles, where her parents had settled after a short stint in New York. My grandparents spoke no English when they arrived, and it's tough to teach old dogs new tricks. They spoke only Spanish at home.

To no one's surprise, young Reina Baruch excelled in school. Her string of straight As, which she never bragged about, but which my father never failed to bring up, always made me assume someone must have dropped me on my head and knocked loose all that genetic sense. Let's be honest; whatever wisdom I arrived with at birth probably slipped right out of my gigantic ears. But that still wouldn't explain why Jaz and I suffer from the same butt-won't-stay-in-the-chair syndrome. My mother is far too coordinated to have dropped us both.

A more logical deduction: We take after our father, street smart but not from the Poindexters. More than once it has struck me what a shame it is that, as a species, we can't choose which traits we inherit from which parent. In a heartbeat, I would have swapped my father's inability to study for his capacity to grow a beard and socialize with other humans like a pro. I'm thirteen already—most of my friends have at least *some* scruff—and instead, I'm left with the mere wisp of a mustache, and I get flustered at the thought of talking to my own shadow. *Plus* I get no grade higher than a C minus.

Before I left for Tucson my father badgered me with tales of my mother's success in Jewish school. "Ma chose a religious institution on her own, you know. Her parents were fine with keeping her in public school."

"I know, I know," I said, sulking. "I'm so darn lucky that I have your support. I'll be living on a barn floor crawling with scorpions. You cool with that?"

"Your mother shared a classroom with twenty other girls, Izzy. More fangs and venom there than any pit full of scorpions."

My mother did well enough in school to skip a grade. Eventually, she got a full scholarship to UCLA.

So . . . I could do this, right? Surely, I'd survive.

But she also told me her early life was not without its hitches. She hit her first wall in college. Returning to a classroom filled with both women and men was daunting, to say the least. And the necessity of getting up in front of two hundred of her peers every time she wanted to ask the professor a question—that thoroughly unsettled her. She simply chose not to get up.

She had the knowledge. She had the discipline. The drive. But her early schooling had failed to prepare her for the "real world" of UCLA. So she decided to drop out after only eleven months.

She wouldn't see another classroom again until a few years down the line. Now fully observant, she came back "home," ending up in a Jewish day school—this time, as a kindergarten teacher.

These are the things I'm thinking about while the nurse is literally gluing the skin of my arm back together in a bright, white room with speakers playing a Muzak version of "The Real Slim Shady."

"So, as long as the edges of the wound are nice and straight," she says, breath smelling of peppermint, "and less than, let's see, I think it's five centimeters, you get the glue instead of stitches. Good, right?"

OK, now it hurts.

HEAD OVER HEELS

Here's how it—my existence—happened: Needing a break from the commotion of the Big Apple, my father booked a quick vacation to California. During his stay, he stopped by a Jewish day school to visit the principal, an old classmate. He spotted, he once told me on the way to the Aventura Mall, "this beautiful, exotic, Latin-looking teacher on the playground with her class." I could see it. "Izzy," he said, "I haven't been able to get her off my mind since." Thank God for that.

"What if I didn't decide to see Yankel that day? What if I got held up at brunch, or traffic on the 405 was backed up, or—?" I never would have come to be. No me. "Izzy, this is the funny way *HaShem* works sometimes. All the time. Everything for a reason. Everything for some big reason we have no idea how to comprehend. The good things, the bad things, the things we can't figure out. We just have to trust. You'll see. It's impossible to miss the signs if you're looking. Impossible."

I always loved that story of their meeting, and I thought a lot about that whole idea of fate. I sometimes looked at my mother doing dishes or talking to a friend, and I tried to see her that way, as though for the first time, laughing on a playground of eighteen noisy kids. And I tried to imagine how this would happen for me someday. I won't know her. I won't suspect I'm about to meet her. Some weird, circumstantial accident will bring us into each other's orbit. Something like a late bus or an ocean wave that drops her in my lap. Something I'd later be able to trace back endlessly through a series of moves and decisions that I had no idea had been leading me to her, a story I'd be able to share with my own kids. That's comforting. That's cool.

But there's something about my father's story that has always troubled me, too, or made me wonder. Yes, some elements of destiny were surely at work, and God has that covered—the Book of Life and all. But what about something I once heard a rabbi at my old school in Miami say, something I couldn't quite grasp when I was ten: *Agency*. Agency means that whatever God throws our way, we still have to act on it, create the vessel. We have to exercise our will. We always have choices, and we can go one way or the other. So my father could've flown home wistfully wishing he'd talked to my mom. He could have forgotten her and married someone else, and maybe he would have had a perfectly happy life with perfectly good *other* kids who looked something like me but with freckles and ginger hair. Or maybe he'd always sense something big was missing, that he had at some point hooked a left instead of right. That he hadn't fulfilled his destiny.

That's not what happened. Instead, he told his friend. He used his agency. He said, "There's something about this woman, I tell you. Something—I can't explain."

"I got this," his friend told him. The next day, Yankel sent his British wife to share the revelation with my future mother. They were on the playground again. She leaned toward my mother and dropped the bomb. "Reina, you knocked that fellow's socks off yesterday."

"Izzy, would you believe I wasn't observant enough for her? Of course you'd believe. I wasn't. I was a nice guy, not–too-terrible-looking, a little chunky maybe. But not her cup of tea. Plus, I was Canadian. Let's say she turned me down. She wasn't interested."

If it ended there, my father would have told some other son some other story of some other mother. But a year later, the same British woman, my father's friend's wife, invited my mother over for a cup of tea. And when my future mother entered the living room, she found said tea; and behind the steam wafting from a mug, there was my father, sitting on the couch, with a silly grin on his face, and dancing eyes, eagerly awaiting an audience. By then, she had significantly "mellowed" (my father's way of putting it), and decided to give this guy a shot. "It didn't hurt that now I had fringes poking out of my slacks and a *kippah* on my head," he said. "You see, she liked that I came with strings attached." He laughed. "Get it, Izzy? Because *tzitzit* were poking out of my—"

"—I get it, Dad!"

HAND IN (LATEX SURGICAL) GLOVE

March 2002. What I like about my nurse is that she tells the truth. She said it would sting when it was going to sting. She said it would hurt, and it hurt—but I was ready. A few months earlier, when I broke my arm, a different nurse treated me like a three-year-old looking for a lollipop. Before the shot, she said, "Mosquito bite." Are you kidding me? I was thirteen—not three. I was ready, like my Uncle Julio had been when leukemia landed, to face the world without having to climb the Boloney Wall adults put up as a rampart, thinking they're protecting you. I've talked with friends about this. They all agree. We're not stupid. We know when a divorce is imminent. We know when Grandma's headed for the grave. And, spoiler alert, we know that Fluffy's not romping on a farm upstate.

I knew about the leukemia. I knew my mother's older brother had very little warning. After months of inexplicable exhaustion, he went for "tests." Adults going for tests is even scarier, apparently, than the tests we kids have to take every other day. The doctors found his blood "teeming with cancer." I remember hearing that word coming from the kitchen. A terrible word, *teeming*. I looked it up. Endless whole-body scanners; a swarm of "mosquito bites"; the constant tang of the powdery surgical gloves on every doctor, nurse, and radiologist who touched him. I'd been to hospitals. They're kind of exciting if you know your stay will last no more than an hour. The vending machines in every hall are always loaded with treasure. honey buns were my favorite. But a long-term habitation would be terrible.

I knew, without them saying so directly, that I would have to say good-bye to Uncle Julio—that he would have to say good-bye to me. "Months?" my mother whispered from the kitchen.

"I'm sorry, Reina," my father said softly.

Kids get good at deciphering the whispers of grown-ups. So much of our existence depends on that which is whispered.

So no more awaiting my uncle's brief cross-country treks to Miami. No mornings resting my head on his stomach as he slept on our black leather couch, concentrating on the concert of gurgles, half laughing and half astounded at the alien dialect of his intestines. No more sitting at the kitchen table with him before anyone else woke up, watching him drink black coffee and scrunching my nose at the bitter smell. No more awaiting the same exact line of questioning he employed every time without fail:

1. "So, how are you getting along with Jasmine?" (Brothers and sisters must stick together—you have no idea how important this is.)
2. "How are your grades in school?" (How are you going to get a free ride to UCLA like your mother? Don't think you can just look an educational opportunity in the eye and turn away from it.)
3. "Tell me about your friends." (What's in your heart?)

See, we're not stupid babies.

Once, Uncle Julio took point two to a dramatically new level, promising to buy me a rocket-red Ferrari if I graduated from college. To seal this oath, he removed from his luggage a large model for motivation, candy-apple-colored, shining in the sunlight streaming through the window. "Izzy, you keep your eye on this, and sooner than you think, you'll be looking at the real one in the driveway. You have no idea how fast life moves."

He would die within the year. The shortest year of my life.

He would leave behind his wife, my aunt Denise. He would leave my cousins, Jake and Suzanne. He would leave my mother and their mentally challenged sister, Sara, with only the scale models of what his life might have become. How many lives in ruin at the randomness, the speed of mutating cells? But none suffered the loss worse than my grandmother Susana. For her, the loss of her firstborn left a screaming chasm where once stood a rock. She could not fill this hole with weeping. She could not cover it over with memories. She could not build a bridge to the other side with comfort from a god she probably left on that island to the south, if she'd ever known Him. The only way out was into the hole with her whole self.

She died a year later, hours after a drunk driver plowed into the car in which she and my grandfather were riding. What if that light on La Cienega and Olympic had stayed red just five seconds longer? I consoled myself with the knowledge that—even if I would never tell anyone this—she must have welcomed the chance to escape, to drive headlong into that tunnel carved out by her son's departure, to join her baby wherever we all go.

Is it better to die from a busted-up body or a broken heart? Either way, at thirteen years old, it's becoming harder to understand the idea of God's plan—to understand that everything that happens, as my father assures me, happens for a good reason. What good reason did *HaShem* have to rain that rubble down on my mother; my *mother*, who'd dedicated her life to Him, and brought us all along for the ride, so certain in her belief that He would shelter us from all such pelting out of the blue? What can I do to protect her? What can I do to prevent more pain? How to be a good son? How to take the place of a big, gurgling, loving man like my uncle? What hope? What God?

HAND TO GOD

January 9, 2009. I have no memory of this exchange, but months later my mother tells me about our discussion when she first arrived at the hospital. "Izzy ... Izzy, can you hear me? Come on, wake up now."

My eyes dart around the room. A recovery room. I find her face. I smile. "Ma."

"Oh, Izzy ... I'm so sorry."

"Ma."

"Yeah?"

"You know I have to go back, right?"

"God willing, Izzy," my mother says.

She looks behind her to unleash a rebuke on whoever blessed my journey back to combat only a day after my injury. She's surprised to see that no one else is in the room. She's more surprised at the calm that follows, despite knowing all too well the hand I've been dealt.

RAISE YOUR HAND, YOUNG MAN!

But the hand!
The boy's first outcry was a rueful laugh,
As he swung toward them holding up the hand
Half in appeal, but half as if to keep
The life from spilling. Then the boy saw all—
Since he was old enough to know, big boy
Doing a man's work, though a child at heart—
He saw all spoiled. "Don't let him cut my hand off—
The doctor, when he comes. Don't let him, sister!"
So. But the hand was gone already.

1999–2000. Sure, good yeshiva boys are banned—well, let's say, strongly discouraged—from reading any secular poetry. You want poetry? Read the Psalms. I learn the lesson about contraband books at the start of this, my fourth-grade year. Rabbi Becker catches me with a book called *Everything Men Know about Women: 25th Anniversary Edition* by Dr. Alan Francis, in consultation with Cindy Cashman:

Famed psychologist Alan Francis has written a landmark book on men's understanding of that most complex of creatures: women. Based on years of research and interviews with thousands of men from all walks of life, he presents the most complete picture ever revealed of men's knowledge of the opposite sex.

"Fully reveals the shocking truth!" —*Daily News*

DISARMED

Perhaps you can imagine the look on the rabbi's face when he clocks that cover as he ambles by, blathering on about the completion of Solomon's Temple in 960 BCE. I can count the fillings in his molars. The look is more regretful than angry. Clearly, he's failed me. And imagine his horror when, even as he yanks me by the elbow out of my seat, I'm smirking. Incorrigible!

Then try to picture the Mole's two faces as I sit across that monster desk from her, my shoes scuffing the floor. For the first time this year, she cannot speak. Where will she ever find enough Lemon Zest to wash my soul clean? Maybe Costco.

Now imagine her surprise when she creaks open the cover of the book, peers sidelong inside, as though some subway rat might be crouched in there, ready to pounce—and finds instead all 128 pages completely blank.

I'm grinning from ear to ear. Fighting the urge to let loose some jazz hands. She glowers, though I can tell she's faintly amused.

They can put me in prison. They can demand I learn by rote all kinds of prayers. But they cannot take away my sense of humor, my rebel soul. They can try—but they won't succeed.

So I find that Robert Frost poem, "Out, Out—," in a book of American verse that someone's left open on a table at Borders, a bookstore.

Best not consider what Dov and his minions would say if they saw me reading poetry. Porn would be better. Poetry would further peg me as the outsider. I must eradicate whatever makes me unlike all the other boys.

Suppressing my self becomes a full-time occupation requiring constant vigilance and cutthroat execution. I've got to try to keep them laughing. Maybe not Dov, but the others, chuckling enough to distract them from hating on me. My self-deprecating humor tends to head most of them off at the pass, blunting their attacks. Here's the thing, though. The shtick that worked so well at camp among the secular or non-Jewish kids doesn't fly so well in an Orthodox school. I had hoped my clowning would buffer me here, too, add a layer of protection to my sensitive skin.

Not to stereotype, but *all* of those Ortho-kids are smart. All of them, relentless. Once, my mother asked me if I was being bullied. I didn't know how to answer. Most bullies in Jewish day schools aren't the type to give you wedgies and swirlies, to knock your head into your locker. I could defend against that. I'm more juiced than the average Jew, and I've always been tall. But bullies they are. The typical bully in this other world uses not his fists but his *intellect* to wreck you. His words. Advanced psyops that slowly make you think you're going crazy. You get a waterboarding of words that'll break you over time, until that afternoon you load your gun and shoot yourself in the face.

So, sure, I can get a good laugh acting the class clown. And in the moment, this usually gives me a pass. But I know they're all laughing *at* me rather than with me. The self-deprecating jokes do not so much deflect the way Kevlar does. They just turn the aim inside. They make me my own bully. I, too, am on the outside of the circle, pointing and laughing at the lone weirdo in the middle. Still, it's better that I be the one to strangle my own soul. Genius, actually.

But this kind of genius comes with a heavy price. Rabbi Becker, Mr. Martinez, and, worst of all, the Mole, don't suffer fools with glee. For every utterance I eke out, every prank I pull, the long arm of yeshiva law skull-bashes me on the *yarmulke*. The punishment's worth it—at first. I don't have a choice. I have to pass the time somehow, expend the bundles of my excess energy. This new school has added hours of study, hours of listening, and hours of praying, to a day that's already too long after twin monotonous slogs down the highway with my mother and sister. Transferring schools last year was like transferring prisons, and this one gave me one *fewer* day (Sunday) on furlough. You have to figure out who you are, or who you could best pretend to be, during such an endless and unpleasant sentence. It's that or you lose your *self* to conformity. It makes me detest the best little *yeshiva bochers*, all good little boys who make their mommies and their Mole so proud.

I can't even sit still for a single minute of any lesson. When forced to concentrate for longer than about forty-five seconds, I start to spaz. Strictness and stricture are supposed to bring discipline and order. But they only exacerbate my antics. Even if I know an answer, I always accidentally blurt it out. "Raise your hand, Izzy! Your *hand*," snaps Rabbi Becker, for the umpteenth time. I keep forgetting. Soon we're in the realm of constant outbursts. We're in the neighborhood of "problem child." We're dipping a toe (OK, we're hip-deep) into "special." Nobody wants to be that kind of special, but I *Just. Can't. Stop.*

Then, one afternoon outside the Mole's office, I overhear her saying to my mother over the phone, "ADHD? No, he's just *chutz-padik*. Insolent. Rude." She's saying, no, such kids don't require counseling. They don't need subtle behavior modification. They need a nice *patsh* on the *tuchas*. And the occasional soapy snack.

Spare the rod, and all that. And I quickly discover that parents of yeshiva boys rarely contradict their child's principal. If you get busted during English or History or, God forbid, Torah class, you're in for a stern talking to when you get home—or, in my case, when your mother comes to pick you up early after you've waited an hour under the eye of the Mole.

Why is this happening to me?

I am not a stupid kid. I've looked into the future. And, like Frost's boy whose arm refuses to decline a meeting with a buzz saw, *I saw all spoiled.*

AN ARM AND A LEG

Yesterday, a Friday in July 2008, we shipped out to B'kaot, our advanced-training base. The company's completed unpacking, and we've just been relieved for the Sabbath. When I get to my platoon's room—the first time we've had our own four walls since the start—I pick up my cell phone and see that I've missed four calls from my mother. There's no message. I call her back right away. "Hey, Ma, everything OK? You scare me when you call so many—"

"Izzy." The ways she says it stops my tongue like a dolphin caught in a net. One of my sisters must be dead. Or my mother's got breast cancer. Or the house burned down. Or—"Your father's in prison."

What?! It's the first time in my life when the facts are staring me in the face, but they just don't register. It won't be the last.

Silence on the line for an awkward half minute. "Ma. What are you talking about? He just flew back to the States this morning. He can't be—"

"It happened at JFK. Izzy, in front of all those people. Cops. The FBI, I don't know. They arrested him . . . right when he landed. I've got to go buy—and I have to get Jaz to the—"

"Ma! *Why*—in God's name—would they do that?" I'm staring at a black scorpion with yellow markings—a deathstalker—as it crawls up the wall by the clock. Yellow means *uh-oh.*

She reads me a headline from the *New York Daily News*: "A Brooklyn Developer Accused of Swindling Some 40 Crown Heights Families Out of Millions Was Ordered Held without Bail Tuesday Night after Returning from His Israeli Hideout." Her voice sounds so small when she says, "I don't know any more than that."

"Shit." I stare at the clock. "Shit. OK, everything's going to be fine. We're all going to be fine, including Ta."

"I'll let you know when he calls. Just concentrate on what you're doing over there, so you can stay safe."

She hangs up without saying good-bye. I leave the phone against my ear and watch as my potential deadly ride home skitters behind the new air-conditioning unit blasting overhead. I'm holding my breath, as usual. In the distance, some troops are bellowing in response to orders given so softly I can't hear them.

The floor is falling out from under me. My mind begins to run wild. *Arrested? What could he have done? There must have been some giant misunderstanding.* I suddenly feel very, very trapped. Far away from my family when they need me most. What can I possibly do from here? *"Concentrate on what you're doing over there"? "Stay safe"? Are you serious?*

I need a plan. An escape. But the most obvious method has just left with all its venom. Supposedly, it can't actually kill the average healthy adult male, though they say its sting is excruciating. *I could just go over there and—* No. Ridiculous plan. But I can't control where my mind's running.

The sun starts to go down as I listen to my heart and the lulling rhythm of the AC.

In the mess hall, I can't bring myself to speak with anybody. After an uneaten supper, more training. I go through the motions as robotically as possible, in the hopes that I'll stay distracted.

Fuks has us doing push-ups on our fists while he pares a persimmon. "How many is that, Recruit?"

"Forty, Sir," says Amir, eager for more.

"Forty? That's it? How about another forty? Count 'em out, boys."

"Forty-one . . . forty-two . . ."

"I'm dying here, sir," says Oren, a comically thin private from Afula, south of Nazareth.

"Sure, look at you. You're a scarecrow. There's nothing but skin between your knuckles and the concrete. You gotta eat more snacks, Oren. They're free."

"Yes, sir."

"Forty-six . . . forty-seven . . ."

"Izzy, slow down. Keep to the count."

Huh? I'm shocked into oblivion. So much so that I can't even appreciate the banter.

That night I lay in bed, staring through the ceiling into the abyss. I think of my father in his cell, staring up, too, and this provides me little comfort.

Huh-ummmm, goes the air-conditioning. It's the first time the platoon's been able to choose and control the weather. A true luxury.

Please, please, be OK, Dad.

Huh-ummmm, says the AC again.

Are you alone in a cell? Or with some scumbag criminal? What if—?

Huh-ummmm.

We're all thinking of you, Ta. You're not alone.

Huh-ummmm—Clack! Rattle-rattle-rattle . . .

I'm startled back to the here and now. Kobi, who sleeps on the top bunk below the AC unit, has stuck his finger into its port. He's trying to shift the slats in his direction so the cool current hits him directly. The unit sputters a few times before dying out. I already know it will never work again.

It doesn't get any worse than this, I think. The rock has clearly hit bottom.

NOSE IN A BOOK

It's May 1998, and I've mostly survived school with the black-clad aliens. My mother has taken a detour on the way home from school to pick out a literary gift for a friend. When we get out of the car in front of the mega-sized store, she says, sternly, "You two stay in sight."

Right.

She knows I have a tendency to wander, both within and outside my head. So, moments later, I've disregarded her instructions. She's preoccupied with her shopping and I'm free to drift aimlessly through the maze of towering shelves. Dull books, dull books, Robert Frost, more dull books—then it happens. I stumble across a section with a range of radically colorful book jackets. Somehow they say to nine-year-old me, *Come closer, Izzy. Check us out, boy.* An overwhelming sense of urgency grips my every bone: Some knowledge that in these volumes I will discover the infinite wonders of the world. *Yes, herein lie the secrets to life itself,* they say. Reverentially, I approach. Inscribed on all the spines I see the word "Scholastic," with an open book insignia. *Open, please!* Not sure I love the word "scholastic," or that I'm pronouncing it properly in my head, but these books look nothing like the solid-colored, dry, and dusty volumes at my school.

I hear my mother's muffled voice somewhere through the stacks. "Where's your brother?" she's asking.

"I dunno," says Jaz, probably ogling unicorn coloring books or whatever little girls do at Borders.

I'm mesmerized by the titles. *Goosebumps: The Horror at Camp Jellyjam. Freak the Mighty. Star Wars.* Of course I've heard of that one. Then, like a dog discovering the rear end of another dog, I know that life will simply not go on until I've sniffed all the mysteries here before me. Soon my tunneling vision leads me directly to the centerpiece of the entire Scholastic display: *Animorphs*, it's called. The stark-blue book covers depict a boy's face in a series of increments transforming into that of a lizard. "Some people never change," it says. "Some do . . ." *Awesome. I have to have this book.*

"What have you got there?" my mother asks, her hands on my shoulders. She snaps me out of my reverie. Without a word, and with burning shame, I hold up the book as though it's a *Playboy*. In her face—I've learned to gauge every climate by her subtle expressions—I see relief that's she found me (70 percent) and relief that it's not a *Playboy* (30 percent).

"Hmm. K. A. Applegate. *Animorphs: The Invasion*. Izzy, doesn't this look too scary? You remember your little shower problem last year, don't you?" She flips through a few pages. She frowns. Not the direction I want this to go. I shake my head from side to side with exuberance.

Scary? No way. I got this, Ma.

Astoundingly, moments later, I'm in the bright, hot parking lot with this blue book in hand, the morphing boy. I hold it like a brick of gold. Something tells me that my life will be forever altered again. It's true. Halfway home and some ten pages in, I am certain. I am hooked. Transformed. Shape-shifted. I'm a kid with a secret identity, suddenly. The epic battle to save Earth from the alien Yeerks is my calling. I am instantly drawn to Jake, Marco, Cassie, Rachel, and Tobias, and their alien companion, Aximili-Esgarrouth-Isthill (awesome, but everyone calls him "Ax"), who bestows on them the power to transmute into any animal they touch. Imagine.

"Wow, you're really into that book," my mother says at the last red light before the Bay Club buildings. "When I was your age, I loved to read, too." She's pleased. Amazing. And there's not a prayer over fruit or bread in this whole book.

Now for the difficult part. Each day becomes a delicate balancing act of monumental importance. In one monotonous, dreary reality, I wake up; brush my teeth; get dressed; eat my boring corn flakes; endure the endless ride to school; suffer the stifling, yawn-inducing tedium of all my classes; try to remain out of the sights of Dov and his bully brigade; avoid the Mole like she's the bubonic plague; and somehow reach the end of the day still somewhat sane. But in my other, thrilling, existence, I metamorphose into a Hork-Bajir, and I help vanquish the evil Yeerks—all, of course, for the greater good of humanity. Will anyone ever understand the simultaneous honor and sacrifice it takes to be an Animorph? Jake here:

We can't tell you who we are. Or where we live. It's too risky, and we've got to be careful. Really careful. So we don't trust anyone. Because if they find us . . . well, we just won't let them find us.

The thing you should know is that everyone is in really big trouble. Yeah. Even you.

Much as I love the reluctant hero, Jake (the boy I want to be), I relate much more to the introverted Tobias, who's picked on in school, who suffers low self-esteem—the boy I *am*. If only everyone could see this kid for who he really is inside: Tobias is intrepid, intelligent, immutably strong. I'd like to someday see myself this way.

I die to get to the end of the book, and die again when I get there. So I start again. And soon—but not soon enough—another book in the series, *The Visitor*, comes out, then another and another, until there are fifty-four. My parents rarely find me without my eyes welded to the page. I know from her face that my mother isn't tickled that I'm reading this kind of illusory fiction, but more than once I overhear my father telling her, "Let the kid read. Why do we care what he's reading, as long as he's got his nose in a book?" My mother tells him she's definitely noticed that since the advent of this obsession, I'm sitting still for once. It looks like my "literary" avocation might continue unhindered.

Except for one problem. Scholastic can't publish the volumes in the Animorph universe fast enough. Why does the science fiction series I so love release its dozens of books at such a painfully slow pace? What the hell is K. A. Applegate *doing* with her time? Baking cookies? What am I supposed to do in between the slow churn of the series development—twiddle my thumbs? I need new characters. New stories.

This desperation forces me back to Borders and the library for multiverses into which I can delve. Thus I begin to sleuth beside Frank and Joe Hardy, who always manage to get in—and then slip right back out of—trouble. I find enough spare energy to walk the eerie, cobbled streets of Ankh-Morpork alongside Sam Vimes, the captain of the City Watch. Not long after, I finally sink my teeth into the vast and intricate world that is *Star Wars*. How few saw Luke's potential. How many might question Yoda's sagacity because of his small stature and funny way of talking. How strong the Force is, if tap into its power you can.

But nothing ever affects me as powerfully as the Animorphs. They can transform themselves into any animal they've ever touched. That's cool in and of itself, but so much more than cool—shape-shifting is my special superpower, too. I see that the adventure of my particular life has always required me to rely on a kind of "morpho-doxy." I need to blend in wherever I can. Wear different masks for different people. One for my Orthodox friends. One for my secular friends. Maybe all kids have to learn this skill, I don't know, but I spend almost all my time wondering whether the me I created for the moment is the right one, the safe one. Since that family conver-sion in 1995, I have learned to turn on a dime, and literally become (or pretend to be) a different person, depending on circumstances. This is not meant to be duplicitous; it's a survival mechanism. I might look perfectly comfortable in my own skin, but it's never the case that I really am. The only place I feel truly safe is when I'm engrossed in a world of fantasy.

At least the long ride to school doesn't seem so laborious anymore. On the contrary, with each newly discovered universe, I find it more and more difficult to unbuckle my seat belt, to open the car door and leave my adventures behind. It feels like a betrayal. Of course, I can't even think of smuggling such blasphemous tomes into school—not since the *Everything Men Know about Women* incident a few months ago—but my friends wait for me on their pages, sheltered between the covers and tucked under the front seat of the car. They never let me down the way flesh-and-blood humans can. That's a marvelous fact about books: Their universes endure for all time, outside of time, on my time.

Nobody—myself the least—would have seen this coming, but I've become a "bibliophile," my mother says. I look it up: Yes. Soon my room transforms into a trophy case of sorts, displaying my only recordable accomplishments in this world. Books upon finished books, whole series, classics and modern, run the length of an entire wall. I'm acutely aware, as my mother makes me turn off my lamp and "Put that book away now," that the people in these universes are not fictional to me. They're realer than real. The way dreams are real. They're Everyman thrust into impossible conundrums, having to constantly prove their mettle, which makes them real heroes, something I could never be. Their strength comes from integrity; their reverence, from studied faith in the invisible rights and wrongs of the world. They are resilient, battle-hardened against defeat. Their lives are so much more interesting than mine. It hurts to reckon the gap between us, between our worlds and between our potentialities.

I say nothing ever affects me so profoundly as the Animorphs—but that doesn't last long.

ARMY OF ONE

1999–2000. "Yeah, Ma. *Yes*. Best behavior today, gotcha."

"I love you, Izzy."

Jeez, Ma . . . Not in front of the other kids. Are you trying to get me killed?

I heave the straps of my backpack onto my little shoulders. Another day in the yeshiva trenches. Another day in the sixth grade of hell.

"*Mrab, mrab, mrab,* this is called a 'gerund.'"

"*Mrab, mrab, mrab,* this is called a 'rhombus.'"

"*Mrab, mrab, mrab*, this is the mighty Judah Maccabee—"

Hold on. *The mighty Who now? Mighty how?* The fog dissipates for almost the first time, and it happens during a Jewish History lesson. Rabbi Becker makes a time machine for me with words and images. With it, I can zap out of the present to wander the desert and fight the good fight with some serious badasses, who, unlike Dov, actually want me on their side. Forefathers, saints, prophets, *false* prophets, idol worshippers. Plagues of frogs and the sinful slaughter of the firstborn. Plotting. Resistance. Hell, yeah—this is what every class should be like. This is almost as cool as my science-fiction books. And this stuff, it really happened?

"Of course it happened," sputters Rabbi Becker—and the books back him up. I pay more and more attention, re-create the scenes the rabbi shapes between 1:00 and 2:15 p.m. each day. Then, one day, I find myself actually looking forward to History class. I'm hooked. I sit enthralled as the rabbi outlines the plight and the triumphs of the ancient Israelites, the Babylonian captivity and its rebellions, the exile from Egypt. "This is real," he says, gravely, as though answering my direst question. Why should that matter when I've spent thousands of hours believing in characters born of authors' imaginations? But it does matter somehow. "This happened. And without this having happened, neither you nor I nor any other Jew, from Brussels to Baltimore, would be here today to recall it." He looks at several of us in turn. I'm sure he lingers on me. "These are your people. Your past is your *self*."

Oh, but how unpleasant our past was. Why did the early Jews have to suffer so much? Have I made myself worthy of their ordeals? I don't know. I have to live with them a little more, as I have done with all the Animorphs and the squad of X-wings under Luke's command. Without ever thinking I was learning per se, building skills, getting better at understanding human nature and the grand sweep of time, all my reading must have somehow cultivated an imagination, a sensi-

109

tivity to detail. So this stuff feels not like it's entombed in history, but that it's crying out still in mortal battle, whispering in the desert. I can taste the gritty sand with each sentence sung by my History teacher, with the turn of each crumpled page of my Torah textbook. Having inadvertently trained myself in the art of fantasizing, it isn't long before I paint myself into the picture—your history is your *self*. And before long, I'm beginning to play a part, as though somehow I matter; I depend on them, and they on me. These really are "my people."

But I don't go back as some schnook slave. I do not travel back agnostic. I return ready for battle, armed to the tonsils. I spend hours rapt in questions and the quest to bridge the distance between us. Are we perpetual victims? Or are we bold? Are we destined for destruction, or will we finally triumph? All I need is a real time machine, an M16, and the cheat code for unlimited ammo—and I can change the course of history, and therefore, change myself. Let's turn those pyramids upside down.

So I am ten, eleven, twelve. In the car on the way home, I gaze out the window contemplatively, still cracking those children's books. But the "real world," as my people have known it, has become far more vital to me. "What's the matter, Izzy?" my mother asks one afternoon.

Where do I start?

"Are you OK? You look—"

"He's been like that all day," my sister says. "Devorah told me she heard from Malkie, whose brother's in Izzy's class."

"Whatever, Jaz."

"So's your face!"

"That doesn't even make sense!"

I cannot put it into words. I can't even think about it very straight. It's just that no amount of mind travel, no number of savage ninja assaults in my fantasies, can console me. The weight of some inarticulate disquiet threatens to crush me. My mother has strong faith.

My father, though he might not exactly toe the line as strictly as my mother, has strong faith. They've both probably forgotten more than I'll ever know about the Jewish people. But I don't know how to ask them my questions, to explain this weird feeling I have, that maybe, just maybe, I really do belong, that I really am finally among "my people." Maybe I always was.

BREAK A LEG

1992. Our little tribe. "Oh, Izzy. *Come on!*" my mother cries out. "I just bought you that onesie, and you're cleaning the stairs with it!"

When she tries to lift me from the stairwell, I go limp as a crash dummy after the test. "Don't wanna!" I don't know how to explain my stubbornness. That if my Tatty could build these steps, this whole entire four-story building, the least I can do is conquer the stairs without any help.

We live on the top floor. President Street, Crown Heights, Brooklyn. I know that much. There's no elevator, and the climb makes my little thighs ache. But I've always insisted on going it alone, even before walking was a thing I had mastered on a flat surface. Before I turned four, the climb was a dizzying blur of fire-engine red and grey concrete passing one inch in front of my chin, again and again. Knowing my father had put this all together made me puff up with pride. I've seen other buildings go up with cranes and cement mixers, and whole teams of builders. But that's not how my Tatty built ours. I picture him waking up one morning with a hammer in hand, a tool belt, and nails poking out of his puckered lips, and by nightfall, our building stands before him. Something for the three of us to call home. Something that used to bring me trembling to my knees each time I tried to defeat it. Until I turned four.

My father possesses the power to create something out of

nothing. That makes him a superhero in my eyes. Never mind that he half created me, and now, Jasmine, which I vaguely understand— I'm more impressed that we're living inside something big and solid and safe that he built. Superman and Batman are on the periphery of my awareness, but my father's the one I most look up to now that I'm older than three.

Like all great superheroes, my father always bursts through the front door in time for dinner. Hands rough and eyes smiling, he's a ball of electricity. He tickles Jasmine, blows farty sounds into her neck until she giggles, then drops to the hardwood floor of the foyer to praise my, at best, lopsided Frankenstein's monster of a "structure," one I've piled out of Lego or wooden blocks—or both mixed together. I always worry my constructions won't pass muster with him, but he never fails to quash those concerns. Most nights, my mother has to drag us both by the ear to the dinner table.

Then, one night, when I'm halfway to age five, even though the smell of spiced spinach has begun to waft into the living room, my father doesn't burst through the door. He doesn't come home at all.

I stay in the entrance hall with my blocks, building something I hope will make him beam. And no matter how hard my stomach grumbles and my taste buds tingle for my favorite dish, I don't ask my mother to wrap me a spinach tortilla. Something about the way she paces the kitchen since that phone call earlier holds me off.

When she's nervous, she pulls out the broom and sweeps. Just this morning, I "helped" her with the chore. "Want to help me sweep again?" she asks, and before I can respond or even nod my head, she says, "Sure you do—but this time, you have to use the broom and dustpan. No cheeks."

I try that for a few seconds, then I get on my hands and knees and begin sucking at the floor in front of me like a street sweeper. "Ah, not again, Izzy!" This time I manage only to find a wad of lint. "Never mind about the sweeping, honey. Go back to your Legos."

What a fun night this is turning out to be. Eventually my mother feeds us. Then, instead of insisting on bedtime, she lets me stay in the hall and play with my action figures long after Jasmine's down for the night.

I'm half asleep as my father passes through the door, but I notice it's more of a hobble than a burst. He flashes me a smile, but all I can see are the two gleaming, silver crutches he uses to ease his body over toward me and my evening's work. He tries to bend down and join me as always, but the effort draws out a shudder and a few winces. I'm not used to seeing his face like this, and it does something to my stomach. From the ground, his whitewashed cast, heel to hip, looks larger than life. He looks like one of Vader's Stormtroopers halfway through donning his white, plastoid armor. "That's quite a skyscraper you got there," he says, using one of his crutches to right a stray corner block. "We'll make a builder out of you yet."

My mother wants to tuck me in, but, after a bit of whiny nego- tiation, she lets me crawl into their bed, where she's propped my father on pillows. "But only for a few minutes." I can't take my eyes off the cast. "Shattered in thirteen places," he tells her. "It was the scaffolding. What can I say—they didn't build it so well. And all that rain didn't help any. They say it was three stories I fell—but it only felt like two."

With both of my hands, I massage his cast. I want to make his pain go away. The texture of the plaster hurts my fingers, but I don't stop kneading. "You're making it feel so much better," he promises.

Next thing I know, I'm waking up in my own bed somehow. I run into my parents' room even before rubbing the night out of my eyes. My father is gone. "Your Dad can't sit still," my mother says from the closet "Not even if his leg depends on it. Would you believe he went to work today? Left before you woke up."

She takes me along for grocery shopping after breakfast. And that's when I see the elaborate spider web of ropes my father set up on each floor to help him navigate up and down the stairs. So, yeah—my father is Spider-Man.

MY LEFT FOOT

September 2008. It's only halfway through advanced training up north in B'kaot, and I've already decided to smash my foot. The only question is—left or right? I suppose I lead with my left, but either way, after it's done, I won't be marching anywhere soon. Except home. I've thought about it, and this is my sole solution. I've put out of my head that this is exactly what cowards have done since the beginning of time. Right now I've got only one thing on my mind: getting home fast, crutches or otherwise. Of course, actually going through with this plan will require the endurance of extreme pain. It's a classic conundrum, Amir's version of the catch-22: The pussy longs for home so severely he's willing to break his own leg. But because he's pussy, he can't quite muster the guts. Pussy boys don't possess the intestinal fortitude to follow through on their big plans. But without seeing this task through, pussy boy cannot go home.

Maybe I can find someone else man enough to un-catch my 22.

It's the week leading up to Rosh Hashanah—Jewish New Year. The biblical name for the holiday translates as "The Day of Shouting/ Blasting." There'll be plenty of that as bones crunch.

I remember Lieutenant Fuks came up to me that Sabbath a couple of months ago when I first got the awful news from home about my father. "Why the long face?" he asked. This was only the third time he'd spoken to me since the start of advanced training, so I must've really looked like crud.

I told him, vaguely, what they did to my dad. He said the Israeli military might be able to help. I told him, specifically, that the American government was accusing my father of pocketing millions of dollars. He sputtered, which was the first outside confirmation I'd gotten about the absurdity, the hopelessness, of my situation at home. I also hadn't known that Fuks was even capable of sputtering. Based on the severity of the accusations, he said, "Sorry, looks like your dad's on his own. But I guess you knew that."

I moped around base for the next few weeks, stunned. I completed my drills and exercises without talking to a soul, barely noticed the live ammo whizzing by me as we fought the cardboard enemies who held the higher ground. Everyone assumed the language barrier had gotten my tongue, little appreciating the gravity of my woe. A wall had been built especially for my family, seven hundred feet tall and made of ice, just like the one that bounds the northern border of the Seven Kingdoms. Everyone else on base was focused on hurtling over our puny, seven-foot training number in full gear. But the Ice Wall at home was insurmountable. Heads were bound to roll.

Not that the hurtles in advanced training were so puny. All the nonsense in basic training about discipline, routine, and responsiveness took a back seat to the actual, difficult combat training: long marches, challenging shooting ranges, and weeks drilling in the field. All of this served as a decent distraction. I might have been the only soldier who found himself in the paradoxical situation of preferring the purgatory of advanced training to the hell of real life.

Now we've spent the week at Yad La-Shiryon, the Armored Corps Memorial Site and Museum at Latrun, twenty minutes outside Jerusalem. The British-era Tegart fort includes one of the world's most extensive tank collections, with a theater where our commanders opened up a free channel of communication about the morality and values the IDF expected us to uphold for as long as we wore the uniform.

We also learned about heroic tank squadrons of the past. I was struck in particular by one badass, Lt. Zvika Greengold. The reservist got off his kibbutz couch on Yom Kippur 1973 after hearing Israeli fighter jets streaming overhead, which was unheard of on a high holy day unless something real was going down. Zvika scanned the frequencies on his military band radio; heard the frantic reports of Egyptians attacking Israeli positions on the Suez Canal to the south; hitched a ride to a vital crossroads; commandeered two bombed and bedraggled British-built Centurion tanks hastily ditched and unmanned in the corner of a base full of wounded IDF troops; radioed Brigade HQ, and informed them he intended to lead a "tank force" in a battle against the *five* Syrian armored tank *divisions*— more than two thousand Russian-made T-62s. Talk about Greengold and Goliath.

Owing to the massive demobilization for the solemn day of fasting, Israel had only about 188 tanks total defending the perilous gateway in the Golan Heights. Zvika commanded from two to a max of some sixteen tanks, and he had to keep switching out as more and more of them took fire. Too soon, the "Zvika Force" was dwindled down to one tank. For thirty hours, despite shrapnel wounds and terrible burns over half of his body, despite some of his comrades ditching and turning tail, Zvika single-handedly held off the invading forces. Without the lieutenant, Israel might have lost the Six-Day War. For his inconceivable bravery under fire, Zvika Greengold stood proud as he received the Medal of Valor.

Many years later, during the weeks leading up to Yom Kippur 2008, I would not be standing proud like Zvika. In fact, I wouldn't be standing at all. Not once I broke my own foot.

With Rosh Hashanah coming up, we'd all be granted four full days at home, days without marching, days without patrolling, but most important, days *with* our families, which everyone needed desperately. Maybe no one more so than I did since I received the news of my father's arrest.

Well, we wouldn't *all* be granted those days. Back on base, we have to decide amongst ourselves which two of us will stay on-site for the holidays. Two recruits from each company must remain on the training base at all times to prevent any theft of military gear—more on the questionable value of that later. We were reaching the end of the week, and so far we had only one sacrifice. It's Oren, the guy who's still rail-thin, no matter how many snacks Fuks rams down his throat. Fuks revoked his leave after he busted the poor kid playing Snake on his brand-new iPhone 3G while he was supposed to be on guard duty. "And next time," promised Fuks in a cool monotone, "I'll shove those thumbs straight up your ass."

Time's running out now to make a decision about the second sucker who'll have to remain. So, one afternoon, we assemble in a platoon-sized circle. Each person gives his reason for not volunteering. Some of the reasons are legit—parents calling it quits, an opportunity to make some shekels on whatever contractor job, "troubles" with the girlfriend. Others are idiotic: "Don't wanna." Or, "I couldn't give less of a damn about you guys, so why should it be me?"

And then it comes my turn. The sun is burning all our faces, causing everyone to squint. What can I say? Remembering Fuks's reaction, I don't want to tell them that my father's been put in prison for supposedly stealing $18 million. That if I have to stay, my mother and sisters will be spending the holidays alone for the first time ever. No Ta. No Izzy. Neither man nor puss to hold down the fort. The wound is too fresh to poke like that. I opt to stay silent. What are the chances it'll be me anyway? Omnipresent entities don't let that kind of thing happen—God, no.

The Circle of Confession clearly isn't leading anyone to volunteer. Then Oren, who's getting bored and, anyway, has nothing to lose, suggests a lottery. "Sure. Everyone puts their name in a helmet, and the person who gets picked out first stays on base. With me." As though a weekend with Oren is adequate recompense for missing out on leave.

This kind of lottery's been banned by the IDF since forever, I suppose because we should all be clambering to volunteer to support each other and the greater cause, *blah blah blah*. For lack of a better option, though, Fuks turns a blind eye. He tells us that brass frowns on lotteries because they don't really give the chosen soldier the option to decline.

So Fuks waits for us all to agree before we toss our names into the helmet. Some are more reluctant than others, but there they are, thirty-five crumpled slips of paper. Seriously—what are the chances? One in thirty-five. I got this. I feel safe as we all peer into the sea of white shreds, and Oren, who's milking his fifteen seconds of fame, slowly reaches in.

Two minutes later, the other soldiers have shuffled back into the barracks, and I stand there under the glaring sun, in disbelief. My name, *IZZY E.*, materialized out of that heap as though God were deliberately screwing with me.

A couple of days later, I watch as all the other soldiers don their dress uniforms and leave giddily for the holidays, for home. Some of them are empathetic—"Sorry, bud. I'll drink a Goldstar in your honor. Maybe two." Others spout obnoxious words as they leave the bunk—"Check your karma, dude. You musta really pissed the Big Guy off."

After I snap myself out of the immediate funk, I start to contemplate ways of getting myself home. By the time night falls, the base is a ghost town. Oren's off playing Snake on his bunk while I spend the first hours of the holiday guarding the perimeter. I need to get home. They're alone right now. And it's my fault. I try to drum up the guts to break my pinkie with the stock of my rifle against the concrete wall. Can't see it through.

I spend the next day fantasizing novel ways of wounding myself bad enough to get sent home, but not so bad as to cause any permanent damage or too much pain. I could smash my front teeth in. "Came out of nowhere, Sarge, a brick with the Syrian flag!" I could gouge my leg with a kitchen knife—*Whoops*. Aiming for the PBJ and hit the ACL.

It's not until the *next* day that I discover the courage and then the opportunity to go home to my family in their hour of need. Oren and I fall under the command of a sergeant major. We don't even know his name. He's a bully, a mouth-breather with a bulbous belly. We call him Master Sergeant Soprano. But this career soldier can't bear the idea of any of his men napping idly on base, playing Snake, or playing with his own snake, as it were, in the empty barracks. So instead, he has us cleaning up the many parade grounds on base. And for the last three hours, he's ordered us to lug massive chunks of sidewalk from one place to another. Each slab must weigh almost a quarter ton. It takes all our strength in tandem to heft each block. It starts to feel like an absurdist prison camp, like something out of Kafka or one of the Russians.

Oren and I break from our slave labor, and I break down and confess to him my dilemma.

"*Prison?* Damn. For how long?" He stubs a half-smoked Marlboro Light against the heel of his boot, then tucks it behind his ear.

"I don't know. But my mother's freaking out."

"Oh, sure."

"Look, I need a ticket home," I tell him, feeling the heat creep to my face as I speak the words aloud. "It's important."

"No sweat. So what's on the menu? Broken nose?"

"Settle down, Oren. I'm fugly enough without your help."

"Right, the ears. So what are you thinking?"

"Introduce one of those big rocks over there to my foot. It'll swell up. We can say one of these giant concrete turds fell while we were moving it, *as ordered*."

"Yeah. That's good. They'll have no choice but to send you home."

"Right."

"Just promise you won't forget the hero of this story, Izzy. Promise you'll tell your grandkids that it was ol' Oren, your bestest, bestest pal who saved—"

"Damn, Oren. Fine. Just do it."

"All right, all right. Which foot then?"

"The right, I guess. No—left."

I look around for witnesses. Nobody here but us chickens. I lean on a light pole for balance. I thrust out my left foot and commence cringing.

Oren stands beside me with a smooth stone in his double-handed grip. It's nearly the size of a volleyball, like the one I won years ago for holding my breath in the pool. I hold my breath again now. "You sure about this?" he asks. He's tipping forward from the heft of it, skinny dude that he is. "You ran this whole scenario?"

I nod and grimace. To his credit, Oren doesn't flinch. But when I see the rock hurtling toward my fragile foot like a comet tracking dinosaurs, my instincts take over. I jerk my leg out of the way just in time. The rock leaves a little crater in the hard earth beside my twitching leg. We stare at it. Oren's got a dumb smile on his face. He scratches where his butt should be, for what seems like a long while. "All right. I see what went wrong here. You need to look away. Then you won't know when it's coming."

"What—have you done this before?" He shrugs, and after relighting his cigarette, he lifts the stone again. All I can think about now is military law, and what happens if the truth about this comes out. I'll be heading to prison, just like my father, because, for the next few years, my body isn't my own. Every inch of this generally useless piece of equipment—including the left foot—belongs exclusively to the IDF. And damaging military property is a grave offense, tantamount to attacking the State of Israel. So, worse than going to war with myself, I'm warring against the entire entity I swore to defend. I'm seconds from becoming a traitor. But what about loyalty to my family?

"I'm gonna count to five so you can get ready, so it's not a complete shock. Ready?"

"Go for it, man." I shut my eyes tight. All black. Oren takes in a deep breath, ready to serve me the volleyball. I'm holding my breath.

"OK, on five. *One . . . two—*"

I hear the sickening crunch before my brain can register pain. The black behind my eyelids morphs red and piercing white. Then comes the rush of adrenaline, mercifully overwhelming the pain. "Do it again!" I hear a voice shout. It's my own voice, but I've retreated somewhere far away to cower from the gremlins crawling out from cracks in the concrete.

"Sure?"

"Just do it!"

Kkrrunnch!

As I scuttle back inside myself, I find I'm writhing on the ground and moaning. Above me, Oren's smiling with that cigarette dangling, satisfied he's done me and the world a solid. I have the presence of mind to recognize how true this is—and what a chance he's taken to help my family. He could be court-martialed, too, for deliberately damaging military property. "You're a—thanks, Oren."

"Anytime. You need another limb busted, hit me up." Oren tosses his Marlboro Light into a clump of bushes that we just labored to clear of butts two hours ago. "Now what?"

The whole lower half of my body is one big throb as Sergeant Soprano arrives on foot to check up on his chattel. He looks down at me but addresses Oren. "What's with him?"

"Sir, one of the concrete slabs fell on his foot."

The sergeant major's shirt, I notice, is partially untucked in the front. From the ground I have a clear view of his belly button stuffed with an odd-tinted lint. Hands on his hips, he surveys the scene, breathing like a leaf blower. Yep, there's the slab. There's the injured private. The foot. I can tell he, too, plays out the whole scenario in his

DISARMED

head. I can smell something burning. He takes it to its rational conclusion—which will be *his* injured *ass*. I see his face turn from vague concern to outright hostility. "You need to be really damn stupid to drop a sidewalk on your foot!" he rants. "I mean—you're supposed to move 'em—not drop 'em on your goddamn—"

"Sir, do you think maybe we should take him to the hospital? Looks pretty bad."

"Do I think—? Yes! Yes, my driver will take him."

An hour later, I'm in the X-ray room.

Not for the first—or the last—time.

DRIVING BLIND

I'm fourteen, on break from yeshiva, and I've been whining for about an hour. I really don't want to go with my father to a parlor meeting in Miami. Why would any kid want to attend an event honoring some random Israeli terror victim? Even a dentist could diagnose my galloping ADHD—how am I supposed to sit still? Listen to some boring speech? And what the hell is a "parlor meeting" anyway? Are they holding a séance?

And then Eyal Neufeld, the terror victim, begins to speak. I'm sitting on the staircase at the edge of a crowded living room, my hands on the railings. With his first word, a hush descends over the room. "Here's the story," he says. "I'm a nineteen-year-old off-duty soldier. I'm riding the 361 Har Meron bus home. We're near the northern Israeli city of Safed. A man shouts just before my stop. Something in Arabic. I turn and watch the passenger who was just sitting beside me stand up and hug another Israeli soldier right behind me. Why this hug? And then they both blow up. Nine people are murdered, ten seriously wounded, and that's the last image I'll ever see—a Hamas killer hugging one of my own."

I'm stunned. Why did my father take me here?

"My lungs and spleen are shredded. My nose, my skull, my eye sockets, my neck, my jaw, and my right hand are all broken or fractured. I'm in a coma for two months. When I finally wake up, I'm blind and deaf. I'm at Rambam Hospital in Haifa, but I don't know it yet. I'm convinced I've been captured by Hamas. I think the mysterious people poking and prodding are terrorists torturing me."

The fuzz on my neck stands on end.

"It isn't until the staff finds a way to communicate with me—big plastic letters—that I realize I'm home. And these strange figures I can't see or hear are trying to help me."

I feel dizzy, and I shut my eyes reflexively.

When I open my eyes again, I look over the whitewashed living room, scrutinizing the well-to-do patrons who've come to contribute to Eyal's cause. I watch their eyes as they watch the blind man. "This darkness travels with me 24/7. It drives me crazy, if I'm honest. I can't escape it. A totally obscure, black, colorless, formless space that is my universe. I may be blind and deaf, but I'm not retarded," he says. "So all the 'ifs' haunt that darkness. What if I picked another seat? What if I jumped out the window after I heard the shout? What if? What if?"

He continues, but I hear nothing more. Until my father says, "Let's meet him."

"What? No."

But he's already dragged me down the stairs and through the crowd across the room. I'm relieved Eyal can't see the way I'm staring at his scars, the weird, deep-seated way his dead eyes look. His hearing aids. I slip from my father's grip and beat a quick retreat back to my perch behind the banister. Everyone is still in "hush" mode, so I can hear the conversation my father's having with Eyal. "Sorry this happened to you."

"Yeah, me too."

"Are they showing you a good time while you're here in Miami?"

"*Showing?*"

"*Oy*, I'm so—"

"Relax. Just teasing."

"So . . . what do you like to do?"

"I'm sorry?"

"What are your hobbies?"

"My hobbies?"

"Sure. Stuff you like to do for fun."

"Well, I enjoy fast cars."

"Really!?" says my father. "Same here."

"I used to dream about owning something, you know, with epic torque," says Eyal.

"Have you ever been in a Z8?"

"The BMW? Not yet, but I hear it's a beaut."

"Listen, Eyal. I've got an idea . . . What do they have you doing tomorrow?"

I'm not present the day my father lets a blind terror victim loose on the racetrack in a silver convertible roadster. Of course he would never put my life at risk even if he hadn't staged his stunt on a *school day*. But while the rabbis blather on about Jewish law, language, and custom, I look out the window at the wind-ruffled palms. And when I close my eyes I can hear a blind man's triumphant howl, the wind whipping through his hair, and that exhilarating torque roaring underfoot.

That's the kind of guy my father is. Always was.

Growing up, we got to spend time together after school while we accomplished our separate, yet equally important, objectives. Like back when I was nine.

"Take that, Batman!" I yip, as Superman's booted foot meets the center of the Dark Knight's tight black spandex.

"Of course," my father says into the phone. "Count me in."

"*Kapow!*" I respond, sending the Batmobile on a perfect trajectory for the stairs.

"Whatever you need," my father says reassuringly into the receiver. Batman moans on the steps of city hall in Metropolis, or maybe Gotham—hard to keep track. "Yes. Sure. Do you want me to mail the check to—? OK, come and pick it up."

He hangs up. "Izzy," he says. "You know what *tzedakah* is, right?"

"Charity."

"Not quite. It means 'righteousness.' We don't separate charity from duty when it comes to the needy. That means anyone—poor, sick, handicapped, refugee—and always without causing them embarrassment, or showing off that you're the big spender. See, giving is something no one can ever take away from you. They can take your money, your material possessions. But once our good deeds are done, that's forever."

I nod comprehension, but inside, a deep-seated fear begins to mount in my nine-year-old head. I'm worried all this giving could start to hurt us—but that's only part of my anxiety. My real fear, what truly scares me, is the likelihood that I'll never be able to keep up with him, that I'll never be able to be as giving. Or to give him the *naches* he deserves. How could I ever compete?

ARMS AROUND HER

October 2008. With my goal of getting home to my family, by any means, finally achieved, I hobble straight from my hospital stint to our apartment in Jerusalem. Only this time, my father's not tinkering or talking on the phone. This time, he's in New York, under house arrest, as he awaits trial. My mother opens the door, and the smells of holiday dinner waft from behind her. "Hi, Ma." We hug.

"Izzy! What happened? Why are you limping? My God."

"It doesn't matter. I'm home."

She's crying. I'm wearing Oren's grin.

Later, we're at the dinner table. I'm supposed to be saying the blessing for the fruit of the earth, but I'm just staring at the plate in front of me, stoned on pain. As if in sympathy with my father, I see I'm also in a prison. I'm trapped inside the skin of a complete wimp—the lowest of the low. Maybe this will be a life sentence. Why couldn't I have just gone AWOL? Just left the base and suffered the consequence for abandoning my post? Instead, I struck the only body I'll ever get. This isn't a video game. I don't get to restart each level, like Mario, wearing new suspenders on his fresh set of bones. What really makes me anxious is how good it felt—how satisfying. As though my troubles had always been awaiting some physical expression. As if cracking open my skeleton was the only way to release the voice inside.

I put the strange fruit down, something red with spikes that I've never tasted. I don't deserve to eat so well while my father sits starved for freedom. I look at my three sisters' faces, one by one. I swear to the universe that if we survive this, I will *never* again be a pussy. The only thought that gets me through this fire is the certainty that I will absolutely keep my vow. That starts with instantly, right now, becoming the man of the house for my mother and my sisters.

"I'm sorry," I say. "Sorry for letting things get this bad."

My mother looks up from her plate. "Oh, Izzy," she says. "So much of life is out of our control. Look what happened to your father. And what about your foot?"

I bite my tongue, hard.

"*HaShem* works in mysterious ways," she concludes.

"*HaShem* is everywhere!" Shoshi exclaims. Six years old, and spreading mushy carrots everywhere.

"That's right," my mother says, praising.

"That's right," I echo for my mother's sake, and I see the gratitude in her eyes. That's when I make her a promise. "Nothing will ever hurt this family again. You have my word."

Later I'll deal with the IDF's marred property—right now, these people need me.

Chapter 6

PHANTOM FUCKFACE

January 8–9, 2009. Soroka Hospital. Waking up in ICU Recovery is about as much fun as being born. *Breech*. And, on top of everything, I was "born" missing a limb. Almost instantly I understand I have a bed-partner. Phantom pain is sharing my sheets, spooning me, laughing in his dream. This Fuckface and I are going to be an official couple from now on. He's turned me into a housewife numbing myself all day on opiates as he's out there partying it up with hotter, younger babes. I wish to file for divorce. But he's in this for life. *I'll always come home to you*, Phantom whispers in my ear.

I keep coming back into consciousness, only to hear everyone yammering about the "soul." Meantime, isn't it my body that's broken? Let's get our priorities straight. One young nurse compliments my inner strength—just because I'm not blubbering, I guess—and says she can tell I have a good *neshama* (soul). "You'll get through this. Trust me. I've seen a thousand—I can tell." Would I get through it? One old doctor says to a younger one—I don't think he knows I can hear—that I'm about to enter "the long, dark night of the soul." I presume this means I'll be lying awake for some months wondering what the hell a nice *boychik* like me was even doing out there on the Gaza border. And what the hell I'm supposed to do now that I left my arm there.

They ask if I've gotten morphine. It's right there on the chart, but I say *no*, and *I can use some, please*. It's the only thing that puts PF to sleep. That gives me time to consider my predicament. I wonder, when I do all the soul-searching I know people must do when they

127

find themselves in my kind of rare snafu—what will I find down there? I suspect tumbleweeds. Maybe a pair of sarcastic vultures cawing atop a dead olive tree limb. A pile of sheep dung entertaining flies by the trunk.

The door to the emergency bunker stands slightly ajar, allowing the florescent bulbs that line the hallway to cast a dim glow inside. Whitewashed walls. Cheap, tiled floors. Fuckface loves the décor. I find it isn't such a cheerful place, nor aesthetically pleasing. But it is *anesthetically* wonderful. Plenty of pain meds swim through my system. Plenty. The grim ambiance and the morphine infusion meld my surroundings into a warbling silhouette, caressed by the fluorescence above. If not for the privacy curtains between each bed, I might be able to just make out the contours of the other four battered soldiers recovering with me in the fortified room.

But I can't. PF and I have the space to ourselves. Within hours, an endless parade of visitors stream in, distracting me from reality five minutes at a time. They all bear gifts. It's only been a few hours since my surgery, and the nurses have had to clear out a closet for all the "Get Well" presents. Lots of junk food: Gummy worms. Almond cookies. Rugelach. Delicious-smelling licorice from Australia. Jerky from South Africa. My stomach is sick, so I can't eat any of it. No one brings me Mike and Ikes.

As the first evening wears on, responding to the visitors makes me more and more winded, so the hospital staff stems the stream. I just want to sleep. During sleep, I won't have to think about the past or future. I'll be . . . nothing. Empty.

The soul: Sure, I believe in the soul. I just don't believe I have one. There are certainly people who have souls. Those three lovely medics in the ambulance, the nurses, the doctors (well, some of them). The visitors who bucked up and kept from crying when they saw me, knowing they needed to be strong. My mother, God bless her, has a soul the size of Cincinnati. What I have, I know, is a black hole surrounded by body chalk where my soul's supposed to be, possibly used to be. And now some helpful CSI guy has erased one of the arms in my outline.

No sleep. The others—the guys behind the curtains—seem to find some peace through their drug-induced comas. Have I already built up a tolerance for the morphine? No way. The drugs are making me want to puke. Or maybe that's just the world spinning now, dizzying me with morose, unanswerable questions: Did I let my unit down? What could I have done differently? Who could love me now? What girl will ever want to—? Is this the final straw that will kill my father, break my mother's heart? If I can focus on something, I can ease the nausea for long moments at a time. But my eyes dart around the bunker, searching, searching. For what?

My soul?

In the sparse light, I can identify, just barely, the outline of the IV bag that hangs above and to the right of my bed. Eyes glued to the drizzle, I watch the bag slowly dispense its cocktail into my body. And I simply . . . breathe. The paradox is that every breath sustaining me feeds Fuckface, too, currently teething on the wound like a sarlacc in the Dune Sea of Tatooine.

When I break my concentration, I notice the hubbub of the hospital ward has died down considerably. I hear only the rhythmic beeping of the life-support machines and various monitors. No. There's something else. Some animal in here, some wounded thing. It's the intermittent moans escaping from the bed across from me. I know now from the nurses' talk, and a glimpse I got when they opened the curtain, that a mangled reservist lay there. I try to muster some sympathy, or empathy, or whatever it's called. I feel nothing. I feel that his whining is going to drive me insane. I need more morphine. He needs way more morphine.

But, screw this moaning son of Satan stationed across from me.

Yes. Where my soul should be starts spinning, a swirling vortex like those dust devils in the desert. My entire mission now is to mute this human air horn. In an alternate dimension, I'd be the cantankerous old man on the floor below him banging the ceiling with a broom handle, demanding he shut off his blasted EDM and let a guy get some goddamn sleep.

No more alternate realities for me. Despite all the drugs in my system, my situation smacks me in the face with the here and now, the truth of my new normal. I've spent a good ten thousand hours reading fantasy and science fiction all throughout my youth. And now I come to find no force field shielded me from a simple mortar. It's the catastrophe on planet Hoth all over again. I couldn't catch the bomb in my web, wind up, and chuck it into the clouds like Spidey. No high-tech bio-suit built by Lucius Fox protected me.

No. Batman, with all his gadgetry and stealth, would *never* lose an arm. And try as I might now, I can't morph my body into something else, something whole, something that doesn't hurt like hell. Damn them all, my heroes of the past. Real heroes look like Zvika Greengold, the tank squadron leader who faced off the entire Syrian Army. Fire from a T-62 burned more than half his body, shrapnel cut him up, but still he fought on for *hours*.

My gaming console is the only war zone where I can boast anything close to Zvika's heroics. For the rest of my time on Earth, I now know, I will never forget that you don't get a second life. You don't get resurrected after that melancholy "Game Over" music plays your blinking corpse off screen. If I ever dare forget that, I'm certain PF will be there to remind me. Dick.

I take a risk and look down at my bandages. They're tightly wrapped in a way that's causing the amputation to pulse, and yet, red and yellow shades of goop manage to seep through the weaves. My eyes move from my left "arm" to my left foot. I cannot believe what I did to myself four months ago. My leg, I notice, pulses, too. I can fully sense both damaged areas but, mercy, these meds are performing their magic. Both spots are warm and fiery, as if my arm and leg are old buddies, knocking back cheap shots of tequila at the pub. I can feel in the twin pulses how each injury's dancing to a different tempo. The amputation throbs strong and slow like the heart of a brave Wookiee, while the pulse in my ankle flutters and jumps like a skittish womp rat.

How could I? How? When at any moment, this *kind of thing could have happened to me—what the hell was I* thinking? *Or did this happen because I—?*

Don't go there, Iz. The first step in your new reality, the only option, is to grit your teeth and keep moving. You've got to honor your vow. The I'll-Never-Again-Be-a-Pussy Promise. Be more like Amir, will you? For once? Now's your chance.

But first I have to try to filter out the cries of my neighbor. It becomes a kind of contest. Who will win the Nobel Peace-and-Quiet Prize? I could trounce this guy with my silence. By my grit.

A visiting soldier told me the poor guy's story, how he was a reservist whose unit had been sent to a rally point on a building outside of Gaza. As he prepared his gear for battle, he simply tumbled over the roof's ledge. Corporal H. Dumpty just plummeted off the three-story building, head first. He owes his life to a wide-open casement window that jutted out on his path to Skull Crack City. This guy can forever trace his lifetime supply of living back to a solid wooden window frame. To some random resident who wanted a breeze, or to get rid of the fish smell in his kitchen. What about me? Am I supposed to be grateful now? It seems as though I should be, but gratitude, I bet, comes from the soul.

His howls pierce the stale air of our chamber. I hate this guy. So what if the window frame shattered his whole leg from ankle to hip like one of those fluorescent tube light bulbs? My father went back to work *the next day* after shattering thirteen bones when he fell three stories. So what if a window frame spun the reservist around so that he landed ass-first and cracked his coccyx? Who needs a totally intact assbone?

You gotta shut up, guy. Please. You're alive. Shut up and deal with it. At least you've still got all your limbs. I'd give my leg now to have an arm splintered in thirteen places.

His reply to my psychic message? A long, pitiful lament, like some Jersey Shore floozy crumpled over a public toilet after a long night of boozing.

My squad mate, Rabbi, resting right beside me, has suffered a shattered femur by shrapnel—and he's not whining. In fact, fifty other wounded men—all undergoing untold agony—lay within a hundred-meter radius of us. Why is this trooper so special, his pain so much more unbearable? Some of these soldiers will never see or walk again—or jerk off with their more maneuverable hand—while Sissy Pants over here, with all his limbs still attached, will likely make a full recovery. He'll go back to playing ball in Gan Sacher Park, or dancing with his girlfriend, with only the faintest limp, if that. A girlfriend who'll be all the more attracted to her beau's "courage under fire." Not repulsed by a gnarly *stump*. God, even the word disgusts me. I'll never get used to it.

More morphine. *Mmm.* What's it like to be absent a soul? I'm not sure I mind the lack. Just because I can't connect with my deepest self, the place where the fear is, the pain, the dark abyss, doesn't mean I'm a bad person. Don't I possess morals? Didn't I just fight and sacrifice for something I believed in? Shouldn't I feel proud to stand up for all the soulful people out there who need defending? That has to be worth something. I might not be Zvika Greengold—who is? But I have so far kept my vow.

Maybe it's the drugs. Maybe it's the fact that I'm not crying that's sent all the pain inside, bundled it up in a concentrated ball of agony and self-recrimination, all targeted at this asshole in his darkest hour. I feel I can travel outside myself. I've already gone. I'm whispering to the injured trooper, right in his ear. I tell him to shut his frickin' pickle-hole—and he won't.

I look at his face. I see myself. Lying there, moaning, so sorry for himself, so pained. Exhausted.

Why can't we sleep?

Phantom is wide-awake, grinning like the Joker. *Why so serious?*

ARM-WRESTLING WITH GOD

Hours pass. The steady blip of my heart monitor punctuates the pitch-black, and the constant buzz in my ears. How long has it been? Maybe two days since they took my arm, and the fumes exuding from my charred flesh show no sign of dissipating. Red has stopped leaking from the bandage. I can't say the same for yellow. Somehow yellow's so much more unsettling.

A blur of more visitors hovers just over the veil of my awareness. The closet across from me is brimming. Multiple DVD players. Game Boys. Laptop computers. Cartons upon cartons of cigarettes—I'll send them to the platoon. All this candy, too. And I'll be damned—Starburst. You're welcome, Amir.

Phantom is going to kill me.

The simplest way I can describe the genesis of this seemingly extraneous pain is by dissecting what happens when you stick your hand beneath a scalding tap.

So what goes down? Your nervous system amps to high alert, sending distress signals to your limb, which instantly warns your brain that, *Uh-oh, our fragile body is in harm's way. Retract that hand!*

Simple enough.

But what happens when the stressor is far graver than hot water? When a part of that nervous system literally explodes, and the resulting twisted wiring leads to a perpetual cycle of warning. Some amputees suffer a lifetime of real pain in a place on their body that no longer exists on this astral plane. Remember—"pain" has no substance or form. It's only an electrochemical signal process.

Retract that hand!

"What hand, Phantom? *What* fucking hand?"

The morphine barely takes the edge off anymore, and despite the darkness, pain is casting deep shadows on everything. I'm trying hard to see past the hurt, but my vision's gone opaque—that's probably the drugs. I keep my thumb cemented to the morphine regulator, which turns into a struggle of wakefulness over pain. When I drift off, though I still can't sleep, I lose my grip on the button. When I lose my grip, the pain returns. If I could just get my hands on some Scotch tape, I'd secure the damn button in place.

It's hand, *not* hands, *you cripple.* That's PF talking. *And you'll never be able to tie anything in place again—even your own shoes. And you'll probably never wrap a piece of tape for the rest of your miserable life.* And that's when it hits me. The pain sharpens the dark horizon of my thoughts.

Wrapping.

Tefillin.

The memory's as fresh as my wound. We all wrapped *tefillin.*

"Oh my God."

"What's wrong?" It's Rabbi's voice from the dark behind his curtain. It muddles my thoughts like a stone hitting the silt at the bottom of a pond.

"Can you remember what we did, Lior? You know, what we were doing *right before*—?"

"Yeah, we wrapped *tefillin.* Of course I remember—it was my idea!" He spent precious minutes circling the tent—right before it began raining death on us—so that we could each attach his personal straps using our dominant arms before entering Gaza.

One small black leather box containing scrolls of parchment

inscribed with verses from the Torah goes on the upper arm, with its strap wrapped around the hand and arm, then through the fingers in a particular way. You place the other box against the upper forehead. "Don't you find it strange," I ask Rabbi, "that right after we prayed, we got slammed by a goddamn rocket?"

No answer. I can almost hear him thinking.

Across from me, the trooper weighs in with another long moan.

"OK, so maybe it's *kinda* strange," he admits, hesitantly.

"Kind of?" I feel a rage growing, something I am powerless to control. "Seriously, Rabbi. Listen. Five months I don't touch *tefillin*, not once since the end of Basic." My jaw is grinding, half from the pain and half from being stoned. I attempt to unclench it. "Then the day I do—the same *hour*, I get . . . I . . ." I'm shaking my head from side to side. The morphine makes a rainbow in front of my eyes, then all those colors bleed into red. Something inside me has been stirred awake. It's the dark and snarling tornado again, and it threatens to tear me open at the seams, and snap up everything around me.

"Oh, Izzy, I—"

"—Five months for me, maybe," I mutter, my jaw locked firmly in place still, "but for some of the others? Lior—they haven't put *tefillin* on once since turning thirteen. Except for *right before the freaking sky caved in on us*."

Tears fill the corners of my eyes, on the brink of rolling down the bridge of my nose. I will not let them fall. I'd hate myself for crying. Maybe I'll get back to that in a couple of months.

It's silent for a long time while I await an answer. Finally, Rabbi says, "Here's the thing, Izzy: We don't always know why these things happen."

I can barely hear him over the typhoon inside me. I can tell my blood pressure is rising, not only from some beeping machine to which an umbilical cord attaches me. But I receive that interesting bit of data via the blood, which flows in the direction of my freshly-sealed wound. It throbs right there like some barometer of my emotions. Each brutal thump threatening to rip open the seams of my stitching, both physical and psychic. "Five months," I repeat, though I can't pry open my teeth to say it. My teeth are the gates holding back—everything.

"It's good you wrapped, Izzy. But it wasn't the *tefillin*—"

"Oh, yeah? Well, God sure picked a hell of time to tear us a new one." Now I really *do* give God the finger, which feels weird, coming as it does from my right hand.

"You're forgetting something over there. Maybe putting on *tefillin* was the *one* reason we wound up in the hospital now instead of getting shipped home to our parents in boxes. What do you think of that?"

Phantom is nodding in consideration of this prospect.

This conversation is over. Rabbi Lior and I lay in silence. For the next hour, I cannot decipher ass from elbow of my disturbing revelation. I assume my faithful friend has fallen asleep and not died. I almost drift away, too.

How do you reason with the blindly faithful? Was it necessary for me to be so black-and-white, denouncing and renouncing God with dramatic finality, to my friend a few feet away in a parallel bed behind an infectious curtain? Did I need to take a steaming dump on his beliefs to solidify mine? He's neither dead nor asleep over there. I picture his grimace as he tries to find a comfortable position. Let Lior lie there, his soul content with his interpretation of the bloodshed and the murder of my arm. How does that harm me? Why should it offend? I can tell by his breathing that he's plunging back into the vegetative state. So I'm left alone in my sulking. Not alone—I don't have God, but I do have Fuckface still, hand in the air, head-banging to Korn. My friend the ad hoc rabbi left us here, alone to brood, so let the brooding begin. Let the freak off the leash.

Seriously? God spared us because we prayed? I should throw this cup over the curtain and whack Rabbi in the teeth. Did GOD do that, Lior? Why didn't He spare you a Jell-O concussion?

Why did his kind words and thoughtful actions rub me so wrong? The tips of my oversized ears begin to burn. I feel nuclear fusion in the back of my throat. My religious friend—for whom I have deep respect and love—has somehow with his words unlatched a Pandora's box. But a kind of reverse Pandora's box, one ravenously waiting to be filled since my soul's departure. It sits, gaping, inside me, between me and Rabbi. No hope for a soul.

A fiery blast is breathing into me from somewhere, spilling into my skull and my chest, and pushing up against the backs of my eye sockets. It feels like a mob of mind-gnomes banging their pitchforks and torches against the portals through which I view the world, trying to escape and burn it all down.

Phantom is tanning his face on the flames, a sun reflector held up under his chin.

Have I always been such a pessimist? A cynic? Some kind of loner? Maybe. One thing a devastating injury affords you is a lengthy hospital stay. Time—which, of course, you never asked for but you're stuck with now—to *get to know yourself.* To entertain those gnomes inside you. To go spelunking in all the empty parts of you where some stray shards of life, brutalized and deformed, yet lurk on the former playground of your soul.

This self-knowledge comes in pugilistic punches in the ring down there, and any one of the monsters can knock you on your ass when startled. Any dragon hiding in your darkest caverns can spring forth, fire and fangs.

Did some old, bearded man on a throne in the sky really keep us alive because we performed an ancient rite, a holy ritual? What if that is the only reason we're alive? Rabbi's right on one count, at least. It could have been so much worse. God's grace? Fate? Random happenstance? Was it meant to be?

It can't be. That timeworn tale smells worse than my charred upper body.

What if my doubt is an even bigger middle finger to the Higher Mind that thought enough of me to save me?

I click the bye-bye button.

Please. Knock me out. Stop this spinning. If I lost both arms, would Rabbi say, "It could've been worse. You've still got your legs"? If I were plopped in this bed a paraplegic, would he counter with, "It could've been worse—all your faculties are still intact"? If I were just a head on a pillow, would he say, "At least you're not blind"? Infuriating faith.

Can't it always be worse? Aren't we always "lucky to be alive"? If that's the best proof of heaven, I'm betting all on black. "Have faith." "Good will come of this." "It was meant to happen this way." "You are not alone." All these banalities delivered by visitors with sincerity, humility, generosity of spirit, bounced off me as the mortar did not. Masses of sheep-people. *Sheeple*, I kept thinking, even as I smiled and thanked them for coming. Easy to do when your insides are a wormhole leading nowhere.

My thoughts are fruitful now in the night. They fulfill God's "ancient prophecy" for the Jews, by going forth and multiplying with dizzying alacrity. I'm struck by how powerful other people's faith can be. And how I'm obviously missing the conduit to access it.

I can hear Rabbi's slow breaths. He's out. Could it be his faith and not the opioid drip that comforts him? I can't deny that believing it's all in God's hands would lift a heavy burden from my now-uneven shoulders. All I need to do is whisper sweet nothings to myself, to "have faith." I can almost taste the immediate relief these comforting clichés would bring, like sweet tea and honey. Believing I am not alone would offer powerful support. But what about being honest with myself? I know just giving in to belief could give meaning to all my suffering—but how will I know if I'm deluding myself, violating whatever individuality made me, me?

And there it is, shimmering like one of those orbs of light from a fantasy book I read as a ten-year-old. I can't know—because none of us ever really *knows*. Not for certain. The best we can do is . . . have faith.

Truth is, I always found the concept of faith most beautiful when it stems *below* the roots of our challenges, when belief comes before the onset of our personal struggle—strong and steady regardless of the hand we're dealt. That's what Rabbi's faith was like. He believed in the same loving God while he was praying before the explosion as he did right after it maimed his leg.

My mother's, too. Her faith did more than just keep her from falling apart after the loss of both of her parents and her brother. Her belief in a higher power made her stronger, more sensitive, more compassionate to those around her. She even prayed for the drunk who slammed into her parents. She dived into faith's warm embrace heart-first. Her faith was not the basis for a wrestling match. Nor was it a crutch. But it saved her from suffering much greater miseries.

Halfway through this long, dark night of the soul, and I'm almost at the point where I'm ready to give in, let the light wash over me. I remember how comforting it used to be when I was a boy, like a favorite sweatshirt, to think of that old, white beard in heaven looking out for me. Though my heart now tells me, "No dice." That if I choose to put the shattered pieces of my body and my life into the hands of some omnipresent entity that I can neither see nor even sense, I'd be doing so for all the wrong reasons. I'd be grasping for security during a moment of weakness.

I trained to become a warrior. I cannot allow the weak tendencies of my past to overawe that soldier's bearing. Not long ago, I promised myself I would no longer be a victim. If I choose the easy way out now, I'll be a victim my entire life.

All of this consideration occurs not at the level of my brain, which is befuddled with morphine, gnomes, and that storm. But in that place deeper inside, that well, that cave I always felt was empty, graced with only the whistling wind and a steady drip-drip from stalactites. Nothing but the remainder of me down there, naked and alone. My body relaxes as I decide with finality that there *might* be a God, but I can never know for sure, and if I can't be positive, I won't use this agnostic "belief" in God as a buttress against uncertainty.

A soldier shuffles by. I can see one leg, two crutches, underneath my curtain.

It's not an easy thing to take on such weight. The burden comes crashing down on my lopsided shoulders. I no longer contemplate the possibility of some all-powerful source of strength to which or to whom I can turn in an emergency. My father could fall off of scaffolding and survive. Get arrested and survive. A rocket could pierce a tent and nearly kill me, but I'd survive. My mother's heart could suffer a crack and still remain intact, like the Liberty Bell.

So I find in the dwindling hours of my long, dark night of the soul that my choice occasions a stunning upside. Inner strength fills the void. A new backbone brought on by the despondency of being cornered and alone. *I can do this. I can take this one solo.* Let Lior rest in his faith. Let the trooper wail in his hopelessness. *I'm a fighter.* And my kind doesn't get to fear gremlins nipping at their nuts or nozzle while they sit on the pot.

Not that I still don't harbor doubts. I just need to lie to myself, over and over, "Izzy, you can succeed; you can matter; you can make something of yourself." If I lie to myself enough, something positive might accidently happen.

BROWBEATING THEOLOGY

January 9–10, 2009. Dawn's breaking, I think. It seems I had less to fear than I'd predicted. Yes, I discovered no deep shaft inside me filled with faith. But neither did I find there any horned demons I couldn't leash. Instead, I heard only the echo of my own questions. And I knew that it was asking not for answers from on high. But from inside. From me. I, Izzy.

My mother is standing over me now. And is that my father? They're on either side of me. I check and, yes, this is a hospital bed—not a coffin or a cold, steel table at the morgue. The closet across from me is so packed now, stuff's spilling out on the floor—mostly treasures of the culinary realm.

What does it all mean, what happened to me?

Maybe there's no meaning. Maybe there is no bigger picture. Maybe there's just me, at the wrong place, at the wrong time. A big-ass mortar, and, tick, tick—*boom*.

No, there is no reason I can prove. There is no longer an arm. That is the only truth.

So, if there is no meaning, no reason, if none of this happened as part of some ultimate plan, then aren't I left to find significance on my own? That's what would happen in all my old books. A boy becomes a man not by going off to war, but by what he does with himself there. What he does when he gets back home.

But many of the soldiers around me were hit during battle inside Gaza, some at extremely close proximity to the enemy—seeing the enemy, fighting the enemy. And me? Where did I get hurt? What did I see? Who was I fighting? Nowhere. Nothing. Nobody. I was sitting in my tent, debating whether or not to call Mommy. OK, so my war's not yet begun. This is my war. The enemy just fired its first, best shot. Now what will I do?

The presence of my parents reminds me that I don't want to live in a soulless reality. Such a reality sounds like a construct that doesn't allow for any sort of cosmic justice. There's karma down here, granted. But I do find it comforting to believe that the good folk will be rewarded in some afterlife, with front-row seats to a heavenly concert of epic proportions. And that the bad folk need to suffer through an eternal loop of Rebecca Black. Now that's justice.

Wait—is my father wearing a Hawaiian shirt? How did he even get here? Isn't he supposed to be in—?

It must be the drugs. I remember the most frightening nightmare I've ever had. It wasn't conventionally scary. No mental institutions with long, eerie hallways and flickering lights. No little dead girls with knotted hair and dirty hospital gowns, mouths wide-open, no girls climbing out of haunted wells or television sets. The most dire dream I've ever experienced felt all too real. And it actually changed my behavior dramatically in the waking world.

I must've been thirteen. I dreamt that my father had passed away. It was unclear how, just that he was wearing a tacky, green button-down shirt—something he'd never wear in real life—when he died. The dream spanned the many months that followed, months that I lived fatherless. When I awoke, I found him alive at my bedside, trying to wake me up for school. From that day on, my demeanor toward my dad shifted from that of a recently pubescent douche to a dedicated son. The day prior to that dream may well have been the last time I ever truly disrespected him. That one long, dark night granted me a deep appreciation for how lucky I was—and still am. You have to go through the long, dark night to find the dawn.

My parents are mysteriously gone now from my bedside. I don't need any more gifts or the platitudes from nurses. I don't need all the undeserved praise. Now that doctors have done what they can to save me, I need to find the thing inside me that makes me Izzy, that will do for a soul.

Then it hits me.

Match and point: Izzy, one. God, zip.

Sheets rustle beyond the partition. "Izzy?" It's Rabbi, startled awake. "Did you say something?" he asks.

I did. "*Ach sheli*," I try to whisper in his direction. My throat, devoid of moisture, manages only a painful croak. "Brother," I repeat. And doing my best to hide all emotion from my voice, I state unequivocally, "I'm going back."

"Back?"

"I'm going back to combat."

The trooper is still moaning lowly.

This is my faith. My deepest conviction.

It's been days since a mortar took my arm, and I've decided somehow without even realizing I've decided, that this is not the end. This here is just the beginning. *There* is the meaning. I must go back to the fight. I won't ever be satisfied playing the extra in someone else's movie. "You fall asleep over there, Rabbi?"

"No. Just thinking."

"Thinking . . ."

"I'll be there with you, Izzy."

"With me?"

"Guarding your six, brother. I promise."

I hear my friend roll over. Slowly he starts to snore.

That's me, front right, with fellow reservists. All smiles, despite days on end without a shower.

Accepting the Award of Excellence from President Shimon Peres.
Can't believe I nearly got arrested minutes before.

First hug from little sis Shoshi, days after injury. How am I already standing?

Hanging out with Chief of Staff Benny Gantz. Drinks at your place.

Command School, navigation training. It's a miracle I passed.

I'm not a badass, but I play one in the field.

Izzy Company attains combat status after a sixty-two-kilometer hike. Proud of my guys.

Minutes before boarding the "Shimshon" C-130 transport plane.
You'd think I'd have enough miles to upgrade.

During a weeklong drill. Fun fact, I'd have killed for a Pepsi.

Tending bar in Laos as a one-armed pirate. No acting required.

Tanks for reading.

Chapter 7

FORCING MY HAND

January–March 2009. So here I am, not quite swimming, in the sweat-laced pool at the Orthopedic Rehab Center of Sheba Hospital in Tel HaShomer. I'm paddling in circles, feeling entirely sorry for myself. I can imagine the relief of letting go, simply sinking. Of course I'm a master at holding my breath, so these do-gooders would rescue me before I could drown.

I can just see how the scene plays out: There she is, the hottest nurse in rehab. She notices me go under, and now she's stripping out of her scrubs. Dear Lord, she's got on a matching bra and panties. Frilly blue. Nice. She's getting ready to dive in after me, her breasts barely contained by Victoria's Secret as she sprints in slow motion toward the edge. But here comes ... Vlad. Oh, God. The male nurse, balding with a beer gut, shoves Nurse Frills roughly out of frame and—revert to normal speed—"Cannonball!" We're on the deck now. Oh, geez. Vlad's giving me mouth-to-mouth, cursing in Russian between each nauseating gust of Marlboro breath. I can taste the tooth-rot in his molars. And there's Phantom slow-clapping as I cough up toxic pool water like the whole thing's an '80s teen drama.

Anyway, I guess it says something that I dived right in, despite the nurse's warnings. As soon as I decided-without-deciding that I would go back into combat, I grew entirely impatient about this interminable "journey" I'd have to undertake to get there. I'm a destination kinda guy—*Screw the journey*, I say. I'd rather not go batty waiting in line. Israelis can't even comprehend the concept of queuing up. Just try boarding a bus anywhere—Eilat, Jerusalem, the Golan Heights—you'll see what I mean.

DISARMED

Anyone who's been in the military will relate to how hard it is for me and the other wounded vets to reintegrate so suddenly into civilian life. The first few days, my roommate, Benny, and I both wake up at dawn, wanting to be useful, expecting there isn't a choice. But, for all intents and purposes, the military no longer has any use for us. We "report" to the nearly empty "mess hall" (the hospital caf) when the nurses say it's time. We show up wherever and whenever we're "ordered to"—as if our leave might get revoked otherwise. Our bodies might be broken. Our "uniforms" might now consist of shorts and track shirts that bare our respective unit logos. Our transport might be wheelchairs or weak knees. But our brains and autonomic nervous systems still belong to the IDF.

And then, after a couple of days, all that structure collapses. And it's like you're in the middle of a deflated bounce house. It feels more confining than the rigid discipline you're used to. All of a sudden, this new normal comes through loud and clear. You realize you're obsolete. Despite how great the staff is at Sheba, no one *really* gives a damn if we show up or not for our various appointments. Lives are not at stake. No comrade will be forced into an extra eight-hour shift of guard duty if we're not there to relieve him. It feels like coming out into a wide-open field, scarecrow and all, after marching through a narrow tunnel. You expect it will be a relief, the ability to turn left or right. But it scares the stuffing out of you. Maybe I get a little glimpse of what goes wrong with so many American soldiers when they get home. Maybe I understand just a little bit why an average of twenty-two of them each day wind up committing suicide.

Every kid can't wait for school to end, but within a few days, most kids grow unsettled, bored—liberty weighs heavy.

Everyone, from the doctors and nurses to the rehab staff and visitors—even the janitor—offers wise, well-meaning advice on my psychological and physical recovery. Most of this counsel falls into the take-it-one-step-at-a-time variety. But I know myself—and the pre-military Izzy starts itching to spread his wing. I've never been the kid who likes to color within the lines.

On top of that, every dose of morphine feels like a concussion grenade lobbed into the tank turret of my mind. *Ka-boom!* Lots of white noise. Hard to focus. Paradox: I know these people want to help me, yet I can't seem to get myself to be a good, "compliant" patient who does what they advise. They're all starting to remind me of the Mole.

My mood can change faster than a recruit can load a mag into his rifle. It started back at Soroka Hospital, where I spent my first five days. One night, I was dozing alone in my room when a Red Alert went off—rockets had followed me from the border and now they were landing near the hospital grounds. As soon as I heard the explosions, I started chuckling. By the time the explosions reached a crescendo, I was cackling so hard I tore my stitches. I laughed the whole time they rolled us veterans down to the bunkers.

Three days into one-armed life, I sat up and got out of bed for the first time. That was the day my father first walked into my room— not a moment before. In his embrace, I can't really explain, I felt some sort of electrical transfer. Like he was recharging my power source. For hours after, I buzzed all over. My father got out of house arrest to fly overseas and see me.

Just five days after the injury, the doctor announced he was moving me to Sheba in Tel HaShomer. They brought a wheelchair to roll me to the ambulance. I insisted on walking out of the hospital on my own two feet. Two of my favorite nurses cried. They drew a heart on my hospital gown, using a thick, red marker. Enclosed within were both their names.

Now I've been here at Sheba a few weeks. I've already done three push-ups on the drab, tiled floor of my room. I'm ready to be out. They say I'll need to stay at least several months. Might as well make the best of it.

I rarely show up to occupational therapy. The acute phase starts with range of motion, pain control, and training in "adaptive techniques" for basic living. Enough with the spoons and strings and balls already—when are you going to put a rifle back in my hand? A grenade? I declare OT "boring" and refuse to keep going. But not before picking up perhaps the only useful thing I learned there: How to tie my shoes one-handed with a "straight lace," same as we were taught to lace up combat boots. This is my first big accomplishment. With the straight lace, when medics need to slice off your shoelaces quickly, they're cutting through only half the amount of lace—no X at each pass. In basic training, you learn to thread a single lace like a snake back and forth until we got to the top of the boot, where a couple of loops later, your boot is tied. Now, because there's only one string at the top instead of two, I don't need to fumble around trying to tie a bow with one hand. I can just make a simple loop that sits snugly and can be released with a quick yank. Works in combat and works for a one-armed civilian. Probably seems like a small thing, but, to me, it means a lot that I can tie my own laces and don't have to buy Velcro shoes like some old fart in the pro shop.

And what if I did need Velcro? No one here's making fun of me, no one's aiming for the jugular. Of course, I slip into the class-clown routine anyway; except this time, I'm not trying to protect myself. I'm just enjoying life, lightening the mood. Not a little of this attitude do I attribute to the fact that I'm heavily doped on every prescription painkiller known to man. *Druuugs!*

Every morning, way too early, the doctors come to do their rounds. A gaggle of white-coated sheep trail the head doctor, Zivner. They all shuffle in with their clipboards and stethoscopes, their spectacles and foam cups of what I can only presume must be terrible coffee. Zivner quizzes them relentlessly. "What are the usual indications for nerve injury after amputation, Doctor Mizrahi?"

"Development of uncontrolled . . . trophic ulcers . . . in an anesthetic upper extremity?"

"Was that a question?"

"No, sir."

"Very good then. Onward."

On my good days, I jump into the herd of lab coats in my shorts and flip-flops, following them from room to room, cracking jokes all the while. Zivner doesn't exactly play along, but that doesn't stop me.

"Dr. Taubin," Zivner asks. "What course do you recommend for the private here, after his recent above-the-knee amputation?"

"Oh, wait!" I cut in. "I know, I know! Is it dropping acid and taking a salsa class?"

"Dr. Rivlin, this next patient, a gunnery sergeant, has lost his sight after an IED exploded in front of his patrol. Would you—"

"Lots and lots of Internet porn is my prescription," I interrupt again.

Why doesn't Zivner kick this pesky patient to the curb? Maybe because I never fail—OK, I *rarely* fail—to crack up the other veterans. And maybe he gets that this is good for me as well. If you're looking to lift the spirits, laughter really is the best medicine. Of course, when you put a bunch of mostly young, mostly male, mostly immature soldiers in a tight space, they're going to laugh at one thing more than any other. That one thing is dick jokes. But the second thing is tasteless antics about their disabilities. We go after each other like it's an Olympic sport.

"Hey, Netanel, before losing the leg, you were an expert in Krav Maga, right?"

"Yeah, yeah, Bloom. What about it?"

"You must be stoked you can continue your service."

"What? There's no way I—"

"Because now you can practice *partial* arts."

"Partial—you better run for your life, *nudnik*; I'll practice partial arts all over your ass. Izzy, help me catch this bastard. Don't just stare at me, all *stumped*."

I enjoy every moment of this rhetoric, even love when the spotlight swivels my way. In my Jewish school, they pinpointed your embarrassing difference and niggled you there with cruel jabs intended to hurt. Here in rehab, everyone pokes fun at the very thing that makes you part of our unique family, the thing that gives you membership into this elite unit. The idea here, one we never had to verbalize, is to diminish hurt you might otherwise feel if you felt alone.

Early on, a vet asked me to hold onto his prosthetic leg, and directed me to pull it so he could "adjust" the fit. Turns out all he really wanted was to click the release latch so that I'd go hurling backward with his appendage in hand, landing hard on my ass—but only after toppling a food cart. Zivner happened to be strolling past, a carrot in hand. He opened his mouth to say something but, instead, took a chomp out of his veggie and walked away muttering. "Prescribe *myself* morphine . . . pain in my ass . . ."

My and Benny's room becomes the default party central. Most days, the other vets swing by with the latest—"Can you give me a *hand*, Izzy?"—or stay there to hang out and talk about nothing. You learn a lot about people in rehab. Maybe even more than you do in a barracks, and out on patrol. Take, for example, innocent country boy, Benny. Grew up on a moshav up north. Total sweetheart. Not a drop of black in his heart—too much soul to leave any space for it. Reedy like a stork, even more so than Oren, though I've never seen Benny standing, of course. He talks softly and never scowls, despite extensive injuries. There's an old adage in the IDF (which rhymes better in Hebrew): *Rockets target the first sergeant.* Meaning that it's always the guys in the last few months of their service who get hit the worst. Benny was one of those guys. He was one month from turning in his uniform when Cast Lead launched. Worse than the mortar that tore up his limbs is that his own battalion took the shot. It was "friendly fire." Whenever there's a crowd in the room, I look over furtively at Benny to make sure he's not too tired or mentally stirred up. Looking out for him is a good excuse for not attending the skirmishes raging among the gnomes in my own mind.

A good portion of everyone's visitors camp out in our room, too—especially the foreign, English-speaking teens. A parade of socially conscious, often stunning females looking to bring cheer to us sorry lot. At night, we all head down to the raucous lobby to play poker.

"Nice *hand*, Izzy."

"I'm still twice the man you are, Fuks."

Some nights, it feels as though all of Israel has shown up to serenade us with cookies, cakes, music, and laughter. One thing I have to say about Israelis and the people who travel here—they're great at keeping in touch with their wounded vets. In my experience, not one injured soldier ever had a day without visitors, many total strangers.

In the first three months after my injury, every single senior officer or politician who comes to visit me in rehab—and all of those I encounter in the lobby—hear my simple request: "Sir, can you help me get back to combat?"

"You've done enough."

"You should be very proud of your sacrifice."

"Look—be realistic, Izzy."

And more than once: "Are you insane?"

DEALT A BAD HAND

March 2009. Rehab's not all fun. My roommate, Benny, is a radio operator. He lost his legs. But the rocket took his balls, too. The entire region down there's a total mess. We're not at the point where we're making jokes about it yet.

One night, Benny shits his bed. I wake up to him moaning, "Oh, man. Oh, man. What's the matter with me?" The nurses are already here to change him. I stumble over to his bed. My face wants to scrunch up from the stench, but I force it to relax. I'm looking in Benny's eyes, and I can see he's in a tailspin of abject hopelessness. My territory. There's feces covering his entire lower half, but his contorted face tells me the situation upstairs is far more of a muddle. So I sit with him while the nurses clean up. I hold Benny's hand the whole time, trying not to shift the IV needle protruding from somewhere above his knuckles.

"There's nothing the matter with you, Benny. You're a goddamn hero, man. A flippin' rock star. Don't you forget that for a second. This . . ." and I motion with my eyes . . . "this is no big deal, I promise. You've survived worse . . . crap."

Benny snaps out of it. Smiles wanly. He sighs a few times and we sit there, waiting for the clean slate. When it's done and I look away from Benny for the first time, I see the nurses are staring right at me. I can't read their eyes. Is it respect? Pride? But in that moment, I'm not thinking about my own pain, my drug-addled brain, my troubles at home. My Phantom. I'm thinking only that I still have this capacity, I have one hand left to hold Benny's—or any brother's. I can do what the nurses do, and think of others before myself. Which makes me experience a little surge of something nice, something familiar. Yes, this is exactly what my parents would do. What they have done their whole lives. *Tzedakah.*

Back in my own bed, though, I can't help thinking, "There, but for the grace of God, go I." It's hard to feel sorry for yourself with a missing arm when the guy beside you lost his legs and his ability to leave behind a legacy. Benny's talking quietly to his mother now over the phone while I open a letter from . . . Curls, the ambulance medic, wishing me well. Wow. Her words comfort me, and I can almost hear her voice again. And I hear Benny's soft voice, comforting his mom; he bolsters her the way I did him. I just spent umpteen months worried I had no balls, and here was Benny, proving it takes something far deeper inside to be a man.

The next day, and from then on, the nurses smile at me in a new way. No matter how loopy the drugs make me, no matter how temperamental and morose I can get, they treat me with patience and kindness.

Despite that, I, too, have very bad days. Days I can't manage the usual dance. Nights I'm covered in my own metaphysical feces, keeping Benny awake. Mornings when I can't rise for the agony. When the shades have to stay closed, and no one can make a sound without stirring my ire. Afternoons that belong to Phantom. *Whatever doesn't kill you, Izzy, simply makes you . . . stranger.*

There are days upon days when I ignore every doctor, nurse, rehab specialist, and visitor. I can tell Benny's parents despise me for this person I sometimes am. How bad an influence I am on their optimistic son. They must be thinking, *What the hell is this guy's problem? All he lost was one goddamn arm*—and their beloved son lost his ability to ever walk again. I want to be there for him. To bust his . . . chops. To aid his recovery. I just can't. Not always. After a few weeks, they stop talking to me altogether. When they come in to visit Benny, they ignore me.

No problem. I can turn and face the wall. Give them the cold shoulder, too.

THE LADIES LEND A HAND

Everything below my belt is still intact, thank all that is merciful in the universe. In fact, as a more-or-less normal twenty-year-old guy, I'm constantly reminded of my junk. First day here at Sheba, this super babe of a nurse—I'm talking a straight ten—asked if she could help me shower. Her exact words were, "Can I give you a hand, Izzy?" Of course my shorts almost tore open at the seams, and I very quickly refused, simultaneously cursing myself and clearing my throat overmuch. Something similar had happened a few days earlier, at Soroka on the third day after my injury. I was taking my first shower in weeks, and two nurses were rattling the door handle, urging me in earnest to open up and let them in, so they could—and I quote again—"Help scrub those hard-to-reach places." I've never had so many tantalizing offers. You know that Muppet lab assistant, Beaker? His was the voice I heard as I responded lamely, "No, thanks! I, uh, think I've got everything covered." My heart thudded, like back in the old days when I feared the gremlins would get me in the bathroom while I was naked and most vulnerable. This might've been worse.

Now, I'm not a complete novice with girls. I lost my V-card nearly four years ago in my Mini Cooper. We were parked a block away from her house in Miami when the magical moment began. Everything went great. That is, until the time came to say "See ya later." Like a total douche canoe, I had left the AC running during the act, and now the Cooper wouldn't cough back to life. I would have been dead, too, if my friend—a real pal—hadn't reluctantly and groggily dragged himself out of bed and arrived with his jumper cables before dawn. Her father would've crushed my head with his bare fists when he came outside for his Sunday paper.

Anyway, to call me confident with the ladies would be like calling me Enrique Iglesias. Sounds cool, but just isn't true.

When I was thirteen, I got the only birds-and-bees talk that was forthcoming. This occurred just days after I saw my first nude human-female-person. I was walking home alone from synagogue in my penguin suit, not yet officially a man, according to Jewish doctrine. The entrance to my complex in Aventura Lakes had a bridge, and lining the water on each side of said bridge were the backsides of all the houses on our block. I was in the habit of glancing into our living-room window as I crossed the bridge, just to see what I should expect when I walked in the door.

But on this night, I couldn't help but notice movement on the second floor of the house to the left of ours. That's where Spanish Princess lived. I called her that because I had no idea what her name was, nor she mine. She was nineteen at least, I figured, and would never in a million years deign to consort with a *pisher* like me. It was her in the window—definitely her. I removed my Borsalino hat, holding it to my beating chest as if in prayer. She was walking around her bedroom wearing nothing but a towel. Then the towel dropped—prayer answered. Spanish Princess was completely naked behind the plate glass. I could have performed my first magic trick if I'd dropped the hat a foot and held it up still with no hands. It was the show of my life. If I were Superman, I'd never save the city. I'd be too busy X-ray-visioning.

So, a couple of days later, my father and I were in our garage. He was helping me fix my bike. I was daydreaming about that absent towel next door. My dad was always the epitome of genuineness and caring—if not particularly good with words—and I'd expect no less in his counsel about girls. He said, "If you just 'fool around' with a girl, you'll hurt her. Women are fragile that way." End of subject. I remember thinking it was so simple, but profound. Yes, archaic, too, and kind of sexist—but not necessarily in a bad way.

A few minutes later, our hands greasy with the chain, he said, "Do you have any questions?" I said no. With that one sentence, he set up how I would consider women for the rest of my life. Of course, more often than not, I'm the one in considerably more danger of getting attached and/or destroyed. Yet my father's advice stuck with me. It doesn't hurt that I'm terrified to talk to women, especially when I'm interested in pursuing them, especially when I'm not socially lubricated to the brim.

Most of the aforementioned encounters occur in a bar or club setting. Almost all of them happen when I'm drunk. I don't know why, but it's the only way I find any measure of confidence. I don't know what it is. I know I'm not hideous per se. But the truth is, I can't blame the average woman for holding her nose around Sober Izzy. Inside, I generally feel about as useless as tits on a bull. You can try to fake it, but that kind of self-loathing seeps out and fogs like a fart in a stalled Mini Cooper.

Which is why I'm so appreciative that Katya doesn't push this issue. Katya is my super-hot, super-smart, super-blunt therapist at Sheba. The mission of getting me to agree to see a therapist was a lot like Sergeant Soprano's slab-hauling tasks at B'kaot—thankless and grueling, with a good possibility of a vital appendage getting crushed. For obvious reasons, it's a requirement that every wounded vet meet with a shrink. "But I'm going back to combat, so this rule doesn't really apply to me. I don't need a therapist."

"Yes, well, how about you just *humor* me," says Zivner, trying not to sound impatient with his patient. "Meet Katya. She's a med student doing her dissertation on—what are the odds—amputee soldiers from abroad, trying to return to combat. You could wind up the star of her paper. Nurse—would you call Katya in, please?"

And in walked Katya. And, OK, maybe I do need a therapist. Yeah, I *definitely* need a therapist. What was I thinking, not wanting a therapist after such a traumatic incident? But Katya was so much more than a pretty face. Soon enough, she got me talking. Over the next many months, we talked about life in general (not terrible); my fears (crippling); my tendency to see the world as black-and-white ("helpful"?); and my many, many problems talking to human-female-persons (thinking about writing a ten-volume tome, are you, Katya?).

"You're talking to *me* right now, aren't you, Izzy?"

"Yeah, but I mean, attractive fe—I mean, women I'm attracted to. Not that I'm not—Please shut me up. This is exactly what I'm talking about. Besides, you're married."

"Izzy, what do you want, when it comes to women? I mean, imagine your dream life, where you're perfectly adept at expressing your wishes. And tell me."

It's been changing.

I'm thirteen and Orthodox, studying at a Chabad yeshiva at the edge of the Tucson Mountains. Despite the heat, I wear a black hat and suit, as is the custom. All around me are black-clad men, mean-spirited cacti, majestic mares, and little else. I already know how everything turns out: Family. Life. The afterlife. I'll be married shortly after my eighteenth birthday—that's only five years off. My wife will be far more pious than I am—just like my mother and father. She'll cover her knees and elbows, her hair—and still pull off sexy with ease. We'll have six or eight children—all boys—with long, loopy sideburns and IQs of 130. They'll all have an enthusiasm for Torah study far exceeding mine, which will give their mother and me tremendous *naches*—lots of pride.

I'm nineteen, secular, and stationed at the foot of a mountain in the Negev desert. Despite the cold, I wear nothing but my combat vest and olive-green fatigues. All around me are cardboard targets, spent bullet casings, and little else. I already know how everything turns out: Family. Life. The afterlife. I'll be married shortly after my twenty-fourth birthday. That's only five years off. My wife will be far smarter than I am. She'll wear a tank top and faded skinny jeans and still pull off modesty with ease. We'll have three or four children—all boys—with boundless energy, and muscular, athletic frames. They'll each insist on serving in a combat unit like their father, which will give their mother and me tremendous *koved*—lots of honor.

"And when you're twenty-four? Can you project that far ahead?"

"God, no." All I can see is the military. And Katya's green eyes . . .

"Tell me more about dreams—your sleeping dreams."

"Are you planning an X-rated thesis?"

"Those aren't your only dreams. What else?"

"Well. I had this one crazy dream a few weeks ago. I was back in combat. Armed to the teeth. I was leading a squad of soldiers through Judea and Samaria, on a hunt for a certain terrorist. I was a tough-as-nails commander, getting stuff done. My men looked to me, trusted me. When I woke up, I could feel my blood pumping in my temples."

"A precognition of your future?"

Marry me, Katya. Marry me, too.

It's not until a day or so later that I realize I'd had my first one-armed dream. And I *rocked*.

Then, one afternoon, the woman of my dreams goes away. I'm told Katya's term with me has ended. She breaks my heart, just like the rest of them. Someone tells me I was her first . . . well, patient. For all I know, I was her only patient. They send me down to "the dungeon," a floor below rehab, to meet her replacement. I knock on the door timidly. A squat, middle-aged troglodyte looks up from her egg-salad sandwich. I take one look at her hairy knuckles, say, "Oops. Wrong office," and bolt back upstairs. I'll be faithful to Katya. She was my first. I want her to be my only before I return to combat.

I replace Katya with CAREN. Sheba's Computer Assisted Rehabilitation Environment is awesome, and I immediately fall for her. She's a real-time, multi-purpose, multi-sensory system for diagnosis, rehabilitation, evaluation, and recording of a patient's ability to balance and control his own movements. In other words, a live-action, virtual-reality video game. Sign me up.

CAREN consists of a movable floor you stand on. As the system manipulates the platform, a sophisticated motion-capture routine measures and logs your movements. She's taken me surfing atop killer ocean waves during vicious thunderstorms. She's taken me dune-buggying down steep desert cliffs. CAREN requires my full attention, my full concentration, as well as a complete awareness of my stability, balance, and movement. I'm at the center of a feedback loop that I can influence, predict, and conquer. Best of all, I get to compete against myself.

But, just like the old days with my Wii and my PlayStation, I'm still playing with myself. Alone in a room. When real life is somewhere *out there*. I prefer this virtual reality. But I find that at the CAREN station, my mood is as unstable as it is in my room. My mood still swings like the jewels Benny lost. Back and forth, or "black-and-white," as Katya rightly diagnosed before she left me for her husband. From happy, dopey, jokester to vampire emo-boy. She taught me these are both me. Always have been. And, truth is, the whole me is itching to get out of this place, to launch my first foray back into the real world. Only, I'm still afraid of what I'll find out there.

YOU GOTTA HAND IT TO THE GENERAL

Late March 2009, about 9:30 p.m., Sheba Hospital rehab ward. The night I first meet General Galant—"call me Yoav"—is a white night. That is, according to the black/white binary Katya diagnosed me with. I'm in a tremendous mood, feeling dumb and high—basically punch-drunk on pain and the meds meant to deflect it. We got word that a special visitor would be making the rounds tonight. I hear the Hebrew words "*Aluf Pikud Darom*," which mean nothing to me. All I know is that I'm feeling silly. Benny is cracking me up, he looks so nervous about the visit. He climbs into his wheelchair and does his best to sit at attention, which isn't a thing. My no-legged roommate sitting so upright, all serious, gets me giggling. By the time General Galant walks in with his entourage of underlings and direct reports, I'm so loose that I open with "Hey, man, what's up?"

I see Benny nearly poops himself again, yet somehow manages to sit up even straighter. An officer nervously thumbs through a folder. He soon introduces me by name. The general looks at me a second. Everyone behind him is quiet. And then he breaks into a smile. Everyone behind him sighs and gets comfortable. "Tell me, what's up with you, Izzy?"

"I want to get back into combat, sir. Can you help me with that?"

He pauses a long while, doesn't lose the smile. "Sure. If that's what you want."

What? Did he just . . . What?

"I'm not just asking to return to the military, sir. You understand? I'm talking about active duty, about *combat*."

"Yes. If it's possible, you and I will make it happen together. And call me Yoav."

Once he leaves, Benny tells me this Yoav is the officer in charge of all the Southern Command. He's a former military secretary to the prime minister. Cast Lead was his charge, and he was here visiting the soldiers who were hurt by turning his battle plan from maps and strategy to a win in the field. He looked us each in the eye, knowing our lives would be difficult, knowing he would have to continue making such decisions. But it was obvious how much he cared. Not only because he visited but also because he engaged with us on a human level and spoke with us so plainly. We'd had visits from various higher-ups, and some came just to tick off the task on a checklist of stuff they were supposed to do. Not this guy, though. This guy's special.

He returns to our room at the end of his tour and asks what I'm doing for Passover in two weeks. I tell him, "Season two of *How I Met Your Mother*. Right here in rehab."

"No," he says. "You're coming with me on a tour of the bases. We'll spend the holiday with the soldiers protecting the border. Good?"

He leaves, and one of his logistical officers asks me for my number. I give it to her, look at the others, and then say, "Really? You're the only one who wants my number? No other takers?"

Even Phantom's thrown off. *Izzy, what da heck?*

She gives me the kind of smile you give a twenty-year-old American who is stoned on painkillers, and also very, very dumb.

What a lost boy. But I have an overwhelming, awesome feeling that with this one conversation, I've found my Tinker Bell. I've got the fairy dust I need to see my mission through. No Captain Hook. No new villains in the brig to muck up the works.

CAPTAIN HOOK TAKES A WHIZ

Early March 2009. For the first time in twenty years, I feel claustrophobia setting in. I'm in a seedy Tel Aviv club with streams of sweat pouring down my forehead, penetrating the eye patch that covers the whole left quadrant of my face. The sting of it's got my right eye squinting, blind as if from pepper spray.

I resort to a cliché, self-motivating shtick: "C'mon, Izzy. You got this."

No. I do not. The smell of other people's vomit overawes my nostrils. Urine, bright yellow from ravers' dehydration, lies in acrid puddles, covering most of the TP-littered floor. Think about all that planning you did to get here, Izzy. Why panic now? For the love of Jor-El, it's just a frickin' button . . . Why can't I—?

Outside, I can hear the girls knocking on the door, wanting to know if I'm OK.

Izzy, you are pretty damn far from OK, my friend. "Fine! Almost done," I say.

Minnie and Annie, two British girls I came to call pals after a couple of friendly hospital visits, informed me of their plans for Purim a few days prior to tonight's execution. I loved it. We put in a serious effort, at least a good hour of scheming. For someone as stoned and distracted as I am, that's nothing to sneeze at.

Soon, we acquired the proper garb—people dress up for Purim, a lot like Halloween. It's surprisingly easy to find both an eye patch and a prosthetic hook in a rehab hospital. Boots, too, were easy to come by. Straight-laced, of course—I borrowed them from Benny. And a flowing shirt from some Titan of a guy who took a sniper bullet to the knee. I hijacked enough pillows from Benny and others to build a believable Izzy-shaped lump for my bed. For several nights, I covertly memorized the routine of the nightshift nurses who walked the Sheba halls.

The only time I risked blowing operational cover was for the sake of veteran safety—my own. The morning of the mission arrived, and with it, the doctor responsible for the day's rounds. I'd never seen the grizzled guy before, and figured that meant I wasn't likely to see him again. Besides, I decided, I had no choice. I needed to know the possible repercussions before undertaking this risk I'd been plotting for my prison break. "Hey, Doc," I chirped. "Good morning."

"*Mornink*," he muttered back without looking up, his pen scribbling madly on my chart, his eyebrows dancing. So he was Russian.

"Say, Doc, if I were to have, I don't know, maybe . . . a drink or two. What, uh, would happen, you know, given my condition?"

The scribbling stopped, and he maneuvered the top of his pen up to his square glasses, pushed them higher on his nose. "*Wodka?*" he inquired, hopefully.

"Sure. Let's say, Vodka."

He glanced down at my chart, studied the plethora of drugs listed there. He flipped a page. Another page. Another. And just when I thought he'd nix the very idea of mixing alcohol with all of my meds, he looked back up at me, nodding. "Two *wodkas* never kill nobody." I smiled. "Really, three-four *wodkas* never kill nobody neither." I got the vibe that he'd personally conducted meticulous research into this area. "No five."

"No five?"

"Five *wodkas* maybe kill you." And he made his way to Benny.

I didn't tell him that pirates don't mingle with *wodka*, that they prefer rum once they've escaped their chains below deck. Or maybe scotch. Probably both. In any case, the doctor's prescription was clear: I could drink again.

So night arrived. I lay, costumed, beneath my bed sheets, with my stack of pillows hidden on the floor beside me. Once the nurse scanned my room to her satisfaction—Izzy, sleeping. Benny, sleeping—I got up and remade the bed with the feather-based me as stand-in. Or lie-in. Now shift one pillow this way for the missing arm, *et voilà*.

"Smooth sailing, Captain," whispers Benny, giving me a wink.

Out I sneaked through the quiet halls, through the back door of the orthopedic ward, and out the side entrance to an idling taxi. I opened the back door and cried out when Minnie yanked me inside by my puffy shirt. Minnie and Annie, both dressed in costume as well, were giggling with excitement. Likely with *wodka*, too. "You're free," Annie shouted.

"Time to party," yelled Minnie.

If I had known during that ride how rapidly my freedom would turn to torture, I'd have given anything to swap places with the pillows resting soundly in my bed.

Now concentrating on the task at hand inside the cramped stall becomes nearly impossible. For one thing, Phantom's on the toilet, crapping, so the place stinks like roadkill. And the constant, impatient rattling of the door handle, along with the fists slamming on the thin barrier wall, don't help either.

The partygoers, all loud and blotto, are growing increasingly impatient, and understandably so. They start to whack the stall harder, to rattle the handle faster. The bass of the megaspeakers—"I Kissed a Girl"—vibrates the beads of piss and puke on the porcelain between Phantom's knees. The more it all thrums, the more I freeze. The more I freeze, the more I lose whatever dexterity I might have had in my fingers. In hindsight, it's a good thing I finished only half a drink before my bladder sent me here. I can't imagine how any level of drunkenness would have contributed to my manual ineptitude.

DISARMED

There's nothing funny about a full-grown man struggling with all his might just to close the top button on his jeans—not even on Purim, while he's dressed like a pirate. My heart is jumping like the subwoofers; my five remaining fingers, turning into sausages. I begin for the first time to dread my future outside the comfort zone of rehab. What kind of life can I look forward to as a useless, clumsy gimp? Back to combat operations? I can't even close my flippin' fly.

Phantom flushes, yawns, doesn't wash his hand.

Finally, I manage to cinch the button and buckle my belt. I unlatch the door with my sore and cramping arm. My costume's drenched in perspiration, the eye patch swimming in sweat. Club music hits me as I emerge from the restroom: "P-P-P-Poker Face!"

I'm all ready to apologize to the throngs. Then it happens. All their stares of drunken agitation melt away the instant they get a good look at me, what's left. Something overtakes them then, the shame at having hounded a poor cripple. Impatient to piss when this feeble sucker has no arm. Shame and pity. The truth of those eyes detonates inside my chest with the precision of a well-aimed mortar. I want desperately to make a self-deprecating joke—but I come up short. So, bowing my head, I make my way down the hall with all the grim ceremony of a man marching in his own funeral procession. The crowd of mourners—all sexy cops and shirtless lumberjacks, all fairies and also "fairies"—parts for me, just like those kids on the basketball court at the JCC parted for Fart Boy. One vampire with a lisp offers a mumbled apology.

After passing the rows of onlookers, I scramble straight for the exit. My night is over. I jump into the closest taxi without finishing my first drink or sending word to my friends, Minnie-as-Sailor and Annie-as-Tinker Bell. Anything but pity. Anything.

It isn't pity in Lieutenant Fuks's clear, blue eyes the next morning. He'd visited me at Soroka, and a few times now at Sheba, to play poker. Our bond would never be broken after what we'd been through together, timeless like names scrawled in wet cement.

BRIK BY BRIK

Aaron Brik. He who'd quarterbacked my bloody ER encounter when we were students at yeshiva in Tucson starting in 2001.

Brik joins us late, a few months before that spectacular pass that ended in my laceration. We begin as enemies.

He was kicked out of his previous yeshiva, in Brooklyn, for spray-painting a couple of security cameras. When his principal called him into his office to level the accusation, the twelve-year-old denied it. More than denied it. He was utterly appalled at the very idea that anyone, especially an authority figure, a rabbi, no less, could even think him capable of, not to mention willing to, debase himself in such a breach of honesty, integrity, morality; *Why, if my father could only—*

The principal, without a twitch, swiveled his monitor so it faced the accused. A freeze-frame of Brik's grinning mug, centered on the screen, a can of Krylon ColorMaster Gloss Black clearly gleaming in his hand.

"Umm . . . I'd like a word with my lawyer."

What he got was the boot. A few weeks later, they unceremoniously dump him among us twenty-five frontiersmen.

Within days, we're Cain-and-Abel-level foes. I can thank cacti for that. One evening, after we finish our daily twelve-hour dose of nonstop Torah fun, a few of us decide to explore the nearby terrain. The only interesting place to scout is the golf course neighboring our secluded dormitory. So six of us carefully creep over to the weak spot we discovered in the barbed-wire fence, and make our way to the highest of the green knolls on the course, which is closed for the evening.

A bright desert moon obscures most of the stars but gives us great visibility. The grass has been trimmed, and its scent strikes me calm. Once we find a suitable plot of Kentucky blue, we all plop to the ground. We're talking smack about the rabbis, reminiscing about home, and telling stupid jokes:

DISARMED

"Hey, Brik."

"'Sup?"

"What do you call a kid with no arms, no legs, and an eye patch?"

"Easy. You call him names."

"So you heard that one. How about this . . ."

At some point, the distant, spooky sound of baying, as though carried on the clear air from some foggy past, begins to reach us, one by one. We ignore it.

"Guy walks into a zoo," says Brik. "The only animal in the whole place is a dog."

"How is that a joke?"

"Because it's a Shih Tzu, man. Get it? A *Shit Zoo* . . ."

With time, the noise of howling and barking grows more insistent. I don't know who's first to panic, just that I'm last to react.

It's obvious that someone has let loose a pack of attack dogs to tear us to bits. Coyotes. No—wolves!

No one actually speaks those words, but our eyes evince that's what everyone is thinking. We all take off as one. Running, panting, *yarmulkes* threatening to fly off in the breeze, aiming headlong for the barbed-wire fence.

Do you know what a jumping cactus is?

Well, if the cactus is the prick of the plant world, the knobby, yellow "jumping cholla" is King Prick. It doesn't actually "jump," of course, although you'd be forgiven for ascribing to it malicious intent. When you step on the soft, compressible soil in which it typically grows, the cactus *leans* toward the "compressing entity"—say, a fleeing teenager. Then the spiky cholla segments pop off the main plant and jab into said compressor-kid. This gives the appearance of it biting or "jumping." Even a subtle shift in the wind—say, caused by a group of terrified teenagers running from an unseen canine enemy—and it'll sway toward you, closer and closer with each passing kid. All the plant requires now is the slightest purchase on a nerdy boy's fragile flesh in which to sink its wicked fangs. Super-sharp needles with microscopic barbs dart deep inside your muscles and tendons—they can even reach bone.

Five boys run past one such plant unscathed. Back and forth it sways. And then I pass. "*Ahhh!* God! I'm hit!" In the moonlight, I can just make out this alien form hugging my leg, digging into me with its probes. "It's got me, guys! Save yourselves!"

Each foot-pound forward sends the spines burrowing deeper into my thigh. But I'm far too terrified to stop moving. The dogs. Oh, the dogs. I'm holding my breath. By the time I reach the fence, the tines have rendered me immobile. I can't even lift my leg, let alone jump over the wire. Four of my companions have scaled it and continue running for the dorm.

Only Brik stays.

No. Not to help.

He's laughing so hard that he runs out of breath and has to lean down and hold his knees. "You bastard," I groan, over and over. "You evil bastard."

The dogs, probably just some neighborhood mutts conversing with the moon and each other, are quiet now. The only sound in the desert night is that dick Brooklynite laughing. Laughing so hard, he's choking.

Yet eight years later, 7,457 miles away, Brik is here with me now. He's spent a week at my bedside, after flying over from the States to be with me. "Perils of the desert," he says. That must be an expression.

"*You* were my only peril in Arizona," I say. "Whenever I get a pang in this leg, I think of *you*."

"I've missed you, too. Of course none of the scars or broken bones in your arm are still attached to your body, so I'm assuming at least *those* don't bug you anymore."

"Bastard."

On the last day of his visit, he's wearing an even more mischievous smile than he usually does. "So, I'm joining up, Izzy."

DISARMED

"The Girl Scouts?"

"No, Ass-wipe. The IDF."

"I pity the IDF."

FEAR THE WALKING MEDS

Rabbi Lior brings his Nissan clunker to a stop a short limp from the front gate of the kibbutz Ein HaShlosha, on the border of Khan Yunis, Gaza. My Ground Zero. I roll down the window. It's mid-April 2009, and we're on another unauthorized outing from rehab. All around is the evidence of recent rocket attacks. I can see the place where, a year before the mortar took my arm, Carlos Chavez, an Ecuadorian volunteer, was shot and killed by a Hamas sniper while working on the kibbutz. I stood guard at that gate for hours on end.

I'm not used to it being so warm here. I'm not sure what crops grow in these vast, green fields that surround us, but the sunbaked vegetation puts a pleasant scent in the air, which sedates me.

Rabbi hobbles around sans crutches to open the passenger door for me, but I'd rather not budge. How the hell is he standing on a three-month-old shattered femur? I don't ask him, because I know exactly what he'll say. He puts his hand out to help me up and out. A strange shift in reality has been dawning on me lately. At first I felt luckier than all the leg amputees, because while they were stuck in bed or confined to a wheelchair, I was running around playing Ping-Pong and "diagnosing" my "patients" alongside Dr. Zivner. But over time I came to realize that they would soon resume their normal lives in a way I never could. Counterintuitively, I'd much rather have lost a leg than an arm, because the prostheses for legs are so much better, both functionally and aesthetically. In fact, you wouldn't even know a guy had a missing leg unless he was stripping right there in front of you. I will only ever have the use of one real arm, but most of those guys can walk around on two legs, and some of them can already run again. Many are totally indistinguishable from fully assembled humans. You know, people whose parts aren't sold separately.

I follow Rabbi. Injured and drugged, we're stumbling toward the rickety gate we both called home not so long ago. My flip-flops are slapping against my heels in rhythm with every step. Then, without warning, Rabbi stops his forward hobble, and I smack right into him. "What the hell, man?"

"I, uh . . . I'm not so sure they're going to let us in." He motions toward the base. The First Brigade—Golani—took over from our brigade, Kfir, soon after the end of Operation Cast Lead. We see their flag now, a green olive tree on a yellow background, waving in the breeze. I wonder if they'll recognize us as friendlies, or if they'll assume we're just the world's worst thieves.

In Tucson, Brik once told me that convenience-store workers are not allowed to act against shoplifters. "Seriously. It's company policy. You could walk right in and openly take as much candy and soda and crap as you want. Maybe you want a Big Gulp? They won't react." The two of us sat on a curb outside the local 7-Eleven. Oh, it crossed our thirteen-year-old minds, all right. But I couldn't bring myself to do it. Not out of any real moral imperative. Mostly because of my father. I could handle the manager, police, a judge—but the thought of my father's quiet disapproval prevented many a youthful misdemeanor.

Most people probably assume that Israeli security is among the best on planet Earth. And it is. So it would likely come as a surprise that the IDF has major issues related to theft. Unarmed bandits and thieves have infiltrated many military installations, often stripping them clean of valuable non-weapons-grade material. Mostly Bedouins. Some Arabs. Some Israelis. Sometimes both, working together. Hurray . . .

With my own eyes, I've witnessed theft by the ton. Spent casings from shooting ranges and ammo dumps seem to be the easiest steal— all of that can be sold for scrap. But live submachine-gun ammo, even live tank shells, also disappear in mass quantities. An emboldened bandit will literally steal the engines off an F-16. Almost impossible to believe—but entirely true.

I've got to hand it to these thieves: they've got balls. But most of them are stealing gear we leave outside base. Stealing from inside is an entirely different, far more complicated, story. You might have to cut through wire fencing, evade guard towers, or bust locks. But the main reason robbers succeed is not their guile at burglary—it's that their opponent is so poorly prepared. There are millions of pounds of metal scattered around the Negev desert, with only recruits a few weeks into training responsible for all of it. Which means, essentially, no one's responsible. Ninety percent of them don't yet understand the meaning of "to guard." In short, it does not mean playing Snake on your iPhone, Oren.

Having said that, these thieves, especially of the Bedouin variety, also seem to have an innate ability to case the surrounding terrain in search of easy entry points—vulnerabilities—and escape routes. They plot. They certainly don't waltz through the front gate while wearing T-shirts that proclaim, "I'm Smiling Because I'm about to Rob Your Sorry Ass Blind."

Neither Rabbi nor I considered the possibility that a different unit now guarded this territory, that they might not allow random civilians to enter whenever they decided to stroll in. The scope of the guard's rifle glints in the sun. "Damn. You might be right, Lior." We face the front gate from fifty meters away. The infantryman on duty stares right back at us, unmoving and seemingly unmoved, his brown beret buttressed on his head. "Oh, hell, it won't hurt to try," I mutter. I take the lead; we begin our short trek to the front gate. I try my level best to project an air of confidence as I trudge forward. Not easy in shorts and flip-flops—especially not while doped up and struggling just to walk a straight line. I nod self-assuredly at the guard as we reach him. And, with a drug-induced sense of authority, I march right past him, Rabbi hobbling at my heels.

The unblinking soldier mumbles something as we go by that, to me, sounds like, "This isn't really happening."

I interpret that enigmatic phrase the following way (and this is purely speculative, possibly achieved by my abusive absorption of both morphine and comic books):

The guard, let's call him "Shmulik," has been working double shifts patrolling the border. He's not been sleeping, because he has nightmares. Not his fault. He recently read the Walking Dead *series of graphic novels, which his brother sent him from Haifa. Sleep eludes him now, as whenever he closes his eyes, zombies amble by. He sees their knotty grimaces, their lifeless eyes, hanging skin, spilling guts, and so on. Their trawling and ungainly gaits.*

He intends to study psychology at Ben-Gurion University, so he knows exactly what's going on here with his "zombiphobia": The walking dead of his nightmares are stand-ins for the real terror lurking nearby. He's haunted by these zombies because they're far less terrifying than the militants crawling through the intricate network of tunnels he knows very well are underneath him. The scariest Walkers are the ones whose arms or legs have dropped off; they keep plodding anyway, slowly, deliberately—no stopping them . . .

Coinciding with his reading of The Walking Dead, *Shmulik and his entire unit recently sat in the mess hall to hear from their captain all about the events that transpired at Ein HaShlosha a month before Golani took over the base and its border fence from Kfir after Operation Cast Lead. Guard duty was meant to be a welcome change of pace for the exhausted unit, which had spent the entire operation deep inside Gaza.*

Golani itself took tremendous losses of their own during Cast Lead. Many soldiers were injured, and some were killed when a tank shell "friendly-" fired from an Israeli armored division collapsed an entire building on top of them—Shmulik knew some of those guys since Basic.

The captain reminded them all that the Haruv Battalion of the Kfir

Brigade had been posted on this base before Golani. That unit suffered casualties of their own only a few tents from where Shmulik now straight-laced his boots. The higher-ups decided to use that "damned" tent to store their weapons cache. No one wanted to sleep in the same spot where that one poor bastard got his arm ripped off by a mortar's molten shrapnel.

Walkers don't exist.

They don't.

Rumors began to spread about that one wounded soldier, and the captain declared them all true. He was an American kid, and he never lost consciousness. Holding his severed arm up by the fibers of his uniform shirt, he stumbled through the smoke the way one of "them" would. Somebody even saw him raise his arms up afterward, so the limb went flying.

Shmulik donned his vest and adjusted the brown beret this morning, trying to clear his mind of that image. He navigated the new layer of concrete barriers that had been added since the incident. The military always reacts too late.

The sleep-deprived soldier felt lucky. He always managed to land the day shift, giving him the comfort of clear visibility. But this wasn't a mistake—he knew his buddies were bending over backward to make sure he got posted only in daylight. They were worried a night patrol would unhinge him. And just as he was thinking how grateful he was for those friends, for a world where zombies didn't exist, he heard a voice cry out in the distance, "What the hell, man?"

He narrowed his eyes. Two figures. Wobbly legs. Unearthly gait. Foggy eyes. A missing arm. He practically wet his fatigues. The two phantasms shuffled by.

"This isn't really happening," he said.

Well, it was either that, or the guard just didn't give a damn. If you ask any soldier from a different outfit, they'll tell you those Golani guys are known for that. Many of them are milling about as we stagger past; none seems to find our presence particularly concerning.

We make our way directly to the tent flap where Kobi found me in two pieces, a look of horror in his eyes. I find that my mind's not ready to cope with this place. Why did we come? It seemed a capital idea at the time. I blame the drugs. And maybe Rabbi pushing me for some spiritual "closure."

I peek inside the tent. Mountains of expensive weaponry, highly organized, filling every inch of space. Someone has done a bang-up job erasing the damage caused by the mortar strike. Who gets tasked with cleaning up the mess that the wounded and dying like me tend to leave behind? Did the chunks of my exploded elbow wind up in a Ziploc bag? Or were they just mopped up and dumped along with the scraps from supper?

Rabbi clears his throat behind me. I let him slip past into the tent. Phantom follows, nudging me inside. Phantom whistles, impressed with the cache. Then Rabbi whistles. "We should not be in here with such gear." He exits the tent and limps toward the bomb shelter where the excruciating tourniquet once held what remained of my blood inside my body.

When I don't follow, Rabbi stops, turns, and smiles. "After you," he says.

One step, two steps, three steps forward. My fear's in there. Fear I didn't realize I've been clutching all this time. Yes, it was Lior's idea to come here. And for my benefit. Bastard.

But I take a deep breath, hold it, and enter the concrete bunker. Immediately, my knees wobble beneath me. Without conscious intent, my body has lowered itself to the ground. Now I'm kneeling on the very spot where Chen the medic toiled to keep my insides inside me. The spot where Fuks, blood on his cheeks like some cannibal, shredded my fatigues with his teeth.

I start muttering under my breath. Then growing louder, I recite much of the dialogue that occurred on this ground that day. Things I haven't thought about since. Things buried deep in my psyche. The

DISARMED

words pour out of me like someone's pressed a button on a tape recording. Rabbi steps outside as I vent. He knows I left more than my arm here. He knows we had to come back. For me to pick up my self. By the time the words taper and cease, and the images fade to grey, I feel a complete sense of peace. Just like when the syringe pushes sedative into the bloodstream. Rabbi Lior's cure. Too bad neither of these last forever. I stumble weakly outside. "We're done here, Lior. We can go."

BROTHERS IN ARMS

One week later. April 2009. The night is messy with color and pain. I would have preferred to sink into the abyss of misery and morphine. But I look out through a gauzy yellow haze. The doctor's upped my pain meds of late, telling me that phantom pain often gets worse before—if ever—it gets better. They've added meds tough enough to tranquilize a baby rhino. Nevertheless, Phantom's in full force tonight, flaring out his fiery fingers all over my left side, suffocating me with his very existence. I have to get the hell out of this bed.

Somehow I summon the will to crawl out from under the sweat-soaked sheets. Benny's not in bed, and I stumble out of the musty room to look for him. I wind up in the lobby, boisterous to the point of nearly disorderly, with Israeli citizens doing their willing duty to raise the spirits of the half-dead. The recent operation in Gaza has flipped the sign on most hospital beds from "vacant" to "*ocupado*." It's packed. I shamble aimlessly through the colorful crowd, through their cookies and flowers, offers of affection. I walk arm-in-arm with Phantom, his terrible tendrils wrapping barbs of thorn into my missing arm. His touch is a mixture of frostbite and dagger that makes it impossible to enjoy the laughter here, or the lone acoustic guitar some guy is playing while the throng slowly sways.

Someone hands me a flower with yellow petals. When I look up, I see her. This woman smiles so much it makes me uncomfortable. "That's my husband, David, on the guitar," she says. "He comes here every week to play for you guys." How long have we been talking?

"He's good," I tell her. "Soothing." And he is, now that I really listen. All around me, mouths are moving, but I can't distinguish the words they're saying. I'm starting to get very, very sick of this stoned feeling.

"I'm Shachar," the woman says. "Hey, where do you stay on weekends? Do you go home?"

Everything around me morphs into a Dalí painting. The clocks are melting. The floors are tipping precipitously like the CAREN platform, so I compensate by climbing. Shachar's smile becomes a monstrous lemon wedge. I pretend I'm OK. "No," I say. "I stay here."

"Alone?"

"Alone." The truth is an anchor, a real thing in this surreal space.

Even if I wanted to, I can't form the words to tell Shachar why. Beyond not wanting to cause them any pain in the midst of my father's plight, I absolutely do not want my family to pity me. They're living less than an hour away, at the Wolfson Towers in Jerusalem. I could easily get there by bus. But I don't want my mother or sisters to see me struggling to feed myself, to dress myself, to *be* myself again. Truth is, I'm ashamed to go home. "I'm—I let everybody down."

"Nonsense," says Shachar. "From now on, you're going to stay at our home on weekends."

"Sure," I say, figuring I'll never see this woman again. She points with her chin to her husband. "Know how we met? David was nineteen and serving in Givati, wore a purple beret. He couldn't play guitar yet, but he was already a combat officer who led troops into battle. I was the secretary on base, which meant I was in charge of our only working phone. We met when he asked me if he could call home. It's good to be the gatekeeper."

Somehow I wind up back in bed. Phantom's shooting spitballs at the wall. Benny's struggling in our en suite bathroom, and a nurse is knocking on the door. "Can I give you a hand?"

And here I thought you and I had something special . . .

Eventually, I'm going to have to wean myself off all these drugs.

That Friday, the rehab empties out, as usual. I have the place to myself, which is fine by me. I'm planning to spend the weekend watching old reruns. I'm on season four of *How I Met Your Mother* when a smiling woman bursts into my room. "Ready to go?" she asks.

"*Huh—?*" Oh, right. It's Shachar from the other night. I try to fight her off, but she literally drags me to her car by my shirt. It's a daylight abduction, and I hunch, stumble, mope until she has me belted fast beside her. On the way to their house, she tells me all about her son, Ido.

"I've got three boys," she says. Her hands grip the wheel at 10 and 2, but she watches me instead of the road. "Ido's in the middle, thirteen years old. You're going to be using his room. This was all his idea."

I wonder whether I, as a typical teenager, would have ever in a million years spontaneously volunteered to bunk with my sisters in order to free up my bed for a random wounded vet. I highly doubt it. My *only* personal space? For a complete stranger? Ido moved in with his little brother across the hall in order to accommodate me.

What starts as one weekend turns into several, evolves into longer and longer stays. In late April, I insist on pulling out my own stiches—thick, painful-to-remove staples—as the nurse videos with my phone. I'm so sure I'm going to make it back to combat that I'm already working on my reputation as the crazy Hollywood drill sergeant. And, suddenly, I'm living full-time in Ido's room. For four months. While I work on getting more comfortable going home. Not once does Ido complain. He's proud of his contribution, and rightly so. His heart, I come to understand, has a tendency to beat for more than just one body. It beats for me now. Just like his father,

David's, when it commanded a platoon of thirty young men a lot like me a decade and a half ago.

I do spend Passover in April with General Galant while he visits the troops on the Gaza border north of Ein HaShlosha. Soon after, he starts inviting me to his house on weekends, where he throws lavish barbeques for all his family and friends. I feel like a little bit of each. It's become increasingly clear I've found my advocate. Someone who can put a purple beret on my head.

Chapter 8

TWIDDLING MY THUMB

June 2009

Yoav,

First off, I would like to thank you for the interest you have shown [for] my wellbeing from the moment that we met. There's no doubt in my mind that you care deeply about the soldiers you command. Even if for whatever reason they are of no further use to the cause we serve.

You may correct me if I'm wrong when I say that in my case one of the reasons you took interest in me is because you saw the potential in my specific situation, and my will to use that potential to its maximum.

. . . [A]fter the injury, all I was worried about was getting back to my unit and completing my mission. In hindsight it's pretty obvious to me I won't be making it back to the shetach krav [field of combat]. I will however do everything in my power to get as close to kravi [combat] as possible.

Every-time I tell someone of my plans to return to combat the first thing they ask me is, "Haven't you done enough?"

This question only strengthens my resolve . . . my hope is that when civilians and soldiers alike see that an American boy who volunteered to join the infantry got hurt and returned again even stronger . . . they will be inspired to do a little more . . .

My goal is to motivate those around me, and if that means sitting on Bach Givati or Bahad Echad [Givati's training base or the officer course training base] for the duration of my service, training other soldiers to enter combat, I would be honored to do so.

I don't see the harm in placing me in combat training. I am willing to be tested rigorously on anything you have a hard time believing I can accomplish. If it be the bochan maslul [combat obstacle course] *or loading, aiming, and shooting an M16, I am up for the test, and I without a doubt will find a way to pass it.*

At the end of the day I am here to serve, and if you see fit to put me somewhere non-combat, I will respect your decision, knowing you did everything in your power to put me in the best place for me as well as the army.

I hope our friendship will continue to grow only stronger.
Thank you for everything,
Izzy Ezagui

I plan to hand the letter to General Galant when I see him today. He's invited me to join him for another visit to the disabled vets still in rehab after the traumas they sustained in Cast Lead. I spot him with his entourage of military personnel waiting outside the rehab center at Sheba, my former residence, now that I live in David and Shachar's home. Seeing him, whether alone or in public, always makes me queasy.

But he gives me a big smile and a warm handshake, which quickly sedates the feud going on between all my organs. The disabled vets unlucky enough to still be in rehab this long all have serious-enough injuries to require daily PT and/or treatments, preventing them from being able to live at home. Benny is one of those guys. The entourage, with me included, goes straight to the trauma ward, home to all the soldiers hurt badly enough that they won't ever again lead a normal life. It's weird to be on *this* side of the general's visit. I'm making progress. Then we head into the CAREN suite. All the bigwigs are much impressed by the ultramodern technology. The engineer who runs the whole operation tells Yoav how the system works, and how much progress the various patients are making. I'm smiling. "Who's got the high score?" Yoav asks her. Good question!

The technician turns to face me. "Want to tell him?"

"It's me," I say.

After the visits, I ask Yoav if he has a moment to talk about my mission. He tells me to wait a moment while he calls over another high-ranking officer. The three of us sit down in a conference room. Yoav introduces me to the officer, Dr. Ishy Icholov, one of his direct reports. "Ishy's the head medical officer of Southern Command. I wouldn't make a decision like this without his counsel. I want you to tell Ishy what it is you wish to do."

I smile at this Ishy. He doesn't smile back. "Sir, my goal is to return to combat. I can see myself as a commander, training other soldiers for combat. But really, I think I can—"

"Ridiculous," says Ishy, cutting me off. He swivels to face the general. "Imagine the poor colonel or major who'd have to take responsibility for a one-armed soldier." He swivels back toward me. "Don't you see, son? You'd be a danger to yourself—and the soldiers around you."

"But, I've already—"

"For example, how would you show a soldier how to load a rifle if you can't do it on your own?"

"Well. Off the top of my head," I say, "I could use another soldier to model the maneuver. I would have him hold the rifle and I would explain exactly where his hands need to be, what actions he needs to do, and the correct stance he needs to do it in. I would . . ."

Yoav is slowly nodding, but his expression reveals nothing. It's clear this "Dr. Notgudenuff," though, isn't even hearing me. "I mean, I can see you passing officer training, passionate boy like you," says the doctor. "Then *maybe* you run an intelligence unit or something like that. But combat? I'm afraid you'll never make it back. In fact . . ." He again faces his superior. "If this is attempted through Southern Command, I'll make sure the notion is quashed."

I shoot the general a look, which says, "A desk jockey? I'll go insane." This time, the general's eyes tell me this isn't over yet; there might be other options. I hope I'm not reading him wrong. That this meeting is simply Yoav's way of putting out feelers. Just because the doctor says "no way, it's impossible," doesn't mean the general has to agree with him. If the guy running Southern Command wants something to happen, it's not like some underling can really "quash" that initiative, no matter how open the dialogue is in the culture of the IDF. Right? But as for gauging just how on board the doctor will be with this mission, I think we've pretty much got our answer. The question is: How persuasive was he?

I thank Dr. Notgudenuff for his time and consideration, *blah blah blah*, and the three of us stand up to leave. Then Dr. NGE says, smiling for once, "You'll make a fine intelligence officer, Izzy."

"Right, sir."

As we get to the door, I slip Yoav the letter I wrote yesterday. I don't know what I'm expecting, but would it be too much to ask that he open it up and read it right there in front of me? Maybe the orchestra—conducted by John Williams—then swells? And when it reaches a crescendo, maybe he says, "You got it, kid. Screw that small-minded doctor douche. See you in the field."

Sure enough—he *does* open the envelope and take out the letter. He's reading it right on the spot, just as I had hoped. So awkward. But nothing approaching so melodramatic a reply comes my way in the ward today. He smiles, nods, folds up my dream, places it in his shirt pocket. And walks off.

Weeks go by. I'm starting to lose hope. Then, Galant invites me on an extensive tour of the southern front, along with a large group of the Who's Who in Israeli politics and armed forces. On a bus near the Gaza border, in the middle of the afternoon, this older guy walks down the aisle toward me and says, "Hey, you're a hero, kid."

A little melodramatic, no?

"Excuse me?"

"Are you Izzy Ezagui?"

"Yeah, but I'm no hero, sir."

"Bah," he says. Then huffs. "As you like it." He limps back to his seat. I've met plenty of heroes. What's the old man know of that?

I go to look out the window and see that the corporal sitting beside me has his mouth open. "*What?*" I ask him.

"Do you know who that was? That's Zvika Greengold ... *The Zvika.* You know, leader of the Zvika Tank Force in the Yom Kippur War? He ought to know a hero when he sees one."

KEEPING MY NOSE CLEAN

July 2009. I don't feel like a hero. I feel more like an addict. The strongest of the many meds I'm on is called Duragesic. That's a fentanyl transdermal patch, at the highest available dose, which releases 100 mcg per hour. I've been on this patch for six months already. Just to give you an idea, fentanyl is about ninety times stronger than morphine. In fact, they prescribe it only after you've been on morphine or oral opioids (like OxyContin) long enough for them to cease doing the trick. I'm doing all three.

One night in Ido's bedroom, I have an epiphany. The phantom pain is never going to abate. So I'll either have to stay on these mega-drugs forever, or learn to live with my new life partner. And only one of these options will allow me to return to combat. I decide right there that I'm going to have to re-enlist along with Phantom, both of us drug-free.

While living with the Dans, David and Shachar's family, I'm still supposed to go back to Sheba twice a week for rehab. On one of those visits, I approach Dr. Zivner with a direct request to help me lower my dose incrementally. "You're kidding yourself if you think you can quit the opioids with your level of pain."

Believe it, Izzy. You're totally my bitch.

"Izzy, we've got guys from five wars ago still on fentanyl. Not to mention withdrawal's not some walk in the park. There's no good reason to add that kind of stress and suffering to your plate right now." It's clear I can't do this under their guidance. No problem. I'll manage my own extraction from the world of opiates.

I start by cutting the patches in half. That shouldn't be *too* tough, right?

What can I say about withdrawal that won't sound cliché? You've seen movies depicting heroin withdrawal? You know, guy shaking, sweating, screaming at so many horned demons? Vomiting nonstop on his pajamas. Writhing around and trying to make deals with the devil for just one more hit? Well—morphine, fentanyl, and heroin all derive from the same opium poppy. For six thousand years it's been a universal analgesic. And for just as long, we humans have gone through hell when we've tried to kick it.

The Dans are, unsurprisingly, concerned. Shachar is horrified at what I'm going through. I keep waking them up at night with random screams, and I'm unable to keep anything down. She calls the hospital to ask what the hell they're thinking by weaning me off these drugs so suddenly. They ask her what the hell she's talking about. She asks me what the hell I'm thinking, going against the doctors' orders. All the while, Phantom, having used my intestines to string his piano, performs an opera with my body.

PULL MY FINGER

Shachar wants me gone, and it's hard to blame her. She's probably worried I'm going to die in Ido's room. She's probably right. Very few things get me out of bed anymore. One of them is an "invitation" from Dr. Notgudenuff. Seems the gatekeeper has not forgotten me. Without telling me why, he says he wants me to visit his base a couple months after our first meeting. I take the three-hour bus on pins and needles. Maybe he's changed his mind?

Nope. He's brought me out to reiterate that his gate is locked: "I hope you've got this nonsense about combat out of your head. You cannot pull it off."

The look on my face tells him everything he needs to know about my attitude toward his obstructionism. "Let me guess," he says, "You heard about Yakir Segev, so you think you can do it, too."

Maybe. For seven years, Yakir was a combat soldier in Egoz, a prestigious guerrilla warfare unit. He advanced to the rank of captain and fought with distinction in the 2006 Lebanon War. All this despite the fact that he'd lost his arm in a traffic accident when he was three years old. He's a legend in the IDF.

"Well, Izzy you're not Yakir. He had his entire youth to prepare for the military. You've been living with one arm for, what, six months? And it's not even your dominant arm. Not to mention you're on significant meds. You have to stop this foolishness, son."

I sit there quietly. Fuming. I say nothing to the man intent on deterring me. But on the return bus ride, I realize NGE's not really my nemesis. No, all he's managed to do is start a new fire under my ass. Maybe that's why Yoav had me meet with the doctor in the first place. To get me to affirm my commitment, bolster my resolve. Well, mission frickin' accomplished.

First I have to make sure I'm completely off these meds. This half dose ensures I'm still partway loopy on drugs yet still in a world of hurt—it's the worst of both worlds. But the thought of quitting cold turkey gives me the shivers. I don't think I'm quite ready for that yet.

THE ROBOT WITH A HEART OF GOLD

August 2009. Ian Ash knows something about pain. And he knows something about the ways we try to medicate the pain away. The Jewish philanthropist suffered unspeakable abuse between the ages of eight and eleven. I'm sitting on a plush sofa in his four-story condo on the Miami waterfront. Ian's heard about my father's plight, and he's decided to help. In fact, he won't rest until "justice is done." I shouldn't be surprised. He's all about justice. He recently spoke publicly about his own abuse, and even confronted his abuser, and encouraged hundreds of others to do the same—nearly unheard of in Orthodox circles. With a few key others, Ian spearheaded a grass-roots movement to change the "grandfather culture" of Orthodox Jewish communities, which tend to care more about their image than the victimization of their own most vulnerable citizens.

I worked for Ian's neophyte company for a brief time when I was a seventeen-year-old schnook and he was a twenty-year-old entrepreneur. I worked for his partner. My only interaction with Ian was when he interviewed me in Miami while he was still studying in yeshiva as he began to build his vision. He offered me a customer service position in his online electronics business. That job didn't work out. I got pissed off about something or other—Ian tells me it was over my pay—after just a few months. I gave Ian's partner one week's notice and I quit. Never saw Ian again.

Until he decided to save my family.

Ian's father lives in Crown Heights, where he sits on Community Board 9. He gets involved in a lot of Jewish community causes: food for the needy, safety patrols. That kind of thing. He also gets involved in my father's case.

A rabbinical court in Crown Heights found my father guilty of violating Jewish law. In Orthodox Judaism, a *beis din*—a house of judgment—consists of three observant Jewish men. One problem in my father's case was that the lead rabbinical judge had no business presiding in any matter related to the real estate development in question—this rabbi held property in one of the buildings. He ought to have recused himself.

The conflict of interest, among other wrongs and biases, concerned Ian's father. So he asked Ian if he'd meet with someone, "just to hear about some injustice in Crown Heights."

"I figured this guy, Eliyahu Ezagui, must have done something wrong," Ian Ash tells me. "It wasn't for me. So I told my father, 'Look, if you need a token contribution, I can help. But this is not the kind of cause I'm interested in. This guy was indicted, for God's sake.' I assumed he must have done enough to deserve what he got."

But Ian's father was persistent. So he arranged for a meeting in Miami about the case. Not with my father, who was living under house arrest in my first home, the building in Brooklyn he built for us on President Street. But with an advocate.

Ian saw what few people cared to recall. My father was extremely charitable. He counseled people having marital issues. He advised estranged parents and kids on how to reconcile. He gave and gave and gave to charities and individuals in need. He'd built synagogues for people, single-handedly, and he had single-mindedly rescued Crown Heights from dire circumstances. Even the mayor acknowledged that. But as soon as the book got thrown at him, almost everyone dropped him like the wrong end of a lightsaber. "This could be me," says Ian Ash. "Suddenly the scapegoat for people's bad investment decisions."

Like my father, Ian also gave of himself and his wealth for the betterment of the community, even as he strived to increase the reach of his businesses. "Maybe I need to prove to myself," he says, "that someone will help his fellow man, will come out of the woodwork to help someone when the chips are down."

Who does that?

"Truth is, I'm terrified by the fact that these people abandoned your father after all he did for them. Well, I'm not going to abandon him—or you."

A few weeks ago, I flew from Israel to New York so I could maybe help my father. We needed money for a proper legal defense. Such a sum was extraordinary to me—hundreds of thousands of dollars. Where were we going to get that?

The two of us huddled on twin mattresses in the tiny front vestibule where I used to play with my Legos, sharing some kind of depressing bachelor pad. Years before, my father had split our old apartment into two. The large part in back, where our bedrooms and the living room were, he rented out. The front hall, he kept for himself, for all the times he had to travel back to Brooklyn for his real estate business. By now the bank had foreclosed, so we weren't even supposed to stay there. One night, he reminded me of a time when I was five, and he used to travel between our home in Miami and his work in New York. "Ma hated the northeast weather and all those roaches in Brooklyn. What's love? It's schlepped on a plane every single week, back and forth, out on Thursday and back on Monday. One night, your mother and I were talking over the phone, and I asked her to put you on. You said, 'I don't know who that man is.' Well, that was it. I came home the next day and reduced my work trips to once a month."

And then I flew away from him, leaving him in Brooklyn. It was for a good cause, though. Ian Ash's dad sent me to Miami.

Before I know it, I'm staying in one of Ian's spare bedrooms. He says I was (re-)introduced to him not as Eli Ezagui's son, but just some kid helping out with the case. I was supposed to knock on wealthy people's doors and simply, humbly, ask them for money. Ian gave me a list of wealthy Jews whom he knew personally throughout the city. I don't remember much of this. In any case, it didn't take long before we realized we knew each other from years ago.

So I went around like a beggar trying to save my pops. In the end, we raised enough capital to get a good lawyer on his case, which I obviously could never have done without the likes of Ian, his father, and other benefactors.

In the meantime, within days, it felt like I was reuniting with my long-lost brother. People comment all the time that they think Ian and I must be siblings. Brothers, yeah.

Ian's three years older, yet his life experiences cast him in the role of mentor to me. At the same time, we're both a little lost. A lot lost. Maybe we can find ourselves together. He tells me I'm probably one of the most intense people he knows. Every interaction, every random event in the universe has *meaning* for me. Too much meaning. He tells me I'm perpetually disturbed. Never at rest. Constantly struggling and grappling. And, much like him, I always focus on what's *wrong* rather than what's right. "You've got ten great things going for you, but one small thing that's not, and you'll work on that one thing forever. It must be miserable being you." Who but a brother can diagnose a guy so aptly, and still love him?

I start jogging around his exclusive little complex. First once, then a few times. Lots of vomit. Before long, I'm doing circuits that total miles. "You know I'm going back to combat, Ian."

I can tell he thinks the very idea is crazy. But he never gets in my way, never discourages me. Even through the withdrawal.

At Ian's, I keep trying to wean myself off the fentanyl by halving the dose I place on my back.

Yeah, I'm *trying* to get off the Duragesic—but a little Jack and Coke tends to ease that transition. Lots of random people pass through Ian's home. One such rando, a guy who's forever doped on boatloads of heavy drugs—let's call him "Munch"—keeps needling me for a hit. We're out one night, and he insists my patch can't possibly be that strong. He bets me that he, of all people, can handle it. He lists all the many drugs he's done in his life—coke, acid, shrooms, E, Special K, some other stuff I've never heard of. I bet him that my patch will floor him. He won't listen. So I cut one in half and hand it to him, 50 mcg an hour.

The next morning, Munch comes up to me with a goofy grin and a greenish pallor to tell me, "You were right, bro. That patch was so strong, I puked. Oh, man. Some of it's still in my hair. I had to flush that junk."

Same story with my father. When I was staying with him, he sneaked into my stash. "I just wanted to know what it felt like to walk around like you. So, I cut a patch in half and stuck it on my back. *Oy gevalt!*" He vomited all night.

Yeah, get to know your stoner son, Pops.

Ian and I open up to each other in a way that neither of us has ever done. I always felt close to Aaron Brik, but maybe we were just too young or too inexperienced (or a little embarrassed or uncomfortable) to really talk about important stuff, to be this raw. Anyway, Ian and I realize that each of us is trying to figure out who we are and what we're doing in the world—and we're both at a point in our life when we're willing to admit that.

Having said that, I see Ian as more like a machine than your typical human specimen, whereas I'm a hot mess—and not the sexy kind. This is not to say that Ian doesn't feel. He does—more than most. Maybe it's a response to his molestation as a kid. He became very calculated in his behaviors and his speech. If you ask him a question, he'll actually wait and think before giving you a planned, articulate response.

Ian isn't inherently wild. When wild does happen, it's a premeditated *decision*. For example, he understands that I'm going through hell and wants to ensure that I thoroughly enjoy my visit. When we hit the clubs, instead of dancing, he does high jumps on the dance floor. Or he repeatedly shouts random nonsense on the street— "*Shmendral! Shmayunki!*"—just to see how people will react. Weird stuff, but all very deliberate, computed in advance.

We spend about a month together. He rolls out the red carpet, pulls out every stop in his effort to show me a good time, despite these activities lurking far out of our respective comfort zones— or specifically because they lurk there. We hit the hottest parties.

I'm like Turtle from the show *Entourage*. I drive Ian around in the Porsche and, on occasion, when the hour gets late, we end up at a strip club. He pays strippers to climb on top of me without warning. And I'm always flustered, because (a) girls, and (b) multiple girls. "Um, yeah, hi . . . That's my lap."

"You're in strip club, little man," says a blasé Russian dancer. "Where you want I sit? On face? We don't do this thing here." She swings around, and her dark ponytail smacks me in the eye.

Classy.

I turn to Ian, trying to see him through my surviving optic nerve. "*You* do this, man?"

He nods, motions with his gaze toward something above and behind me as another pair of hands—slender and spray-tanned—grasp my shoulders.

Da heck?

"Hello, baby," says another robotic Russian stripper. This one's blond. "You very handsome, baby."

"I, uh . . ."

"You need relax, little man," says Ponytail. "You need *wodka*."

Ha. I'm pretty sure I know this chick's cousin, a bushy-eyed doctor in Tel Aviv.

"I—"

"You quiet now. I dance."

Ian's laughing beside me. I silently mouth the word, "*Why?*" My entire body's stiffer than Jack Dawson chasing the *Titanic* to the bottom of the North Atlantic.

"Because," he says, "you're going back to combat. So . . ."

"So?"

"So you need to figure out how to grasp multiple objects simultaneously. You know, with one hand."

"Really, man? Really?"

"Just trying to help." He winks. "Little Man."

DISARMED

FIVE-FINGER DISCOUNT

Not since Aaron Brik have I had such a friend, the kind who'll go out of his way to shine light in my darkest hour.

Orthodox school policy: no *"treif"* books, no games, and absolutely no music. For the love of *HaShem*, it's 2002, not 1802! I'm OK heading to Tucson without a crate containing K. A. Applegate's oeuvre. I can leave my Wii behind. The only chink in my armor has been carved near the heart by one Avril Lavigne.

Avril's music intoxicates my thirteen-year-old brain and body the way I imagine heroin must. I physically cannot hold myself back from bringing her CD to my new school in Arizona. Some courageous/criminal kids might smuggle cigarettes, liquor, or porn. I bring Avril Lavigne as my sole contraband, jammed in a secret compartment in one of my suitcases. I get away with it, too. For a while. A few glorious months pass before my dorm counselor discovers Avril's album spinning inside my bright-red CD player. I have fallen asleep to the song "Complicated," and my rude awakening occurs when The Man un-complicates things by cracking the CD in half.

Now I'm jonesing. I need my Avril fix before I lose my grip and go postal on this place. During our class's next weekly visit to town, I sneak into Target to re-buy her album, *Let Go*. There she is in her overlarge coat and smoky eyes, her hip out and arms crossed, the whole city blurring behind her. As I'm taking it all in, I feel eyes on my back.

It's Aaron Brik. I glare at him just long enough for him to be sure I haven't forgotten the jumping cactus fiasco of a month ago. I get to the sliding glass doors with my hard-won booty, and, lo and behold, my dorm counselor, anticipating this rookie move, is standing sentry. He busts me for possession with intent of use before I can even leave the store. Again, he snaps the album in two—this time with the case and all. Who is this guy, the Hulk?

That night, fuming and pouting like a little girl who's had her Avril Lavigne album snatched—twice—I hear footfalls approaching. Then a Brik-shaped head pops into view above my bunk. What does this schmuck want? He plops a chunk of square plastic on my chest. "She sounds like crap anyway," he whispers, and walks away.

No one has ever done something like that for me before. For the price of a stolen CD, Aaron Brik buys a lifetime supply of my undying loyalty.

A SHOT IN THE ARM

August 2009. Back in Israel. Ido Dan's borrowed room. Lights off. Door closed. Moaning and sweating. Nightmare images. Random flashes of contorted faces. Vivid hallucinations, evil clowns, mind gnomes, and Hitler's German shepherds. Body heat so intense I need to fling off all the covers—then instant shivering so strong I have to struggle just to reach down and pull the covers on again. Each movement—wiping my forehead dry, scratching a phantom itch—feels as long and difficult as running a 10K. During the rare moments my body and Phantom declare a temporary cease-fire, I veg out on a marathon of *30 Rock*, but after a few minutes, I remember nothing of the plot or Tracy Jordan's antics.

Shachar's mother insists it's time to cut the American drug addict loose.

It takes her a week to pull the pin. Finally, Shachar, tears drying on her cheeks, says, "We love you, Izzy, but it's time to go. You have to *do* something with your life, and that's not going to happen as long we're enabling you."

"The devil makes work for idle hand," says Phantom, unhelpfully.

"You're kicking me out?"

"We're setting you free. You don't need us anymore. Go *live*."

"It's the drugs?"

"Well, that isn't helping, dear. What if something goes horribly wrong? We can't be—"

I get it.

Back to Jerusalem, I go. Back to my mother and sisters. As the poppy wanes, the Phantom rises. I'm in such throes at the end of August 2009, Kobi suggests we go to the beach, to keep my mind off the challenges of withdrawal and pain. The beach where I meet the woman of my dreams, and she discards me after I save her life. In the RAV4 on the way back, still high on adrenaline, I turn down the stereo, shush Phantom, and dial General Galant. I have his private cell. The difference between the American military and the IDF writ in bold print: Can you picture an American GI ringing up General Petraeus? "Heya, Dave. I was wondering if you could help me out with something . . ." Or, "Colin. Yeah. It's Izzy . . ." You might think it's somewhat provincial, but no one's ever accused the IDF of being a second-rate fighting force.

"Hello?"

"Can you really make this happen, Yoav?"

"You work on yourself. Get better, mind and body. I'll work on this end."

"When?"

"Let's talk again in six months."

"Six *months*? But I'm ready now."

"Then you'll be even more ready then. And we'll be more ready for you."

I'm thrilled by the general's all-but-promise. But this wait's going to feel like a prison sentence.

HANDS AT TWO AND . . .

December 2009. The words "suspended license" flash at me—in bold red letters—from the self-service kiosk in the war zone of the DMV in downtown Miami. I'm surreptitiously trying to hide my injury from the prying eyes of petty bureaucrats.

"You self-absorbed, two-armed douche-nozzle," I curse my younger self. "Why would you leave your license in such disarray?" During my final weeks in the United States, before gallivanting off to Israel to donate my arm, I got ticketed twice by eager traffic cops for minor infractions. First for an illegal U-turn—a man's gotta poo when a man's gotta poo. Then for missing a stop sign—if they expect people to see it, they've got to prune the foliage once in a while.

Instead of dealing with these tickets. I left them for Future Izzy to worry about. Granted, younger me could not have predicted that I'd return to Florida minus my steering wheel's ten o'clock.

To renew a license, the instructions explain, a suspended driver needs to retake the written test. Damn. Once the crack staff at the DMV spot my disability, they'll require me to get a special license, which will allow me to drive only retrofitted cars. Renting a car will become impossible. What a tiresome inconvenience this missing arm is turning out to be.

I drive back to Ian's to lick my wounds. I'm reading a fantastic book about the raid on Entebbe. I'm reading every book I can get my hand on about military operations, especially those that required extreme chutzpah. Operation Entebbe will go down in history as one of the boldest hostage-rescue missions of all time. In 1976, armed terrorists hijacked an Air France flight from Tel Aviv and forced the pilots to fly the plane to the backwater capital of Uganda. Idi Amin—the dictator *du jour*—personally welcomed the terrorists, threw them a party, and gave them an airport building to house nearly one hundred Jewish hostages, whom they threatened repeatedly with death for more than a week. A courageous French pilot had remained as well, not willing to leave his passengers behind. As a result, the entire French flight crew bravely followed the pilot's lead, bringing the number of hostages to 106.

IDF officials, with the help of Mossad intelligence, decided to send a team of one hundred elite commandos to the rescue in six aircraft, including two Boeing 707s, and a huge C-130, all loaded with armored personnel carriers. Armed resistance from the Ugandan Army and Air Force was a guarantee. We're talking a big-budget Hollywood-film kind of mission. Definition of "badass." It happened in the dead of night. They called it Operation Thunderbolt.

Part of the audacious plan depended on the team airlifting a replica of Idi Amin's favored black Mercedes along to the mission, followed by facsimiles of the Land Rovers common to his convoy. The idea was to fool the Ugandan guards into thinking their very scary president had decided to stop by for a surprise visit/inspection. That particular part of the plan didn't quite work—one of the airport sentries knew Amin had recently junked the black Mercedes in favor of a white one. They say nothing about military operations is ever black-and-white—but this intelligence failure literally was. *Take that, Katya!* In any case, the Israelis managed to save all but three of the hostages, killed all the terrorists and a number of Ugandan soldiers, and even destroyed a fleet of MiGs on the tarmac.

Well, this gives me a capital idea. Even a half dose of fentanyl can addle a good mind, mind you, and I'm still suffering Phantom's embrace at its tightest. But it *seems* like a great idea at the time. Be bold or be beaten, baby.

What I need is the *equivalent* replica Mercedes for this particular situation. Surely the folks at the Florida DMV would be nowhere near as wary of such a Trojan Horse in their midst as Idi Amin's loyal soldiers. I'm going to figure this out.

"Mercedes, Mercedes, I need a Mercedes," I continually mumble under my breath for the next two days. Then I see it—it's so ridiculously obvious. I imagine a shiny new arm on display inside a red metal box, its front made of glass. Its label reads, "Break glass in case you need to fool the DMV into thinking you have two arms."

After digging my suitcase out of Ian's guestroom closet, I find my curled-up prosthetic gathering dust inside. I've worn it only a few times. I toss the cosmetic appendage onto the bed to inspect it further.

It looks nothing like a real arm. That's why I stopped wearing it. The material doesn't even resemble skin, but...Mossad was banking on expectation only. You know, you're expecting the Mercedes you see pulling up in a convoy to contain your boss—so any minor abnormalities go unnoticed. Yes, the *shape* of the prosthetic *does* match my remaining arm, insofar as it's generally arm-shaped. Generally. I dive back into the closet to find the only long-sleeved shirt I brought with me between searing Israel and boiling South Florida—a worn, grey sweater.

An hour later, I'm convinced I've created the impression that my normal human arm is resting casually within the confines of the sweater's front pocket. The test is a forty-five-minute drive away. I arrive back at the DMV sopping with sweat, jauntily attired.

An hour later, I leave the building two pounds lighter. Five pounds, if you count the fake arm I toss into the back seat, never to wear again. Having committed a new version of armed robbery, I leave with my shiny, new license.

ANKLE BRACELET

It's winter 2010. I'm back in Brooklyn, where I've come to help my father get ready for trial. Back in the decrepit "bachelor pad" on President Street. We have nothing. Just two old mattresses resting side by side, and an old, beat-up fridge.

DISARMED

The trial lasts roughly a month. I don't miss a minute of it. I wake up early every morning to gulp down raw eggs and take the Number 4 train to a gym—New York Sports Club—off Union Square in Manhattan. I use this commute to read books about military strategy, leadership, and operations. I read *The Art of War*, *How to Lose a War*, the *US Army / Marine Corps Counterinsurgency Field Manual*—anything I can get my hand on at the Strand ("18 Miles of Books"). These, for the mind.

And for the body, I work out seven days a week to prepare for my return to military life. My first day at the gym, I meet a trainer named Matt, a buff Puerto Rican in his early twenties, and a US Marine sniper reservist. When I tell him what I'm training for, he insists on training me for free.

"Here in the US military," he tells me, "an injury like yours is a career-ender."

I tell him it's a career-ender in Israel, too.

Matt's a great motivation. "Izzy, you and I are both gonna make general. I'm telling you."

"Yeah, and we'll coordinate joint anti-terror operations. First order of business: A drunk rave in the jungle for all our grunts."

"First, do ten more reps, tough guy."

I shower, re-dress, and head to court in downtown Brooklyn to make it just in time for proceedings to begin. The Theodore Roosevelt United States Courthouse on Cadman Plaza East is an imposing glass-and-steel structure. Presently, it entertains twelve people—unlucky thirteen if you count the judge—who hold in their hands the fate of my family.

Prosecutors are calling my father's case the biggest local subprime mortgage fraud on record. They say he "pocketed" millions, but, in fact, he went bankrupt, lost everything he'd tried to build for decades. He ran out of money and couldn't keep the lopsided rig running.

The government will always find something if they look hard enough. And, when members of the local community started to make a ruckus, look hard is just what the government did. But his intentions were always magnanimous. He wanted to help people.

My mother articulated this, far better than I ever could, in a letter she wrote to the judge in the case, Judge Frederic Block. I've excerpted it here:

It is amazing that a young man without skills or schooling was able to accomplish what he did by sheer will and determination.

The [Lubavitcher] *Rebbe* [Menachem Schneerson, leader of the Chassidic community, whom many considered the Messiah] *had a lifelong struggle with his followers to keep them in Crown Heights. In the 1950s Crown Heights was an upscale and safe community with a diverse population living together peacefully. In the 1960s all that changed. Crown Heights became a bastion of crime. The once-beautiful neighborhood was burnt down and abandoned, becoming a haven for crack houses and criminal activity. The Rebbe pleaded with the people that New York, home to the UN, with its diversity of cultures, was an inspiration to other cities and to the world at large. Everyone had their eye on the Big Apple, and therefore the* [Chassidic] *people had a responsibility to stay put and set an example in order to send out a message that running was not the answer. Being personally affected by the Holocaust . . .* [The Rebbe] *knew what the implications of running were, and he was very firm on this issue. Nonetheless, most people fled, leaving him and about two hundred families behind. Although safety has always been a concern, at The Rebbe's insistence, the community was slowly built up and eventually flourished again.*

On August 20th, 1991, we were living in California the night our daughter Jasmine was born. When we called Eliyahu's family in Crown Heights to relay the good news, we were informed of the pandemonium that was taking place. The Rebbe's motorcade had mistakenly hit and killed a little African American boy, and riots ensued. A young Jewish man was killed in retaliation, and all hell broke loose. People feared for their lives. Homes were broken into, stores were looted, and cars were set on fire. Talk of abandoning the neighborhood resurfaced, and was rampant. My husband told me, then and there, that as soon as I could travel, we were moving back. This was his calling. His fear for all the people in the neighborhood propelled him to take action.

Being that Eliyahu was not a born Chassid, he had a different perspective from those . . . born into the organization and living in the neighborhood. [E]veryone was stuck in a "fight or flight" mentality. Eliyahu had a key to a middle ground option. Time was of the essence, since it was necessary to start building while The Rebbe was still alive and able to instruct his people . . . about never running away from one's neighborhood. One of his main concerns was that the rich would head for the suburbs (which was the trend at the time), and the poor would be left behind in dire circumstances. Rather, he insisted on working things through, and striving to bring about peace and unity.

. . . [H]ad the people run away, it would've had citywide implications. Billions could have been lost to banks and the private sector. Neighboring communities would find themselves threatened, and running as well—history repeating itself. It was dubbed by the former Mayor, Koch, and the media to be the first anti-Semitic "pogrom" on American soil, and an indication of further unrest to come . . . [such as] the Rodney King case that sparked the [LA] Riots in 1992 that so polarized the country.

Touched deeply by the birth of our daughter, Eliyahu felt it was no coincidence these incidents concurred. Although it is counterintuitive to jump into the fire, The Lubavitcher Rebbe had ingrained into my husband that a little bit of light dispels a lot of darkness. . . . If not I, then who? And if not now, then when? *We moved back, which was a message of encouragement to others as it was intended to be. People approached Eliyahu in utter disbelief upon our return, since they couldn't get out fast enough. Eliyahu's mission was to restore a sense of hope and security to the neighborhood. After the riots, during a terrible recession, nobody in their right mind dared to build under the circumstances.*

The people asked Eliyahu to write to The Rebbe, sure that he would be advised not to build. In his letter, Eliyahu clearly indicated the risks involved, and the reasons so many cautioned him that it was not a good time to take on this endeavor. The Rebbe immediately responded in the affirmative.

Please notice in The Rebbe's response underlined [in the enclosed correspondence] *the word "bracha" ("blessing") numerous times . . .* [he also] *gave my husband an order to "build now!" This was . . . unusual . . . because The Rebbe never gave orders, he made suggestions. This indicated the urgency to take immediate action in order to stop the situation from further deterioration.*

Armed with The Rebbe's blessing and an honest reputation, Eliyahu restored peace. He expanded the borders at a tremendous financial risk to himself, by relieving the pressure that was causing much of the conflict. With an eye to the future, he built a building next to Lefferts Park, a project that caught [future] *Mayor Giuliani's attention. . . .* [Giuliani] *was assessing the conditions on the front lines in order to devise a plan and start making much needed reforms. Encouraged by Eliyahu's efforts,* [the mayor] *eventually followed through with his own plan to redo city parks to give people quality of life, and an opportunity to peacefully mingle with each other.*

. . . Today the area is safe and thriving. Even with the collapse of the real estate market, these units are retaining their value. The government brought witnesses on the stand to prove that Eliyahu was defrauding the banks by inflating the prices on the units, but this is what really happened. He provided affordable housing to over one hundred families, and was a constant source of encouragement, as he advised countless others to fight their fears, and move ahead.

People watched my husband struggle for years before the next developer got the confidence to build. Hundreds of units sprung up after that, followed by schools, temples, and community centers. None of this could have taken place if the people in the neighborhood had not joined hands in a group effort. . . .

I would like to mention that Eliyahu was on his own, working thirteen to fourteen hours a day to survive since the age of fourteen. He did repairs and odd jobs, something that came naturally to him. Before going into construction, he opened up a small wood shop in his apartment. He expanded years later into a storefront with his older brother, and eventually they opened up a factory.... Some time later Eliyahu started doing home renovations. He slowly built up his reputation as being honest and hardworking. People knew they could trust him with their money....

[But] *two and a half years ago,* [my husband's business stalled]. *Our dire circumstances forced us to move to Israel. We simply did not have the financial means to stay in the States. Thanks to the assistance that Israel provides for newcomers who become citizens, we had a chance of survival. After ten years of carrying all of the mortgages, being pressured with lawsuits and threats, and having his reputation dragged into the mud—Eliyahu collapsed....*

[He] *flew back to the States, broke and forlorn, to dispel the myth that we had run away to Israel. Knowing his own innocence, he did not foresee the possibility of being arrested.... He was not provided with any documents for over a year while he was under house arrest waiting patiently for the government to finish their investigation, knowing his name would be cleared and he would be set free. I still believe that justice will prevail....*

On January 8th, 2009, my son was injured in the Gaza War, fighting for the state of Israel and global democracy. A frontline foot soldier in Operation Cast Lead, he was hit by a rocket and his arm was traumatically amputated on impact. We were left in a state of shock and pain, beyond what any words could possibly express. The [US] *government allowed my husband ten days to fly in and be with our son, although* [the prosecutors] *remarked he should not be let out of the country because he would never return.*

If anyone had any doubts that my husband would take this opportunity to evade the law and avoid facing his responsibilities, or to give up the fight to prove his innocence, they were wrong.... [H]e flew back as was required by the law. Before my husband's arrival, for days my son refused to move, overwhelmed by shock and pain. Within ten

*minutes of being beside his father, everyone cheered as he rose from his
bed, infused with the strength he needed, just by being in his father's
presence.* [My son] *has had several operations, and a yearlong struggle
to come off the morphine that dulled the phantom pain in his arm. By
sheer will and determination he got himself back into shape,* [to rejoin]
*the Israel Defense Forces. Although this is unusual, despite the odds, he
has a need to finish what he started, and to be a source of encouragement
to the soldiers. Although they tried to persuade him otherwise, he will
shortly re-enter a combat unit, thereby losing any and all benefits due
to him for his injury. I guess the old adage is true. An apple does not fall
far from the tree. . . .*

*I am very proud of both of my soldiers. Even though my life would
be more peaceful if my men were not such high achievers. . . . Although
we have lost our home, our name,* [our credit,] *our stability, and our
peace of mind—no one can take away what we have given, nor destroy
our spirits.*

As the trial progresses, each day I grow more confident that the
jury is seeing how noble my father really is. How, even if he didn't do
everything by the book, he did what he did to help people. Not for
his own gain. His lawyers cart out boxes and boxes of evidence of his
tzedakah, hundreds of checks to good causes and individuals in need.
They say they've never seen anything like it.

As the month-long trial comes to a close, and we're waiting for
jury deliberations, I use some of my scant savings to purchase a small
keg of Heineken so that my dad and I can celebrate the justice of his
inevitable win. I am certain he will be exonerated. Some goon will
come and unlatch the ankle bracelet. We'll get our family back, our
house, our good name. And we'll all be reunited in Jerusalem.

HEAVY-HANDED

February 2010. While the jury's out, I'm lying on my mattress on the floor, and suddenly I see a mortar diving through clouds and heading straight for me. But I can't move. It strikes me dead-on, a brutal and terrifying concussion. My father's watching the news just a few feet away. I'm completely awake but totally paralyzed. I can't even signal to him that I'm in distress. It's all I can do to keep breathing.

Israeli veterans enjoy one of the world's lowest rates of Post-Traumatic Stress Disorder—about 1 percent of all IDF soldiers post-service. In comparison, in America, an average of twenty-two veterans commit suicide *every day*, and up to 15 percent are diagnosable with PTSD—that's a rate of almost 1,500 times greater prevalence. What accounts for this huge difference? Probably the best explanation I've heard is that it has to do with mandatory service. If everybody has to join up, then once you go home, you know that almost everybody understands what you've been through. You don't feel so isolated once you return to the unstructured world in which you're not constantly at war.

But very little is as isolating as being on trial. Even more so is watching your Spider-Man, your loyal, gentle father, facing a firing squad. I've never felt so helpless in my life—not even when I lay bleeding out, waiting for the world to go dark. Members of the Orthodox community in Brooklyn, people who knew very well how my father had helped them and the community, turned on him like jackals. The things they were saying about my father online, behind a curtain of anonymity, were vicious and cruel. They compared him with Bernie Madoff. They wished his entire family would suffer and go hungry—these brave keyboard warriors. They accused him. They cursed him. Called him a pig. Prosecutors were asking for him to get twenty-five years.

In the meantime, my baby sisters, Shoshi and Emunah, in Israel wandered shell-shocked, searching for their Tatty. My seventeen-year-old sister, Jasmine, was angry, lost, and tanking in school.

Thank God for Ian's robot heart. He was more of a brother than even my brothers-in-arms. One day, I'm on the bench in court, awaiting the jury's finding. And I'm recalling an incident when Ian pulled me in close, by the scruff of my neck. We were in some loud club in South Beach several months ago, both of us profoundly drunk. A few minutes before, we had passed a bachelorette party in a hotel lobby, and Ian literally pulled out a wad of hundreds and made it rain, just so the girls might talk to me. Now we're in this brothers' huddle, forehead-to-forehead, no girls or bachelorettes in sight, and Ian is shouting over the music, forcefully, even angrily. "Izzy, your father's going home. You have my word. I'll sell the last shirt in my closet to keep him from prison. My very last penny, whatever it takes."

I'm counting on my brother being right, as usual.

The jury finally files in. We all stand, awaiting their decision. Each "guilty" they call makes Phantom flare. I nearly buckle over right there, almost vomit over the banister and into the court. I watch the people at the prosecutor's table laugh and hug and celebrate the destruction of a good man right in front of them, with no regard for his family. I could kill someone right now.

But when I see my father standing there, upright, expression unchanged, I calm myself. He holds himself with the pride of a man who knows he's innocent. I know then he will overcome. That he'll survive the troubles ahead, troubles which are only just beginning.

They don't remand him into custody immediately. That'll happen in a few months or a year—the time it will take Uncle Sam to get his act together for sentencing. That's when the handcuffs, armed guards, and foot-chains will happen. For now, they lead him away to meet his lawyers, after which he'll continue on house arrest, far away from his wife and daughters. He looks up at me and gives me a weak smile. Crushing.

I book a flight back to Israel the next day. I can't bear to be around him. I'm as broken as my recently busted body can further break. For the next few weeks, I keep daydreaming about a scenario in which the judge will allow me to take on half of my father's sentence, to do half his time beside him so that we'd both be in and get out together having served his full sentence in half the span.

Before the case began, the government was offering my father a few deals in order to get a pretrial plea of guilty. Some of them were as low as six or seven years. The people who were advising my father urged me to push him toward taking such a deal. They said the government wins 90 percent of the time. They said instead of six or seven years he might end up with twenty or twenty-five. They said there is no way to come back from that long a sentence. They said our family would be destroyed by such a long sentence—but that six or seven years was short enough to survive. "He'll still be a youngish man."

So I went to my father and begged him to take a deal. Begged him numerous times. He kept calmly repeating that he would do no such thing. Around the tenth time I tried to convince him, he burst out in very uncharacteristic anger. "Izzy—I'm not guilty! I'd rather spend my life in prison as an innocent, than walk around free as one who admitted to false guilt."

I was so proud of his resolve, even though I was terrified. I went back to his advisors and told them, "I agree with my father."

"You're making a huge mistake," they said.

But it turns out we were right. The judge, who watched the entire case unfold, disregards the aggressive sentence the US Attorney's Office is recommending. In fact, Judge Block scoffs at the suggestion that Eliyahu Ezagui ought to go away for twenty-five years for what was clearly very bad judgment but with good intentions. In the end, he gets thirty-three months—lower than the minimum sentence for the crime for which he's convicted. He'll likely serve less, with time off for good behavior.

And he's going to a minimum security camp in Pensacola, Florida. Literally the opposite end of the state from Miami, where I'll be living after the conclusion of my service. But what's ten hours? I'm the only family my father will allow to visit in the nearly two years he serves. These visits are some of the most profoundly moving and memorable times I've spent with my father. I won't even share here the conversations we had. Suffice it to say, my father continues as my man of wcbs. In my cycs, no green jumpsuit with a number could ever diminish the length of my father's cape.

ARMS DEALER

"Yoav here. So this is the call you've been waiting for."

Finally. It's been a year since the injury.

"Yes, sir. I'm ready. Really, really ready. I just ran across Jeru—"

"Good. Because I've gotten you a meeting next week at Givati HQ outside Be'er Sheva." Givati is the infantry unit in which David Dan served as a lieutenant when he was my age, and where he earned his purple beret. "You'll be meeting the brigade commander, Moni Katz. You're going to have to impress him. He's not sure a one-armed soldier can survive in combat. The only one who's ever pulled off that kind of feat is Yakir Segev, and you know, that's a whole other story."

I know, I know.

A week later, in February 2010, I'm on another bus, this time heading to Sde Teman near Be'er Sheva. The bus is extremely overcrowded, so I find myself leaning on the ledge before the last seat, where the engine releases terrible heat. As uncomfortable as the ninety-minute ride is without sitting on a proper seat, I'm determined not to ask another passenger to give up their spot for the "disabled" guy. If I'm really going to make it back to combat, I can't look at myself as disabled—and I can't have other people see me that way, either. I'm just the same as every other twenty-one-year-old.

But any twenty-one-year-old sitting across from a battalion commander and his assistant is bound to gulp a little. "So what are we doing here today?" says Katz. We're face-to-face at Givati HQ. The only furniture in his spacious office is the bare, wooden desk between us.

"I, uh, want to go back to combat, sir."

It takes him so long to reply that I'm wondering whether I actually made my statement out loud. I'm dressed informally, jeans and a Haruv Battalion T-shirt.

"What makes you think you can do all the things a combat soldier has to do in battle?" I've answered this question a hundred times. But before I can answer this time, he says, "How are you going to do *Pazastz'tot*?"

A *Pazastz'tah* is a training exercise in which the soldier, holding his rifle in one hand, uses his *other* hand to either get down to the ground into a prone shooting position or get back up into a standing shooting position. It's a difficult maneuver, even with two arms, and drill sergeants make their soldiers repeat it literally ad nauseam.

Katz is clearly a man who appreciates a soldier who contemplates his answers before spouting off. So this is what I do, Ian Ash–style. And, after a while, this is what I say: "From the moment I got injured until today, everything I do I've had to relearn from scratch. Even the simplest things like buttoning a shirt, opening a bottle, and closing my belt were impossible at first. But after a while, I always found a solution. To everything. Every challenge. And I usually end up doing it just as well and as fast as before. Maybe better. So I believe the same thing will apply to combat. I understand it will be difficult at first, but not impossible. With time, I'll relearn."

His assistant's writing notes, but Katz keeps his eyes on me. "Right." He turns to his secretary and starts laundry-listing all the logistical details that need action and resolution before I can return. "Izzy, you'll be back in fatigues within the month." It's clear to me this was all just perfunctory officialdom—Katz has already gotten the order from Galant to put me back into service. "That'll be all."

I get up to leave. "Oh, and one more thing," the brigade commander calls out as I reach the door.

"Sir?"

"If it ever strikes you again as a good idea to come to my base wearing your old unit's logo, I will personally kick your ass. Understood?"

I can't tell if he's joking.

"Yes, sir."

I have a lot to think about on the long bus ride home, so I'm happy to find myself sitting on an actual seat this time. Foremost on my mind is something I read somewhere: "You must be careful what you wish for. You might get it." And there's another quote that comes to mind, this one from Kurt Vonnegut: "We are what we pretend to be, so we must be careful about what we pretend to be."

Chapter 9

ITCHY TRIGGER FINGER

December 27, 2009

Yoav,

I am e-mailing you to keep you updated on my progress.

I stopped taking all forms of medication. That means no pills, patches, or painkillers. This was initially against doctors' orders simply because it is not an easy task to accomplish. The doctors are very impressed and can't believe I have done so. We can both agree that nothing stands before a man's will.

Sadly, this does not mean that all the phantom pain is gone. I am seeing a world-renowned specialist in N.Y. next month to deal with the pain. I have heard really good things about him and am hoping to see immediate results.

Once the pain is gone I will be heading to a company called "A Step Ahead." They make prosthetics for the soldiers [who] come back from the war in Iraq. An organization has agreed to pay for my prosthetic. I explained to them my will to return to combat, and they agreed to help me [by making] a prosthetic that is capable of holding an M4, among other capabilities.

I hope all is well by you and that the UN isn't giving you too many problems.

Please send my warmest regards to your wife and kids.

(Feel free to reply in Hebrew)

Izzy

DISARMED

MY RIGHT-HAND MEN

No fireworks or parades mark my return to Givati, south of Be'er Sheva, in March 2010 ("Go straight to the end of the world, and make a left"). In fact, I'm not even going to have a second to celebrate. Moni Katz informs me I've got just a month to pass all the tests I had eight months to pass as a new recruit more than two years ago. He isn't rude about it, just matter-of-fact. Katz won't allow me to salute him—in fact, no officer, including General Galant, will let me salute them anymore. I think I'm supposed to take this as a sign of respect. Like we're equals or something. But it makes me uncomfortable. "One month, Izzy. Do or die. That includes the wall, the rope, marksmanship—everything."

Day one, I'm introduced to two people who'll be my lifeline here—and my gatekeepers. Ofir is the base's lead fitness instructor. He's a tall, handsome, quite smiley lieutenant. He happens to hold the record for the fastest obstacle course run in Givati. He's a physical freak of nature—strong and fast with inhuman endurance. Avishag—"Shoogy"—is the base's lead shooting instructor, also a lieutenant. Short, dark, and very much "one of the guys," she's beloved by everyone under her command. I can tell right away these two are natural leaders. I'll be working with them for two weeks each: Two weeks training on the obstacle course and the one-man drill with Ofir. Two weeks on the range with Shoogy. Then a final test, in front of Katz and whoever else he plans to drag along.

That first day, I go on a run with Ofir. "Not bad, not bad," he says a few miles in. "Good pace. I'm surprised by your level of fitness. This might be easier than they prepped me for." I'm smiling—but I don't have the breath to respond. He hasn't broken a sweat.

I'm rooming with two lovable stooges. The base's Krav Maga instructors, Efi and Dudi, are both deadly dudes, well-versed in snapping limbs and killing with their fists and kicks. But they're also both goofy as ball sacks. I decide that first night to share my dark sense of humor. So lots of one-armed jokes right off the bat. These two loons run with it. They come up with more amputee gags in one night than I ever will in a lifetime. I see Dudi, sporting eight-pack abs, likes to walk around in his tight underwear, farting away, and making little content sounds about it, as though rating the power of each release. And Efi is arguing with his girlfriend over the phone as he lies in bed, a nightly custom. Then they spend several hours in front of a small TV in the room, making grilled cheese sandwiches on a little press, yelling obscenities at the soccer players, and screaming whenever whoever scores a goal. They never once question the crazy, one-armed soldier who claims he's going to make it back to combat. I love them already.

On day two, Ofir lends me his combat vest, with its ammo and water weight. We hit the obstacle course, which is supposed to simulate operations under pressure. Having already served, I know I'll probably never have to do most of this stuff in combat, but I understand why they make us do it. IDF soldiers typically first attempt the course in the middle of basic training. Those who fail have to keep trying until they pass.

The exam begins with a five-hundred-meter sprint, before you reach a high wall. For many, the wall is their great nemesis. I didn't have any trouble two years ago, so I'm not expecting any now. There's also monkey bars, parallel bars, crawling under a low metallic grate, and a dozen other obstacles you have to master. In the middle, there's the rope. The rope you have to climb. After completing the last obstacle, if you have any gas left, you sprint four hundred meters to cross the finish line.

I'm more shocked than Ofir when I go hurtling over the two-meter (seven-foot) wall on my first try, with room to spare. "What the what," he cries out. "*Duuude* . . . A Jew with mad hops."

The parallel bars, on the other hand, take me a night of tossing and turning to figure out. The bars rest at about chest-height. I figure I can grab a hold of one of them, and jump/pull myself onto the other so that I'm seated on the thin rail. Then I'll scoot, scoot, scoot, scoot, until my butt cries for mercy. The next day, I get to check the parallel bars off the list. My ass raises the white flag, though, and I'll never again be able to sit quite the same way.

The rope is where things get hopeless. During this retraining, I can't make it more than a hand-length up the rope. To pass, I'll need to climb three meters—that's ten feet—and hit the beam at the top with my helmet. And that's after completing half the course, so I'll already be exhausted.

Obviously they're not about to offer me the Cripple Course. I would never ask for the booster seat, even if one existed and it was on offer. But that rope climb is going to be my Waterloo. I start to have nightmares about it. I wake up in a cold sweat with all my abdominal and oblique muscles cramped. One night the Stooges hear me, and they both switch on their lamps. "Dude," says Efi. "You should call Yakir." He means Yakir Segev, the one-armed commander. "Pretty sure he's got the rope-climbing record for Egoz—or was it all Golani?"

"No way," I say.

"Yep," says Dudi, taking the opportunity to switch the TV on and check the soccer scores. "Yakir's *the* fastest rope-climber. Like, in the entire IDF."

"He came to visit me in rehab," I tell them. "I've got his cell number. When I kept telling the general and all those politicos I was returning to combat, the first thing they all did was call Yakir."

"Cool."

"Yeah. Pretty sure his mission was to talk the crazy guy off the ledge."

So, the next day, I call Yakir Segev. I go through a long diatribe about how amped I am, and how prepared, but this rope thing, it's going to be the death of me. *Mrab, mrab, mrab* . . .

When he first came to see me in rehab, he gave me thoughtful advice I'd used to get this far. He said, "Izzy, there are soldiers who are slow, or fat, or have horrible coordination. There are guys who are a terrible shot. No soldier's perfect. But the goal of any soldier is to do so well at all the tasks he's good at, that the bad things get sort of . . . suffocated . . . by all the good. See?" That all must be an expression. Right? I expected no less wisdom now.

Silence on the other end.

"Yakir?"

"I'm here. Listen, Izzy. You listening?"

"Yeah, hit me." I await the sagacious nugget.

"Izzy. Just. Climb. The rope. *Just fucking do it*."

Advice from a check-marked sneaker. But of course he's right— it's exactly how I got it done the last time—why should now be any different?

"WHEN YOU LOSE A LIMB NO GIRL WANTS YOU ANYMORE"

A week before my first enlistment, February 2008. I'm reading Ron Leshem's novel, *Beaufort*, which was originally titled, *Im Yesh Gan Eden* (*If There Is a Heaven*). In the book, an IDF soldier loses his arm in the dangerous hills of Lebanon. Before the deadly mortar attack takes Ofir's hand, he gives the narrator a piece of his mind.

> "Aren't you afraid?" [Ofir] asked, "at being on your own? If your arm gets blown off you'll never find anybody who'll fall in love with you and look after you. You'll die all by yourself, a disgusting, miserable old man. Aren't you afraid of being alone?"
>
> . . . Truth is, this wasn't new. A long time before, we'd agreed, Oshri and me, that losing a limb was worse than anything, worse

than death. We weren't the only ones who thought that way, either. All the guys in the brigade said so, it's a known fact. When you lose a limb no girl wants you anymore. And you can't play soccer anymore, or swim. No treks. You're just going to get bumped around like that your whole life, so it's better to die, no doubt about it. When I finished officers' academy I said to Oshri, "If I get blown up and lose a part of my body, just shoot me. Kill me on the spot."

Of course, later on, Oshri loses an arm. His friend doesn't have the guts to follow through on their mercy-murder oath. Poor bastard. Glad it's only fiction.

A week later, my first day at Camp Michve Alon near Safed in the mountainous north. This is what you could call "pre-basic training"—a three-week intensive training. I'm here because all foreign volunteers and recent immigrants are obligated to pass through like it's some predetermined spawning point in a video game. All the bottom bunks are taken by the time I arrive. No ladders or footholds. Pain in the ass to climb. I pass out on a creaky mattress formerly owned by Moses (the 1st). It smells exactly like you'd think it would: Like the cast of *300* slept in it after a hard day's filming. Before I know it, a soft voice tickles my ample ears. "Fifteen minutes. Outside, in formation."

By the time I manage to stretch and drag on my boots, the line to the bathroom loops around the corner. Some recruits are paired up two and three per urinal. That's when I discover the term "crossing swords." In front of the sinks is a tangle of flying elbows, razors, and toothbrushes.

Only half of us reach the courtyard with enough time to start forming up. One overeager recruit counts down the remaining seconds. "Disappointing," comes the soft voice.

I don't dare lift my head to see who's spoken.

"What. A. Terrible. Disappointment."

Here we go, I think. This commander is straight out of Central

Casting, and he's about to rip off our heads and piss down our necks. But the harangue never comes. "Four minutes. Out of uniform, back in formation." The order arrives without emotion. "*Tzeh*" (Go).

Pandemonium erupts in direct opposition to the commander's unaffected delivery. We charge into the barracks all flailing and stepping on top of each other. Rifle-strapped commanders line the perimeter in evenly spaced intervals, each in the black beret I recognize as the signature of the armored division. So our new superiors are tank commanders. "Two minutes," the man in charge says impassively. "Move."

I catch a glimpse of the guy while my limbs are all twisted in my half-on uniform—a redhead sporting Oakleys and a trimmed ginger beard. Hold on—is the commander actually wearing Reeboks?

Sergeant Sneakers keeps up at this drill for the better part of the morning, and, after a decent buffet-style lunch, he splits us up into our assigned squads for the following three weeks.

David, Simon, and I are all from Florida. Noam, our fourth American, grew up in Los Angeles. Stav and Alex make up the Russian contingent. Snape is our South African; Ori, our Aussie, and there are two Frenchies who shield themselves from the rest of the UN with cigarette smoke.

"Thirty seconds. Form two straight lines in the courtyard. *Tzeh*." It's the same low voice that woke us all up. Now I'm marching at a fast clip behind the owner of that voice. He's short, not very muscular, and the stems of his glasses are poking out from behind his ears. He has the closest thing to a bowl cut one could get without breaking any hair-length regulations. We're being led by a total nerd.

"Form a *chet*," he orders, once we reach a clearing splotched with weeds. We shift into the IDF's most commonly used formation—a square missing one of its walls. Commander Bowl-Cut takes up a position facing us from the open side. He shifts his M16 so that it rests against his waist. It forms a kind of barrier between us and him.

"I am Commander Natan. For the next three weeks you are under my charge." That voice: As quiet as Sergeant Sneakers. But is that kindness underneath? "I'm going to do whatever it takes to ready you recruits for basic training alongside the Israelis. You, in turn, will do whatever it takes to succeed."

The rest of his speech is probably poetic and soulfully uplifting despite its atonality, but I can't understand much—should have paid a little more attention in Hebrew class. Yet his demeanor somehow comforts me. Whereas Sergeant Sneakers sounds aloof, this guy sounds like he could be your older brother encouraging you—albeit without much emotion.

Nothing about the next two weeks is comforting or encouraging. Every day, we sprint from one side of base to the other, double-time. Then we stand at attention for twenty minutes under a punishing sun, all gasping for oxygen. Then push-ups. More push-ups. If your palms are not indented with impressions of the asphalt, you're not doing enough push-ups. But Bowl-Cut's worst form of torture—one that, soon after our tenure, will be banned by most units in the IDF—is the universally reviled "second position." Sort of like a frozen push-up. As in, the "up" part of the push-up. And hold for . . . well, let's see how long you can hold. Ass level with back. One minute is brutal. At two, your whole body's bawling for relief. Three's sadistic. Most recruits don't make it past two.

If I ever become a commander, I'll never do this to my men.

So I have revised my initial "nerd" diagnosis of Bowl-Cut. He's a ninja disguised as a pencil pusher. Always on an evenly detached keel. Yet his words—those I can understand—are always motivational. It's obvious he aims to cut off our clumsy edges, to sharpen us like the points of a spear. Once, I catch him smiling at our formation. He's always there for us, until the day he isn't.

One night, a week before the end of Camp Michve, some commander with a minor speech impediment wakes us up in the middle of the night to form up on the parade grounds. Seems a terrorist attack has unfolded at a yeshiva in Jerusalem. Eight young boys are slain, and eleven injured. Only a specific breed of Russian recruit remains unmoved by this devastating news. This is why we're here, after all. To prevent this kind of thing from happening. To defend the innocent. After the announcement, those Russians rotate on the pull-up bars with cigarettes dangling from their lips. The rest of us are broken. I can't help thinking that Commander Bowl-Cut would know exactly what to say, how to comfort us during the lowest point of our neophyte service. *Where are you, sir?*

The next day, a full day since Lieutenant Lisp has for some reason replaced Commander Bowl-Cut, we're all sitting on our bunks.

David walks over to Simon's bunk and holds up the morning paper. "What am I looking at, bro?"

"Here," Simon points. "Who does that remind you of?"

I roll off my cot and join them. Simon's pointing at a collage of images on the front page—headshots of the boys murdered the previous day. Names and ages are printed beneath each photo. One of them is a fifteen-year-old kid with geeky glasses and a bowl cut. I see the surname Natan. Our commander lost his baby brother yesterday. There's nothing I want more right now than to comfort him, to tell him how sorry I am. But I fear I won't see him again. And I won't, for nearly four long years.

ELBOW GREASE

March 2010. It's impossible to get across how strongly these Givati officers and soldiers want their one-armed comrade to succeed. By day three, my roommates are insisting we all climb rope together before each meal to get me up to speed. There's a set of three practice ropes set up right in front of the mess hall so that the commanders have the option of abusing their recruits before grub. So the three of us climb—they both put a hand behind their back for unity, which is the kind of thing that could make a one-armed soldier want to weep. By the third day, we get so into this workout that, by the time we finish and look around, we see lines of recruits and commanders just staring at us with mouths open, wondering what the hell is going on. I find this attention embarrassing. But you can bet a bunch of awe-struck, green recruits eyeing you is an excellent motivator.

How does a one-armed guy climb rope? Most soldiers assume you have to rely entirely on upper-body strength for rope climbing, but with Ofir's help, and all the practice with the deadly Stooges, I discover that's not true. The arms are only placeholders. You have to let the legs do all the heavy lifting. The legs and core.

In about two weeks, I've gained the strength and technique I need to beat the rope. It isn't pretty, but it gets the job done.

OUT ON A LIMB

March 2008. In the middle of my three-week pre-basic training, I get the first opportunity to try out for a special unit. It's all I've been able to think about since deciding to join up, all Jonny, my Canadian friend and fellow volunteer, ever hears from me over the phone. They haven't assigned us our battalions yet, but I know exactly where I'm going to wind up. I'm gunning for Tzanhanim—the paratroopers. I will wear the red beret. If I had a tail, I'd be wagging it right now.

I know this base, Bakum, because I've been here before. All new recruits get processed through the IDF Induction Center at Bakum. No challenge there. But this time will be an actual test.

Step one: Medical clearance. Shouldn't have any problems there. The line is long. One in five of these applicants won't make it. At my turn, the medic shoves a digital thermometer into my ear canal before I can even say howdy. I smile wide and thank all deities for not having to answer questions. Can't have a paratrooper confusing "jump" with "hump." I hear a beep inside my skull, and the young soldier scribbles something on my form before waiving me through to see the doctor.

It's a little, shabby room with a card table and two metal chairs. The doctor's scrawny and so fantastically bald I can see the reflection of my dog tags glinting off his forehead. "Shalom, sir." Dr. Dome motions me to sit. I sit. I smile so wide it hurts. Can't help it. I'm gonna be leaping out of C-130s, helicopters, and who knows what fancy, secret, high-tech planes. All the units are named after snakes. Will I wind up a cobra? A viper? A flying serpent?

Dr. Dome looks down at the form. He frowns, furrows his brows. "You won't be participating in today's *Gibush*." He stamps my sheet and hands it back to me. Calls, "Next."

Another recruit walks in, but I don't budge.

"I'm sorry. What? No tryouts?"

"Your temperature is a point above the maximum allowance. You can't participate in today's test."

"But . . . what does that mean?"

"It means, Recruit, that you need to vacate my office. You cannot, and will not, test today in the *Gibush*." Another one with the emotions of an automaton.

I'm absolutely about to vomit. I stand up on shaky legs. I shove past the next applicant and make a break for the door. Gotta drink. One degree? Come on, I can nudge that down with just a wee bit of water. Right? So I snag a canteen from a nearby pile and fill it so it makes a convex surface over the brim. Then guzzle.

Now back to the medic, my stomach sloshing. Only a few stragglers left. I wave my sheet in front of his face. "I can only test an applicant once."

"Yeah. I know, I get that. I know there's rules. Of course you have to obey—look, please." I communicate all of this in a mishmash of Hebrew, English, Yiddish, and interpretive dance. "You need to help me. This is my dream. This is why I came here from America. You know this is the only possible day I'll ever have to test."

"All right. Keep your pants on." He casts a few sidelong glances and sticks the device back in my ear. I shut my eyes. I pray a little. "And..." He pauses to scratch a new set of numbers onto the form, "You're good to go. Just see the doctor and you're golden, San Francisco."

"Miami."

Back into the doctor's hovel. My head held high, a new skip to my step. I've beaten the system. Maybe I can be an anaconda. Do they have an anaconda unit? "You again."

"Yep."

"I mean *why* you again?"

"Look." I hand over my form. "Look."

"Clever," he says, handing the paper back. "But regulation allows for temperature assessment only once every two days."

"What does that mean?"

"Do you have *special needs*, Recruit? It's simple. Have two days passed since you last sat in that chair?" He pauses for effect. "Exactly. *Next.*"

Another enlistee walks into the room, but—*déjà vu*—I don't move.

"Recruit, please don't make me call the MPs. It's going to screw up the whole day."

"Sir, please. Just hear me out. Just for a second."

The kid behind me shuffles his paper and his boots.

"I come from—I came all the way—just to be a paratrooper. That's it, sir. My entire dream. I beg you, please don't crush my hopes."

Surely the middle-aged doctor is tired of petty bureaucracy, pushing papers. Surely he understands the glory, the patriotic—

His chair screeches as he gets up, leans forward, motions me closer with a finger. "If you're not out of this office in the next five seconds, you're heading to the brig. So . . . ?"

Somehow I muster the Mole's death stare, turn on my heels, and head out of Dr. Dome—no, Dr. Doom's—office.

All is lost.

No one wants to see a grown man, in uniform, no less, blithering on the sidewalk, but I can't stop the tears.

I failed. I haven't even begun, and I've already failed.

A SHOT IN THE ARM

Shoogy spends our first day on the range this April 2010 making me do *Pazastz'tot*, transitioning directly into having me load the rifle. It isn't working. The bullets won't catch properly in the chamber. Meanwhile, I'm pulverizing my only remaining ally—my right arm. After the second day of such abuse, I wake up and my remaining limb is swollen, stiff. I'm forced to wear a sling for a few days. It's nearly impossible to wipe my ass. The base doctor orders Shoogy to ease up on me. She doesn't. I don't want her to. So it's just her and me alone on the range, killing ourselves for my cause. Nothing around us for miles. It's a weird kind of heaven. Infected by Phantom, of course, who's lording over us both like the Mad King, with a brand new throne of human sinew and bone.

Day after day we drill, the three of us. Shoogy never lets up. So I never give up. If at any point she said, "Listen, Izzy. Give yourself a break. You're disabled. You're good enough, all things considered," I'd lose respect for her—and myself.

She gives me a practice test after a week.

Click, click, click—I'm pulling the trigger, if only to vent my frustration.

"Work already, damn it!" I yell at the Israeli-designed weapon in my grasp. The Tavor jams every time I load a bullet into the chamber, because I still can't hold the gun steady with one damn arm. What remains of my left bicep hangs limply from my shoulder, my sixteen-month-old battle buddy.

I've hunkered down in the shooting range every day for a week trying to prove my worth as a combat soldier. But now that idea's sloshing around my mouth like expired milk.

You do know, Izzy, that if you don't come up with a solution to this rifle jam soon, brass are going to strangle your aspirations to keep wearing that uniform. They'll bury your attempts at combat status farther below ground than our rotting left arm.

Instead of lingering on this painful truth, I kneel—lowering my knee until it grinds against the cement slab of the firing line. My troublesome weapon rests atop my flattened right thigh, barrel facing three human-shaped targets, fifty meters away.

I'm not giving up, I inform the three wise men and my gun. "Eventually you'll fire, and you'll fire straight."

Spent 5.56mm cartridges left behind by previous marksmen litter the range. They glint in the sun and force me to squint. These shells taunt me. They mock my inability to add to their golden ranks, the way any worthy soldier could.

Pain jags through my phantom arm when fingers that no longer exist try to cross for good luck. Old habits die hard, and this one keeps coming back to haunt me like a ghost.

I've learned to compartmentalize the pain, to drown out the Phantom—most of the time. So I focus on cocking the rifle. I slide the bolt backward in the smoothest possible motion I can muster. When I glance down, I see failure glaring back at me through a thin slit by the bolt. That means the bullet didn't catch in the chamber. Yet another ballistic miscarriage. I cautiously find my feet and brush the dirt from my fatigues.

Izzy. Seriously. How on Earth are you ever gonna hold that thing in place? What were you thinking? A one-armed sharpshooter? Really?

This isn't the way it was five weeks into basic training when we started rifle drills. Back then, after six days of intense shooting practice and firefight scenarios, the range instructors awarded just two exemplary soldiers with a gift. I was one of those guys. Another recruit and I were allowed to shoot five bullets at a can of Loof (a wet canned meat product commonly called "Kosher Spam," second only to Hezbollah fighters in terms of enemies of the state). I hit it all five times, all dead center. At one hundred fifty meters. "Looks like we know who we're sending to sniper school." I probably would have become a sniper, had we not been called so soon to recoup Rosner's body. Operation Cast Lead cast a pall over all kinds of plans.

Now I see that Phantom's right. Until I figure out how to load without jerking the weapon, it simply won't fire. He whines a long while, and to appease him, I rub what's left of my left arm.

How far am I willing to go? How much pain is this really worth? The solution comes as I knead above where my elbow used to bend, and when it does, I know it's official. I've gone insane.

But I need to try. I must. I've got to use the pain, make Phantom my bitch.

Back to a crouch. Rifle resting atop my straightened thigh. This time, I stare out past the three cardboard cutouts, past the sandy ranges, and into the mountains that jut out behind them. I let my vision blur.

The answers aren't out there, Izzy.

No. You're the answer. I slide a magazine into the Tavor's loading port. My gaze remains unfocused. I distance myself from the agony I'm about to inflict.

If you do this, I'll scream. I swear to God, I'll scream.

I lower my left shoulder to steady the rifle. I let the warmth of my amputation collide with the cool plastic of the weapon. Then the remainder of my arm compresses against it. Phantom's squealing. The ensuing pressure crushes my entire being like a grape under a gorilla's foot.

But I'm committed now. I press deeper into the gun—harder—and my vision darkens. My sight starts to tunnel through the anguish. The force is unbearable, but I reach forward before I faint. And, with my right hand, pull the loader back as roughly as possible while fully supporting the weapon.

My left shoulder springs upward as soon as it's done. The pain lingers, but the darkness that smothered me retreats for the time being. I lift the Tavor to the rivet between my right pectoral and shoulder, and aim at the closest of the paper terrorists.

Sweet, sweet music soothes my eardrums: a drumbeat of discharging rounds. A symphony of lead tearing through the air. I continue firing until the clip is empty of all twenty-nine bullets. And not until the explosions die down and the report follows do I realize that I'm roaring loud enough to lose my voice and probably leave me rasping for days. How do you out-ghost your Phantom? You can't. But if he screams, you can scream back, louder, right in his face, and drown him out. You have to use whatever you've got. If what you've got is pain, then bring on the pain.

I catch my breath and load a fresh magazine. I put pain to shame. Maybe I'll eat a bullet later, but for now I've got to bite it. I again press roughly with my tortured limb. Again my vision darkens. Again I ignore that suffocating pressure that constricts my chest. Forcing myself to hold on, I push and I push. Through the nothingness I flail until something catches on the other side.

Then my vision clears like a windshield with wipers flipped to high. The blur hones into perfect focus. The targets and my future sharpen perfectly through the Mars infrared scope. I can see the individual lines on the black-and-yellow bull's-eye fifty meters away, the grains and cracks on the tan post holding those wise men steady.

Time creeps like a tarantula as I fire a fast clip. The silence between each trigger pull deafens me, temporarily stopping my heart. Only the next pull jumpstarts it again. This throbbing wound, this adrenaline, this will—have all shifted into a weapon. A painfully secret weapon. They have forced me to become a more accurate marksman. A stronger soldier. A better man. Phantom's not my bitch—we're in this together, like it or not.

Will my body ever cease shuddering?

How many days have I toiled on this range not knowing how close I knelt to the solution? I easily could've stopped fighting. I easily could've dropped my weapon and shambled back into darkness. But I never would have discovered the treasures that are now mine. I've now accomplished what any two-armed soldier could. Piles of shiny shells surround me. Both they and I are glinting in the sunlight.

FLATFOOT

March 2008. The night of my return to Camp Michve from my non-start at the paratrooper test, my uniform seems to sag on me. Wearing olive-green suddenly feels wrong. I can't face the UN, my friends, in the barracks. Instead I find a dark corner of the parade ground, where I sit on a concrete slab thrusting out of the ground at an awkward angle.

Alone with my thoughts—*I failed, I failed*—it takes me a moment to realize someone's stepped partway out of the shadows. I see the Reeboks first. "Sir." I jump up and thwack my brow, a painful casualty of my own salute.

"At ease, Recruit." Sergeant Sneakers flickers into view as he lights up a cigarette. "Any reason you've decided to take over my private oasis?"

"No, sir. Sorry, sir." I turn to leave.

"Relax, Recruit. Have a seat."

I've never been one-on-one with a superior before. How are you supposed to act? The sergeant studies the strange American, takes a deep drag off his cancer stick. I realize this is the first time I've seen him without Oakleys covering his eyes. Of course—it's dark out. "Spill it," he says.

"No disrespect, sir. You wouldn't understand."

"Try me."

By the time I finish explaining what went down at Bakum, tears are streaming down my face again. I hate myself for crying. Tears and temperatures—my body's failed me many times today. Sergeant Sneakers drops his cigarette, puts it out with the heel of his right Reebok. He says, "Ever wonder why I wear these?"

"Everyone does."

"Flat feet. The doctor discovered the problem when I went in for my pre-enlistment examination. Do you know what that means?"

"I don't, sir."

"Flat feet are an automatic physical-profile reduction. Automatic," he repeats. "So I also didn't get the profile I needed to try out for the paratroopers, or any of the other units I wanted. They offered me Tanks or Artillery. I chose Tanks."

"Wow." I don't know what else to say.

"I didn't end up where I wanted. But I'm still contributing." He tucks a new cigarette between his lips, lights it. "I look back at my service now, and I'm proud. It'll take time, but you'll learn, as I did. The paratroopers aren't the only soldiers making a difference." He inhales deeply, releases the smoke with a sigh. "We all fight. We all matter. Now . . . Recruit?"

"Yes, sir?"

"Get the hell out of my oasis."

LIKE THE BACK OF MY HAND

April 2010. The day of my first attempt to pass the obstacle course comes halfway through the month I've been allotted. I know every inch of this monster. Still, my stomach is doing loops. Vest on tight. Helmet tight. Rifle swinging freely from my hip for Fuks's sake. Ofir stands with his stopwatch in the morning sun. Some of the female fitness instructors are there to cheer me on. Two of them are straddling the wall I must conquer. Efi has come to run the course with me even though his beloved Blue and Whites are gunning again to qualify for the World Cup.

When Ofir gives the signal—"*Tzeh!*" I dash out madly, so fast that Efi beside me says, "*Duuude*, pace yourself. You're gonna burn out!" But I just smile and ignore him. I need *beast* mode. I actually leave Efi in my dust. But I still hear him behind me, egging me on. I reach the girls at full gallop and simply soar right over the wall like Deadpool. "Hey, ladies!" Even I can tell it's a thing of fucking beauty.

But on the other side, the brute effort I've been making begins to take its toll. Efi's right. I can't catch my breath. I'm not willing to slow down, though. The rhythm of the rifle banging against my hips keeps me going. It says, "*Just do it, just do it, just do it . . .*"

Suddenly, I'm at the rope. I'm dog-tired. There's a random veteran unit stretching for a run right beside the course. I don't know why they're on our training base; they're already active combat. But a few of them notice me. Then all of them. And then they spot the missing arm. They're shielding their eyes from the sun, and they begin to prod one another, to point.

Am I making a fool of myself? Are all these guys about to watch me fail?

They start to cheer me on.

"*Yalla!* You crazy beast. You can do it!"

"Go, Beast, go!"

But I don't make it up the rope the first time.

I don't make it up the rope the second time.

You can't do this, Izzy. Time to give up.

Those veteran soldiers all start to run over. They can see I need more motivation. The third time takes a thousand years of pain and robs me of all breath. I can feel my heartbeat in my neck. My head is throbbing against the inside of my helmet. Finally—*plunk!*—my helmet hits the beam! An upwelling of roars overwhelms my ears from below. There's an obese fly up here with me, and I say, "Hey, fella . . . Nice view from the top."

I drop down into the crowd of vets—they're on the course with me now. They're nipping at my heels as I drag my bones to the next obstacle. "Come on, Beast! You're an *animal!* You're kicking ass! *Yalla!*" ("*Yalla*" means "C'mon!") They surround me. Envelop me. A chorus of "*Yalla!*" Gravity draws my eyes to the ground as we run, and all I see are flashy feet flitting in and out of frame. Their energy carries me along like one of those moving sidewalks at the airport. Blur of yellow, of neon-green, of pink, of yellow again—the soldiers' sneakers. They simply don't allow me to slow down, to collapse, to fail.

We all cross the finish line together. They're going wild. I'm a palpitating mess. All fifteen of them slap my back, roughly. So does Efi. He'd skipped all the hard stuff and was waiting at the finish line. Goofball.

I gulp stale water out of Ofir's ancient canteens. I can't explain why, but I'm utterly dejected. Yes, I made it. But I know it took me almost twice as long to get through than the passing time I need. *So, basically, you failed. It figures. Failures fail*, says Phantom. That goddamn rope ate up too much time. In basic training, I failed the course by ten seconds. Now I'm sucking all over again.

But Efi and Ofir are staring at me stupidly. "All right," I manage to eke out. "What was my time?"

They just keep staring at me, staring down at the stopwatch. "Come *on*, guys."

Then Efi says something that blows my mind. "Dude. *8:30* on the dot. You passed. By a full two minutes."

AN ARMY MARCHES ON ITS STOMACH

March 2008. On to basic training in the Jordan Valley. Having missed my only opportunity to make the paratroopers—thanks, in part, to a combination of my terrible Hebrew and a hornswoggling officer who didn't fully explain the options—I'm exactly where I don't want to be. Kfir. Infantry. Two-and-a-half years of monotonous guard duty and terrible, overcooked food ahead. Welcome to the IDF.

All Kfir recruits must survive eight months of combat training to graduate to active service. Training includes the "basics," meaning discipline, physical fitness, and various weapons and tactics. Specifically, marksman classes, basic field-navigation training, open-space warfare training, helicopter-deployment training, special-weapons and physical-fitness training, Krav Maga, as well as some general education classes. All of this at Kfir's main training base, called Peles, on the Jordanian border.

Welcome to the "Victory in Judea" Battalion. I'll be your host, Satan. I'll recognize you peons by your dark-green beret. Remember, the only thing to fear is Kfir itself.

I come to learn here very soon that, in fact, the "basics" on this base basically consist of four rather-base activities, in a loop, for sixteen weeks. None of them involves jumping out of an airplane at ten thousand feet:

1. Guard duty.
2. Push-ups.
3. Kitchen duty.
4. Repeat.

DISARMED

Guard duty: Countless hours, days, and weeks standing on bruised, possibly suppurating feet. Eyeing the distance for Bedouin smugglers, guerrillas, and other creatures of the night. Ten jammed little piggies. Blistered ankles bound by rough leather boots not yet worn soft. Moth-eaten socks. Flies.

Push-ups: Shredded palm-skin. Congealed blood from broken blisters. A subtle twitch of the arms that sends sharp, dagger-like twinges down triceps. The smell of piss and sand.

Kitchen duty: Flies. More flies. And smells. Loof, like canned possum. Recycled Crisco. Burnt rice. More flies. Huge tubs of dirty trays glued to each other with powdered mashed potatoes, mystery "meat," and sliced eggplant that seems to grow spider-legs before your eyes. Nope, that's a spider in the eggplant. More flies, like a plague on Egypt.

Guard duty: A rock to kick becomes a long-sought treat, though only fleetingly. Counting the cracks in the wooden beam overhead kills a few minutes. Counting again. Waving hello to a scorpion sightseer. Flies. Suffocating silence.

Push-ups: Coolly delivered reprimands dropped from in between the crooked yellow teeth of another robotic boot sergeant. Aching shoulders weighed down further, somehow, by the bully's invective, and personal shame. Flies.

Kitchen duty: Sliding inside from the desert sun's devastating "dry" heat into the steam room of commercial ovens and giant cauldrons of boiling slop. Kilos of flies, alive and dead, dropping into the mixers and pots. Rivulets of human sweat pouring into all receptacles. Loof, all asshole and eyeballs, which only a Russian recruit could relish.

Guard duty: Solitude. Loneliness. Despondency. Flies.

Push-ups: Calcified palms. Core strength. The occasional shared smile six inches off the asphalt, out of view of the commander above. Getting so good you can clap on the upswing. Once for your honor. Once to kill a fly.

Kitchen duty: Psych! It's a gas-mask drill. Put your masks on, *Tzeh! Tzeh! Run! Now masks off! Did I give you permission to choke, Recruit!? Now give me your ID number. Run! Fifty push-ups, then second position ... hold it ... What was that ID number again? Give it to me backwards.* Dead flies, strangled in the gas. No more flies. For now.

Repeat.

Repeat.

SHOW OF HANDS

April 2010. The big test. *Another* big test. The training grounds are barren except for rusty barbed wire and a few dead shrubs, which look like scorched bodies that nearly escaped hell. My leather boots sizzle until I find a patch of shade beneath a steep hill that dominates the horizon. Conquering the arduous incline is my last obstacle before I regain combat status. At least, that's what everyone keeps telling me.

I've jerry-rigged solutions to all possible problems. For example, one day I hit upon wrapping grenade pins in thick hockey tape. Smartest thing I ever came up with considering its simplicity. No damage when I use my pearly whites to pull the pins.

Soon, I'll charge up the untamed ground and attempt to score hits on cardboard enemies that Shoogy set up along the ridge's steepest face. The forefathers of the IDF created this exercise to simulate a worst-case scenario, a literal "uphill battle."

Think happy thoughts. Don't poop your pants during the drill. That would suck for Shoogy, who's going to follow a stride or two downwind.

Shoogy wears her hair in a tight ponytail. She's got her favorite blue "One Shot—One Kill" T-shirt on. I'm wearing Ofir's sleek black vest wrapped tightly around my chest. I've wedged my helmet between my remaining bicep and a few lightly bruised ribs. This past month has left no part of my body anything less than black and blue. *No* part.

My rifle swings freely by my side.

Moni Katz's jeep comes to a stop before us in a cloud of dust. I use my flopping left shirtsleeve to wipe the sweat from my forehead. "You ready?"

I nod. I wedge my helmet on my head, using my thumb and index finger to buckle the clips in place.

I don't bother saluting.

I lift my rifle so it parallels the ground, a sign to Katz that I'm ready to get things started.

"*Tzeh*," he orders.

"Commencing live fire exercise," I alert.

Cautiously, I walk toward the first set of targets. I sweep the terrain with my rifle as my finger hovers over the trigger. I allow my mind to go blank. For once, I don't hold my breath. I can hear the flies buzzing. And just as I breach the three-meter mark separating me from my first cardboard enemy, Katz barks, "Under fire!"

I let countless hours of training take over.

"Under fire, under fire," I repeat, while charging for the first set of targets, firing multiple rounds instinctively from my hip.

Passing the enemy's line of defense, I dive to the ground for better cover. Without a second arm to ease my fall, I hit the sand with a teeth-jarring impact.

"Four enemies at my twelve," I yell, trying to retrieve my lungs from where they've been slammed up in my throat, simultaneously firing at each target in my sights, all roughly twenty meters out. "Moving out!"

I roll out and upward, using both legs to thrust myself away from the sand. Even without a spare arm to lift my body, the force of my up-kick propels me into a run. I sprint forward, firing at a target above me.

Two shots later, it happens. That telling, hollow-sounding *click*. My rifle has jammed. Whatever. Now I can show Moni how I take care of business. In one smooth motion, I release the magazine from my weapon, discharge the shell stuck inside, cock the rifle twice, reinsert the magazine, and reload.

Hot damn.

A soldier should be able to unjam his rifle in five seconds flat. I'm able to do it in three, by pinning the rifle to the ground with my stump and using my hand to go through the motions. Of course, the act sends jolts of pain through my missing arm, makes Phantom sing for his supper. This sends an octane boost of adrenaline through my system, giving me an extra edge.

But my rifle continues to jam after every shot. There are few things more difficult than trying to charge up a hill while firing a rifle and hitting each target. One of those harder things is doing all that while pausing after each shot to unjam your weapon.

And then it's over. All I can think about as I stand there, shaking the desert from my soiled fatigues, is how unlucky I am. Every last bullet? Really?

"Izzy, any thoughts on how you could have performed better?" Katz asks.

"Sir, looking back, I can see that if I positioned myself closer to the center of the hill, there'd be more room for the squad accompanying me. If the scenario was real."

He nods agreement as Shoogy joins us. She's carrying the targets she gathered from the drill. She has a smile on her face. "You see?" She rifles through the targets one after the other. "Besides the first target, he hit each of them four times, center mass."

Moni Katz says nothing. No smile. No frown.

What does that mean? Do I pack up my gear—or do I *pack up my gear*?

FINGERS TO THE BONE

March 2008. First week of basic training, and another opportunity—this will be the last—to test for a Special Forces unit. This time, it's the IDF's elite canine unit, Oketz. If I can't jump out of planes, I'm going to have a sturdy dog by my side. It's a three-day *Gibush*, one of the toughest tryouts in the IDF. I wake at dawn with a wicked hangover—but, wait, I didn't drink last night. That means I'm actually sick. Headache. Nausea. Fever. "Pain is only in the mind," I decide. "Fear is the mind-killer." There's no way I'm missing another chance.

The actual *Gibush*—the tryout—won't commence until nightfall, but my engines are already revving. This is all an enormous waste of energy.

Halfway through reveille: "What's this?" The commander's thumb and finger press against my upper lip, tickling the pitiful growth there that left me with a blessed extra bit of time each morning. "Two minutes," he orders, and off I sprint to shave—another untold number of unnecessary calories cooked.

Kfir's training base is witheringly hot during the day, and it's only going to get worse as the months wear on. Practicing an impressive abundance of caution, the IDF does its best to combat the devil Dehydration. You're not allowed to take a step outside without a canteen connected to your person.

"You don't know?" one of my fellow Oketz wannabes says. "Dudes have died during these tryouts. Sure, a while back, some really determined bro was found all dead and shriveled. His body was dry as a bone and stuff."

This was on Jonny's original list of do's and don'ts: Don't wait till you're thirsty to drink. It's probably too late by then. He said the Israeli military used to be very stingy with water. They wanted soldiers to learn how to fight effectively in the absence of clean drinking water. But that proved foolish. You can't prepare or train against dehydration. You just die.

Of course, I already proved last month that just one canteen lowered this human's body temperature a full one degree Celsius in five short minutes. I'm not about to get disqualified again on any high-temp technicality. I'd rather my dry, withered corpse be found than fail to begin yet another *Gibush*. The commanders make us down five canteens of water in a matter of two and a half hours. No sweat, right? Well, you ever hear of hyponatremia? "Water intoxication" can occur when you drink too much or too fast for your kidneys to piss it out. In some cases, this can actually kill you. So we pee a lot. They don't even have to order it.

Lunch is parched and overcooked. Burnt rice and sticks of something that might be ground beef. Can't eat anything. I offer up my portion to the biggest of the bunch—a recruit who looks startlingly like Arnold Schwarzenegger. They soon take us out to the buses that will bring us to the *Gibush*. "Hey, you ever seen *Predator*?" I ask the big guy.

"Get to the *choppah*!" he shouts good-naturedly, in a terrible impression of the Governator.

They corral us all into a courtyard, where we all simultaneously hush. All of the draftees who signed up for these three days of affliction, all hoping for the same reward, continue to amass into an olive-drab throng behind us. "Man," says A*hhh*nold.

"Yeah. You're all so damn huge."

A*hhh*nold says, this time in Hebrew, "Muscles don't mean endurance. They're not looking for biceps. They're looking for soul."

Before boarding the buses, the boot sergeant makes each of us drown on yet another canteen. All I can hear is retching and the splatter of possibly-beef sludge and stomach acid on the pavement. And then the flies. I, however, hold onto every last drop, aiming to keep my temperature within the strict parameters despite what is obviously turning out to be some full-on desert flu.

The transport we ride in is more cattle car than bus. The commander sits in a separate compartment up front along with the driver, while the rest of us are packed into the back with no means of contacting them. We rumble into the desert.

Try drinking eight liters of water in a single morning. Then get on a bumpy bus crammed with fifty other guys who've done the same. I don't know if the commander really can't hear us vainly bashing on the roof, waving out the window, and shouting—or if he's just having a wee bit of fun while we all nearly burst in the back. Maybe the whole thing's some sort of psychological test. But after a few panic-stricken minutes, we all really, *really* need to piss as soon as possible. But where?

There are two options. One is out the window. Fortunately, the road near base is scarcely traveled. But getting that height is going to require teamwork, and no one's ready to risk taking friendly fire this early on in the service. Option two is in a bottle, and then out the window, a feat that can be completed with a lot less indelicacy. We decide together that option two's at least marginally civilized. So we turn the back of the transport into a relief station. Many recruits are close to tears by the time we finally rig a system. There are only two bottles on the transport, one Coke, one Fanta. They remain in constant rotation. Their contents—sometimes faintly yellow, but mostly clear—are repeatedly flung out the window just so the bottle can be refilled seconds later by another dancing recruit.

When the storm of shouting, pissing, and hurling finally subsides, I try to remember Jonny's tips and go over them for the remainder of the ride south to a base called Mitkan Adam.

The most important was this: "During a few of the most difficult exercises, they're going to ask for volunteers to prepare the food. Don't be one of them," he warned. "It's a test to see who will take the easy way out." Not me.

The only solution is to kick serious ass in the *Gibush* and then get my dog and kick serious ass in combat.

But first I yell, "Bottle!" The sopping plastic orange soda bottle hits me in the ear from behind, spraying blended urine over my chin. "Thanks . . ."

Two bottles later, and all three hundred of us are kipping out at night beneath a massive hangar slathered in bird poop. Jonny warned me not to get too cozy, and to wear my boots to sleep. They'd shock us awake to kick off the *Gibush*. Half of us have our toes out, and the grossly tangible stench of so many feet is thick enough to walk on.

What can I say about the next three days? Only isolated images and senses, scraps of dialogue, and general impressions come to consciousness. In the spaces between, the blackness of exhaustion and hopelessness:

None of the tryout instructors ever shout. These reservists give all their orders, even the most pressing, in deadpan voices just above a whisper. Far more menacing. Contrast that to the blaring horns over the megaphones that wake us up whenever we try to fall asleep.

Hauling sandbag-laden stretchers through the night desert. Screaming calves, dying thighs, the rough-edged pole of the stretcher plunging into the meat of our shoulders.

Those eerie commands. Sprinting a hundred meters over and over again under a punishing sun. Fifteen men at time, half pushing, half dragging, a massive, heavy, awkwardly bundled canvas tarp the size of a circus tent from one side of a one-hundred-meter marker to the other. This tarp serves no function or purpose beyond breaking the spirit of young men. This task, like many, impedes all forms of group cooperation and individual coordination.

Our sedate taskmasters ordering *"Tzeh"* time and again, and forward we go like dogs let off the leash. Each of these commanders once had a devoted canine partner they spent hundreds of hours training and fighting beside. We recruits have not yet earned our place among those dogs—let alone their masters. The vast majority of those who try out never will.

Grinding sand in my teeth. Sweat stinging my eyes. Watching many giants fall. First ten minutes of the first day, first drill, and I'm ready to give up. Already.

A*hhh*nold hunches his hulking shoulders in defeat. "Are you sure, Recruit? Are you absolutely sure?" his instructor asks in that irritatingly calm manner. My own lungs are straining. I'll never make it.

"Yes, sir," he mumbles dejectedly, staring down at his boots. "I'm done."

"Yes, you are, Recruit."

We've been charging back and forth through the desert for less than an hour.

By the end of that very first day, nearly one hundred fifty recruits, who signed up with bluster and pride, call it quits. All this does is increase my odds.

My strength rises from the weakest part of my nature. My resilience is built on the broken dreams of others. But whatever it takes, right?

The longer we go, the more likely the recruit will stay. It's just like actuarial tables. If you survive drill one, that makes it all the more likely you'll survive drill two, and so on, exponentially. So, technically, that which doesn't kill you really does make you stronger. It's a cold comfort while you're digging your own desert grave.

A piercing wail wakes us survivors mid-REM that first night. With boots laced tight, and eyes still glued mostly shut, I haul ass toward the stretchers outside. I know this drill.

There's an ambulance ahead, half hidden in the tree line. Those rigs mean medics, and medics mean the little machine they shove in your ear. On the pretext of needing to piss, I hide and wolf down a gallon of water. "Is there anyone who feels unwell?" asks an instructor robotically. "The medics are going to take all of your temperatures for safety precautions. And then we'll all play."

Mother . . .

240

I manage to lean away from the device so it doesn't contact the molten lava roiling in my cranium. I keep my mouth open—a Jonny tip. I think cool thoughts. The pool back in Aventura. The winters in Brooklyn. Penguins. "Pass."

This hike is twice as long and twice as fast as the prior one.

Two hours of sleep, then we crawl. "If you're in the middle of the pack, you're in trouble," said Jonny. "If you're behind the pack, you're in trouble. Basically, if you're anywhere but the head of the pack, you're in trouble. The final four in any drill spells trouble."

I'm in trouble.

The sand is soft and notched, like the waves of a frozen ocean. But within the first minute of crawling on this choppy surface, you realize why they call it "sandpaper," and why it's able to blast through paint and stain and anything. Blood seeps right through the sleeves of our uniforms. One of the hardest parts of crawling is keeping your head up. Your neck gets stiff after just a few minutes.

Are these other competitors with their scrunched-up faces and flayed elbow skin my comrades—or my enemies?

"*Yalla*, just a few more meters," some random recruit cries out.

"We can do this," another voice replies.

Each man yips his oaths of encouragement as though we're a pack of wolves hunting together. I don't have the breath to contribute. But I do appreciate the camaraderie. I understand the challenge is to get my pack its quarry.

A guy named Oz is in my pack. Oz is in trouble. "Are you experiencing difficulty, Recruit?"

They all sound like the HAL 9000 computer from *2001: A Space Odyssey*.

"Is it time to throw in the towel?"

"Can we get you a popsicle, Recruit?"

I can see he's about ready to crack. Oz is for sure going to be in the last four to finish this drill. So I slow my pace—let him slink past me, and take the bullet for him. Seems like the right thing to do at the time. He knows what I'm doing, and mouths a silent "Thank you" as he drags his weary bones past.

I don't understand the instructions for the dune drill. Fortunately, it looks like it doesn't require much thinking. I can see the monstrous dune out of Frank Herbert's universe; I can see the heavy sandbags heaped at its base. It seems the goal is to carry a bulky sandbag up and down the hill as many times as possible before time runs out, a measurement they purposefully fail to disclose. So, how hard do you work? Are they looking for speed, quantity, what? I'm spent. I'm done. I'm bloody. I'm probably going to crap blood. "We need two volunteers to prepare lunch."

So, so tempting. But I remember Jonny's edict.

Two extremely relieved recruits take their leave for the lunch-prep shade. Good-bye forever, boys.

My fever's peaking now, I can tell. I can feel a strange wave of cold creeping up my chest. "Are you unwell, Recruit?" Practically a whisper.

"No, sir."

"*Tzeh.*"

Boots sunk into sand. Shoulders offended. Elbows sensitive as eyeballs. The uphill slog. The awkward burden. The downhill charge. Lungs full of sand and agony. One time. Two times. Three times. Four. *Guys have died on this tryout.* Where do I sign up for that?

On the fifth, a tiny sound.

Clink.

My ears perk up the instant I hear it. In fact, all activity on the dune comes to a halt as we each turn and stare at the instructor who stands below. He's a burly guy with a shock of hair sticking up from his collar. He holds in his grip a perfect, glowing, sweating can of Pepsi. The sound was him cracking it open. It's so quiet in the desert now I can just pick out the fizzing of foam. Or is that flies? He takes a big sniff. "*Mmm*, who does this soda belong to?"

It's a trap.

"No one? Anyone can have it. Any recruit. Just come down here and take it. Just come down, take it, and walk away. Why continue suffering? Just end your misery. Be the Pepsi Generation."

I'm hallucinating. Fatigue and fever and the oasis of cola . . . I see myself stripping naked—Metallica's playing—and swan-diving into that can for a swim. Fifteen seconds pass in silence. No one moves a muscle. If not for our ragged breathing, the desolate training grounds would sound a lot like I imagine Mars can sound, when the winds aren't whipping.

All eyes are on that bright Pepsi logo gleaming in the sunlight, completely alien to the barren and colorless landscape.

One by one, we recruits turn back to our burdens. We continue to hump up and down the steep incline, pain etched on our faces like the forces of time.

I can't go on much longer. It's simply too taxing. I'm standing now, unmoved, head bowed, eyes closed. So, of course, he chooses me. The instructor and his sacred aluminum chalice are now both inches from my face. My sandbag is dumped at his feet. I cannot, will not, move from this spot. If shade should suddenly appear, if a crevasse opens up in front of me with clear, icy mountain water, I will not have it in me to tip myself in there. I'm in real trouble. I'm about to fail again.

A chorus of instructors converge on my position now. They surround me. And, with their eerie composure, they begin to buzz: "Can I help you back to your sleeping bag, Recruit?"

"Or do you need an ambulance?"

"Ice cubes, Recruit?"

"Slice of lemon?"

The keeper of the can tips it a bit, and Pepsi bubbles on the sand. He says, "You *really* look like you could use a refreshing beverage."

What will they think of me? God, what are they going to think of me if I pack it in?

A tear chooses that moment to forge a path down my dirty cheek. I'm not crying, I don't think. My exhausted body—possibly ridden with Screaming Flyshit Influenza—is acting without my consent.

Major Tuft places the Pepsi can right under my nose. I can't help but inhale deeply. What a rush. Ineffable. Riding a saddled great white shark through a black hole only half captures the sensation. I really am very, very sick. And very tired. And thirsty.

And then I hear a voice. My father's. "Izzy, don't you think there will be plenty of time to drink cola once you make it into the Special Forces?"

What will they think of me if I give up?

Utterly distressing that the only emotion powerful enough to carry me over this finish line's going to be shame. Not pride in my actions. Not some deep, Zionistic fervor. Not even a full understanding of how important my service will be to Israel and the future of the Jewish people. Just bare, naked shame.

My whole spine groaning, I bend forward and heft the sandbag back onto my shoulder. When I do so, a rivulet of blood from my left elbow travels down into my armpit. "What are you doing, Recruit?"

"Yeah, why are you leaving us?"

"Dr. Pepper's more my speed, sir."

"Who is this Dr. Pepper?"

Now I demand motion of my body. For the first time in my entire life, I know I will finish a challenge that I set for myself. I might not have finished school; I might not have raked in a fortune at any job; and I didn't get to be a paratrooper, but I'm going to finish this drill. So what if it's shame pushing me over the line?

I survive the dunes. I carry the spices. I ride the sandworms of Arrakis till they roll over, defeated, and show me their tummies.

I sleep. Meanwhile, my white blood cells are losing their epic battle with the micro-predators that have invaded me.

But only a day to go. Each time the instructors order us to crawl, the grisly scabs on our elbows reopen. I succeed in pushing through. Something might be seriously wrong with me, but if I'm going to die, it will be on the road to the finish line. Just because I cannot bear the thought that I promised the world and myself I'd make it, and I might not.

So I succeed because I'm too ashamed to fail. Right now A*hhh*nold's probably passed out with three empty cans beside him, and I'm here. Because he was willing to give up. And I'm not.

And suddenly, it's over. I'm done. The final whistle blows, and the Oketz *Gibush* is over. I count among the one hundred forty recruits—less than half—who survived.

Now I'm in the exit interview. After sitting outside an inconspicuous trailer for hours, cross-legged, body and mind as numb and blank as the shifting sands. "Have a seat, Recruit."

Jonny warned me how crucial these last few minutes are going to be. "The final meeting has to go perfectly."

Sure. The math: one hundred forty recruits finished the hellish trials. Only thirty-five open slots. That's—well whatever the odds, they're not good.

There's a box of store-bought pastries on the desk. Multicolored sprinkles. My stomach weeps. "Have some cake."

Another test?

"Thank you, sir." My voice is gravelly from the desert and my illness. "But no, thank you."

They're just being nice. That was rude, Izzy. Strike one.

"Do you think you performed well these past three days?"

No, I think. "Yes," I say. It's all I can do to suppress a coughing spasm.

"Any injuries we should know about? We need to know for our records."

Instinctively, I lift both my arms to show them the nasty scars that have encrusted both of my elbows entirely, little blobs of bright blood oozing through as I bend them. "Just these."

"What are you referring to, Recruit?"

"Where? Where is your injury?"

This reaction is so disorienting that I actually glance down at the perfectly obvious wounds still leaking onto my fatigues, just to make sure they haven't spontaneously healed like stigmata. "These. Right here."

"Where?" I scoot closer. "Where are your injuries, Recruit?"

Suddenly, I understand, as though someone's pulled a cord and dumped a bucket of freezing water on my head. "Oh, look at that," I say. I smile weakly and with mock surprise. "I thought I saw something, but it's gone. Sorry for any confusion."

"Good, Recruit. No worries, then."

"You may go, Recruit."

I say thank you and head for the door. But before I get there, I hear these final words lobbed at me: "Say, Recruit. The IDF has nothing but respect for those who volunteer from abroad."

"Uh, thanks."

"But . . . how do we know you'll see this through? Stick around? Maybe the going gets tough, and you bolt, you head straight home for the beach or your pretty girlfriend. How do we *know*?"

Pretty girlfriend? Wish I had one of those—and a ready answer. But I'm not sure I'm actually supposed to answer. So I smile politely and bow out.

I should have taken a piece of flippin' cake.

Back to Kfir's training base. My commander, who must approve my seeing a doctor, makes me wait three days, implying I'm a wimp who just doesn't feel well after the grueling *Gibush*. "What makes you think you're so special you should see a doctor when every other man in Second Platoon has to go back to duty?" He looks at my mates. "Perhaps he's experiencing some anxiety about his new condition in the world. Perhaps his head hurts because the IDF fell on top of it like a sack of shit. There's nothing physically wrong with this man."

I'm in a constant cold sweat. I'm croaking. My skull is pounding. I'm suffering delusions. But I'm not a wimp.

On the third day back on the parade ground, I'm looking down— he's only 5´6˝—at his outdated facial hair, and he's looking up at my pasty, wet face. "Why is this man wearing a coat? It's hot as blazes out here."

"He's cold, sir," says someone faceless in the platoon. I cannot differentiate him from all the other recruits, even if I could find the strength to lift my lids. This person, who I'll only later learn is Amir, shows tremendous guts when he follows with, "He needs a medic right away, sir. Maybe you should take him yourself."

It's obvious that Major Muttonchops can't keep up the abuse anymore, so, through his largesse, I get to see a medic—who quickly sends me to the doctor, who says, "My God, you're more fever than man."

I get a pass home for three days. ("You better come back a brand-new recruit, Recruit.") Three days to consider that final interview. For weeks after the *Gibush*—after I finally beat my flu, and long after I get the news that Oketz passed on me—their question haunts my thoughts. *How do we know?*

Chapter 10

THINKING ON MY FEET

May 2008. It's about two months into basic training. I wake up one morning and see everyone tying their boots extra tight. The tent is buzzing with energy (and wings) like something out of a high school football team's locker room. The whole battalion's getting pumped for something big. What? Seems my poor command of Hebrew has kept essential information from getting through to me again. I ask Kobi what's going on. "Course of obstacles today."

The first thing I notice is that recruits from other units are strapping their rifles to their backs, freeing up their hands to make the obstacles easier to tackle. "I thought we weren't allowed to do that." I say as we prep our gear.

"We're not. Not our unit. Listen."

Fuks nods with his chin toward those other guys, says, "This unit is above that kind of bull. When you need to jump over a wall during a firefight, do you think you'll have time to neatly strap your gun behind your back? Do you think you'll want to?"

Ten minutes later, it's my turn. I stand at the starting line with three other recruits, all ready to give it our best shot. They're going to keep sending us out in waves of four. In a strange way, I feel like I'm representing Team America, and if I fail, I'll let down everybody there. Countdown . . . "*Tzeh*," a commander says, and the four of us balls-out sprint. After about fifty seconds, though, we realize this was not the right approach. We all slow down so as not to burn what's left of our energy. The concrete wall looms larger as you close that third of a mile. Simple physics—the closer you get, the higher it looks. How am I going to do this? I think Spidey. The Man of Webs can walk up walls, and that's kind of the goal here. In fact, there's no real other way to do it. You have to run at the wall with enough momentum that, if you throw a leg in front of you, you'll actually start to climb vertically. I've seen all those kung fu movies—those guys don't have stunt doubles. Even with my rifle flopping and slapping, I'm able to bound over the wall with relative ease. Pays to be 6´1˝ in a land of 5´7˝s. And I idolize Spidey.

Getting up the rope proves much more difficult. It takes me two tries, and I waste precious time. Two of the other guys in my group slip ahead, and I can't stand that. The crawling also goes at a slug's pace. Dragging my heavy vest through thick sand reminds me of failing to get accepted into Oketz. *Oketz* actually means "sting"— and that one really stung. Sometimes your best isn't good enough. By the time I finish the crawl, all I have left is a half-kilometer sprint to the end. I push myself, but all I can manage is a pace slightly faster than a jog. When I cross the finish line, finally, Fuks says, "Fail." And then moves on to the next guy.

My time was 10:40, a full ten seconds above the minimum passing time. Ten seconds, God damn it.

"I can't believe I didn't make it." I tell Kobi, as we lumber back to the tents.

"Yeah, that was one tough course," he agrees.

"But you passed."

"Only by a few seconds. You'll get it next time, Izzy."

"I seriously better."

Next morning, I'm in the middle of a lovely dream in which two lovely ladies—

"Get up." It's Fuks, shaking me awake.

Some Hebrew must be sinking in, because I offer up a curse in his native tongue. "What time is it?"

"Time for you to pass the obstacle course."

"Sir, my legs . . . We just did it yesterday."

"And you failed yesterday. Today you'll pass."

Only eight of the thirty of us need to rerun the obstacle course. We all stretch in silence near the starting line. It kills me to be in this bottom third. The fat kid. The kid who keeps losing his glasses. The kid who gets picked last for dodgeball. But there are one or two surprises among this lot, super-fit guys who, for one reason or another, didn't make the cut. All of our bodies are beaten from the previous attempt twenty-four hours earlier. As I passed Kobi's bunk—he was smiling in his sleep, the bastard—I decided there was absolutely no way I was going to do this thing a third time.

"*Tzeh.*"

The wall's still a piece of cake. Rope goes better. Crawl goes better. Ten minutes and twenty seconds later, I'm crumpled in a heap by the finish line, huffing and happy. Happy that Fuks says, "Well, you didn't fail, but—"

"Thank-you-sir-gotta-go!"

I stumble back to my cot, drop to the concrete slab beside it, and lie there, facedown, until reveille. Amir nudges me awake with his boot.

"Seriously, dude," he says. "Show an ounce of willpower."

THUMBS-UP

30 December 2009

My Dear Friend Izzy,

Good to hear that you are moving ahead. I'm not surprised at your fast rate of progress since I noticed your willpower a long time ago. It is worthy of admiration.

Continue to send these messages as it is important to me that I know your situation and how you are feeling.

Best of luck, Yoav

THE IRON FIST OF COMMAND

I'm starting to feel like a circus freak. *Dance, Izzy, dance!* It's August 2010. I thought I was done with all the testing, thought I was just waiting for Moni Katz's final approval for combat status. But this is the third monthly request dropped on me to "perform" for a litany of high-ranking schmoes. "This one's important, Izzy," Moni says. Some bigwig from Southern Command.

Once again, I'm standing in the blazing sun at the foot of the training hill, wearing Ofir's gear, my helmet in hand. Vehicles soon approach, kicking up a storm of dust. I feel a little like I'm in a Bond movie. The door to the lead jeep opens, and right then I understand that I'm screwed.

"James Bond. You appear with the tedious inevitability of an unloved season."

Of course. It makes perfect sense. The bigwig is Dr. Notgudenuff. Smirking as he strides up to my position.

Now the IDF has 176,500 active personnel, and another half a million reservists. That's a good-sized army (thirty-fourth in the world, but for a nation about the size of New Jersey). So there are many thousands of officers. But Dr. NGE and I both fall under the same Southern Command. And his job—a fact I already know but must have put out of my mind—involves dealing with medical-related issues—especially the non-routine ones that underlings can't handle. Like, say, a one-armed guy trying to get back in the fight . . . Would I have pushed as hard over the past months if I knew I'd eventually come face-to-face again with the one guy who told me "No way"?

No way.

"Sir." I have to will my fist to open so that I can shake the doctor's outstretched hand. His smile is starting to creep me out. Does he actually enjoy shooting arrows through young men's hearts?

"All right, let's see what you can do, Izzy."

I'll show you what I can do, Douche Wrapper.

Eight minutes later, I stand at the top of the hill, bathed in sweat, sand, and euphoria. Both runs, dry and live, went as smoothly as possible.

Five men who arrived in jeeps behind the doctor make their way up to the summit. The doctor turns to them. "What do you think?" he asks.

Honcho Number One, who apparently commands a company of soldiers here on base, says to the doctor, "Well, you're more than welcome to stay and watch my troops perform the same drill, but I can promise you this man doesn't fall short of any of them."

Not even a backhanded compliment. Take that. The doctor turns to the other officers, and they start discussing my fate as though I'm not standing right here, heart racing. I don't know what's worse—the doubts, or the laurels. Some of them are lauding my exploits over the past months as if I were some impressive shit-flinging chimp. Three of the honchos pummel me with a barrage of questions, constantly cutting each other off. "What do you do if a fellow soldier needs a tourniquet?"

"Well, sir, I—"

"How do you take apart your rifle? Clean it?"

"I—"

"Let's say you had to take over for a wounded handler of the Spike missile system . . ."

Then Dr. Notgudenuff—no, it's unfair to call him that any longer. I can tell from his face this is not the same man Galant introduced me to last year—then the chief medical officer of the Southern Command, shuts them all up with a raised open palm. "Gentlemen," he says. "Enough. I don't see anything, physically or mentally, that'll get in the way of him performing his duties. Agreed?" And he actually winks at me. Could he have known that his "no way" would be the single most important motivator that got me here?

DISARMED

No way.

Or . . . ?

The afternoon ends with each honcho shaking my hand and starting back down the hill toward their vehicles. "We'll do everything we can to get you back into combat," Dr. Gudenuff says. "You've earned it, Izzy. And then, Command School. Any recruit would be lucky to land you as their commander."

Who is this guy? That's the nicest thing anyone has ever said to me in twenty-one years (other than Amir's "You're not a pussy"). I could hug him. "Thank you, sir."

I raise hand to brow out of respect as he opens the door to his transport. He does not return my salute.

PHANTOM'S KUNG FU GRIP

All of 2010. People keep telling me how inspiring I am, how "heroic." Even before I jumped through all the hoops to get back into uniform. Do they have any idea how I feel inside?

Ugly. Alone. Worthless.

Always have. Always will. Phantom feeds on more than physical pain. He gorges on the perpetual motion of my shame. That I'll never be good enough, never be worthy of the mantle of a man, my father's level of accomplishment forever out of reach. That I'll never get the girl. There are times when it's almost unbearable to live inside my skin.

BUM FEET

After endless paperwork and a couple more meetings—but no more tests—they reinstate me in December 2010–February 2011.

Holy mother of . . . So I've finally made it back to combat. The dream. Mission accomplished, right? They send me to join a veteran unit. It's Givati, the unit where my dear friends David and Shachar served. I get to wear the purple beret like they did. At the moment, this unit is back from a stint near Gaza to complete six weeks of retraining on some random base up north before heading to Chevron (Hebron), in the West Bank.

Really cold here at night in Tevetz, but the temps fluctuate wildly. In the middle of the afternoon you could be sweating your balls off, and at night find they've retreated toward the warmth of your core. The first weeklong exercise starts with a dash up a two-kilometer incline in full gear. A forty-kilometer trek through the mountains follows. Soldiers are dropping like poop from a pigeon. Hypothermia has the medical choppers working overtime as one frozen soldier after another needs to be airlifted to the hospital, a chattering mess. Dehydration's still a problem; you don't actually have to be hot to die of thirst. And simple wear-and-tear on the human endo- and exo-skeleton takes its toll on a soldier, as it would on anyone.

I become one of these anyones. About thirty kilometers in, I cannot move another inch. Despite all my retraining, I'm not dealing well with this level of difficulty. Every time we stop moving, it's cold enough for me to find myself sincerely grateful my arm's amputated. One fewer limb to worry about thawing when the signal comes to trudge forward.

I'm always looking for some little edge to save me time or aggravation. Lacing up boots, despite how masterful I've become in the one-handed straight lace—still eats up precious seconds, and I'm damn tired of sleeping in my boots, Jonny. So I went on Amazon for a boot-hunt. These were supposed to be the best ones, tested by members of SWAT. They lasted about four kilometers. They have side zippers, which both split like a pole dancer's father, so I had to wrap them in rope just to keep them on. This made me waddle like

I was an extra on *The Walking Dead*. They're also steel-toed, and the combination of the metal and my heavy wool socks has created two miniature furnaces that have flayed the skin off the tops and bottoms of my toes, even as the rest of me shivers. Pure podiatric hell.

They have to drive me back to base. It might as well be into the center of the Dead Sea; the shame is so heavy I'm floating on it. I can't even speak. I'm sitting in my new unit's empty parade ground on a metal folding chair, my whole body numb. Even Phantom sulks. I feel myself spiraling into a mire like used oil through a funnel. Didn't I fight tooth and nail to get here? Is it all over? I'm not the suicidal type, but I don't feel much like living right now. Living with this anchor tied around my neck, choking me, weighing me down. A twinge in the foot I deliberately broke reminds me that I might still be, regardless of all my recent hard work and heart, that one thing I vowed I would never be again.

Then I feel a hand on my shoulder. I look up to see a face I don't know. A young officer. Receding hairline, dark eyes, arched brows, and that look of intensity not uncommon in IDF officers. I wish he would leave me alone. I don't think I can handle explaining my failure. He introduces himself as Ziv Shilon. He's come back to base to pick up more ammo for the drills. "I want to let you know, guy, I was watching you out there, and you kicked ass. Seriously. You'll be back on your feet by next week. Gotta get back. Bye." He pats me on the back, and then he's gone.

That one officer was like a mercenary angel who breathed life back into me, and then disappeared into the ether. This is not a failure. It's a mere setback. I've overcome plenty of those—and one big one. I can do this. I have to do it. First thing first, though: I throw my dilapidated boots in a Dumpster.

IDF-sanctioned boots in hand, I get my head back in the game.

I keep a journal on my phone to document the next few months, my first back on active duty:

Saturday, Dec. 25, 2010, 5:18 PM, Entry 7

    In regards to 13 Dec – 19 Dec

    It was definitely the boots. . . . This time I kicked ass no problem.
Merry Xmas.

Thursday, Jan. 6, 2011, 8:55 PM, Entry 9

    *I can't believe I actually made it. I'm sitting in a field-box smack
in the middle of very Palestinian Chevron. Who would have thunk I
could pull this off? I guess in a way I did, or else I would never have
gotten this far. So here are the basics of what I'll be doing over the next
few months. Our field-box is in the middle of Arab-populated Jabel-
Jewara / Abusnina, both of which I'm spelling way way wrong. Four
soldiers at a time are posted there in rotations that vary (about 3–4 days
at a time). Three times a day the commander and two of the soldiers
leave the field-box in order to do random vehicle searches and whatnot.
When I'm not posted in the field-box I can be called upon to participate
in arrests. Not only that—I would be in the entry team because I'm the
Com. Spec.*

    *I never really took the time to formulate who I am regarding the
treatment of the Palestinian population. People seem to place me as a
softy (lefty) for some reason. For me it's so much simpler than that. I
might just be overly naive . . . but I look at it as follows: Good people are
good regardless of race, creed, or religion, and good people deserve to be
treated with respect. Bad people, such as terrorists, fanatics, and killers,
are to be treated at the opposite extreme. As far as I'm concerned, that
means death. When I say* bad *it could mean Jew, Arab, atheist, or Bud-
dhist—as long as they fit the basic criteria for badness.*

    *Tomorrow my officer will be taking us out to do our first patrol/
search, etc. . . . I'm curious to see my own reaction to my job. I really
want to do the right thing morally but I need to be on edge regardless,
for the safety of my unit and myself.*

    *I'm reading a lot on my off time. Happy that I have grown a thirst
for world history. Even if it happens that I'm interested mostly in
war . . .*

Friday, Jan. 07, 2011, 2:40 PM, Entry 10

Just got back from my first checkpoint car search. I didn't get to interact because my sergeant placed me as the safety overlooking the group, to keep an eye on everything going on around us. It wasn't as exciting as I thought it would be, and I personally feel my guys were too lax with their own security. Allowing the people being stopped to walk straight up to them, and more than one at a time. Also lots of cars saw the checkpoint and reversed to take a different route. It doesn't get more suspicious than that . . . I guess it's because I'm new at this and still "live in a movie" as the guys keep telling me, but we could be doing a much better job . . .

The Arabs' reaction to us varies dramatically from impatience to fear to open hatred. One little boy about six years old walked by confidently with a big smile and a wave, and I couldn't help but smile and wave back. These are people, too, and most of them just want to live their lives. Yes, we do make their life a bit, if not a lot, harder with our regulations and checkpoints, but we do this because when we don't, those few who want to hurt us send in suicide bombers, etc. I can't let the fact that a lot of these people are good blunt the edge that I need to survive this place.

Sunday, Jan. 09, 2011, 1:05 AM, Entry 11

Pulled over a car at the checkpoint today. Our sergeant finally let me perform the search instead of standing behind the group as overwatch. Three Arabs sitting there entirely drunk, haha. They offered me and the sergeant a drink. These men told us that the Arabs make all the damn problems and that if they had control of Israel, all the Jews would be dead.

YOU SLEEVE, YOU LEAVE

August 2011. Camp Dimona near the town of Yeruham in the Negev. The School for Infantry Corps Professions and Squad Commanders is the IDF institution responsible for the training of all the commanders and platoon sergeants of the Infantry Corps. I'm going to get my own command. But, first, we all need to pass the final exam. This consists of yet another combined obstacle course and shooting exercise. After a commander-in-training thoroughly exhausts himself from exertion on the taxing course, he has to run straight onto the shooting range and shoot six shots: three while kneeling and three while prone. They have to hit shoulder-height targets from twenty-five meters away. If they don't hit four out of six, they fail the entire course and need to do everything again. No use diving over and under obstacles if you can't hit the side of an airport hangar from eighty-two feet. With that nerve-wracking prospect weighing on my shoulder, I begin.

And, strangely enough, out of the over one hundred soldiers in my company of potential commanders, I'm one of only twelve to pass on the very first attempt. In fact, I finished the obstacle course in under eight minutes, my fastest time ever, a full 2:40 faster than the first time I took the test as a new recruit in basic training. I hit four shots, for Fuks's sake.

It feels fantastic. All I can say is when a one-armed warrior is flipping mags out of his vest and loading like a ninja, all the commanders, sergeants, lieutenants, flies, and earthworms have their eyes glued on him. Of course, this gives all the other ninety-nine the opportunity to . . . well, let's say, cut various corners. Just sayin'.

On to the awards ceremony. Independence Day. National TV. Fighter jets screaming overhead in tight formation. Shimon Peres is about to hand out awards to the military's most distinguished soldiers. What the hell am I doing here? I'm all lined up to climb the stairs onto the stage. My mother and Jasmine are somewhere out there in the crowd. My other sisters are watching from home, a few blocks away. My father's still in prison, and I find myself hoping he's found a way to watch this on TV, glean some form of pride from afar. Suddenly, various handlers, generals, and their lackeys encircle me like hyenas, all barking orders at me to roll down my right sleeve posthaste. The other 119 soldiers in formation pretend not to hear. Can't show any arm skin in front of the president—that would be (a) rude, (b) improper, and (c) dangerous, if Peres is as allergic to forearms as the generals make him out to be. Screw all that. I say I don't want to roll down my sleeve. On principle. I won't. Now we're into insubordination territory, too.

"Why the hell not?"

"Because I can't do it alone."

"Explain," says a red-faced general.

"First you help me roll down my sleeve, sir. But are you there tomorrow on the battlefield to help me load my rifle? Pull grenade pins?"

"Sergeant, I will help you right now to military prison. You can't be the first soldier ever to receive commendation from the president with your goddamn sleeve rolled up, now can you?"

"I've had a lot of 'firsts,' sir. This won't be the first." I raise my remaining arm in a "take-me-away-Boys" gesture.

They huddle up in a noisy confab. I hear the words "offensive," "obscene," and "indecent," but then I hear "screw it" and "crazy American kid, but I don't want to deal—" from someone who has more important matters to handle. I stand in the line to receive my award, unflappable. I have made it this far without anyone doing anything *for* me. I'm not about stop that roll now. That's why, twenty minutes later, I, indeed, become the first soldier in Israel's history to ever stand in such a ceremony, to shake the president's hand—with a bare arm. And the world keeps spinning.

MAN'S SEARCH FOR MEANING

August 2011. To celebrate our graduation from Command School, and my award, I head to a popular club called Haoman 17, in Tel Aviv. A buddy and I are super-smashed from a little "pregame" at his place, so by the time we saunter into the club, I've lost all semblance of inhibition. I have no qualms acting as if I own the joint. I swagger—stumble right up to two girls at the bar and slur, "Which one of you ladies wants to buy me a drink?"

Cue the *Twilight Zone* script. That brash nonsense actually works. They *both* buy me drinks. Both! And, suddenly, one of them is sitting on my lap, and I've got my arm wrapped around the other's shoulder. My friend's just watching the entire scene unfold with his lower jaw scraping the floor—I've told him often that I'm a loser with the ladies. So the girls invite us back to their neighborhood for more drinks. Turns out they live in an über-posh part of Tel Aviv, and the girl I'm interested in might happen to be the daughter of a big-shot Coca-Cola exec in Israel. As long as it's not PepsiCo—no need to dredge up memories of the Oketz *Gibush*. It's also safe to assume her mother is a supermodel.

We're at her house. "Who'd'a thunk it?" I slur. "I meet the love of my life at Haoman 17."

"Well, I *am* seventeen! So it's perfect." The girls both giggle.

Instantly sobered, I grab my buddy and push him down the hall and out the door.

"Dude—you're only twenty-one, you know? It's not like you're forty. And this isn't America, bro—age of consent here's sixteen."

"Gotta go with my gut and call it a night."

It's a long, and I don't mind saying, uncomfortable, ride home. I'm glad I didn't stay. Glad I influenced my friend not to, either. He still disagrees, but I think of my mother, my sisters, Yoav, and Rabbi Lior. Being heroic is complicated, I see now; it's extremely multifaceted, and sometimes very subtle. For one thing, I realize that to be "honorable" is rarely connected with being "honored." Being honorable has to be its own reward. An internal blessing, even without external recognition. You can be a hero in your own life, with little acts of heroism every day. Not holier-than-thou acts—just trying to do the right thing. Always. And if you don't, you work a little harder the next day until it becomes a way of life. You don't have to save the city from a villain. You can be a hero to just one person—say, your son, or even yourself. And that counts just as much as foiling an evil plot to throw the world into chaos and ruin.

If I could just find that one person, maybe I wouldn't feel so terrible inside, so unworthy all the time.

OLD HAND

November 2011. I now hold the rank of sergeant, and I have my own class of thirteen fresh recruits to season, to put through the paces. Fate brings my little unit to a tank base up north in the mountains. "Form a *chet*," I order, my voice unwavering. How much fun is this? And how grave the responsibility. They form up, and I take a position facing them from the open side. I shift my Tavor so that it rests against my waist. This creates a necessary barrier, distance between them and me.

I don't have to tell my men that I'm going to do whatever it takes to prepare them for success, to keep them alive. They knew the second they laid eyes on their one-armed commander that I would mean business, that nothing would be handed to them. "Second position." I join them down on the ground. It's the kind of thing I believe a commander should do.

A hard-looking lieutenant's been watching me. I don't recognize him at first. Then, all of a sudden . . . *Holy . . . Is that . . . ?* I bounce up on my right arm, and stand to greet him.

"Izzy," he says, striding up to me, his black beret planted firmly over his buzz cut. "Good to see you."

"You too, sir."

"I see you made sergeant."

"And you, lieutenant. And you cut your hair."

"You gonna let these guys hold second position forever?"

"Dismissed," I say, and my men collapse, then scatter at the chance for freedom. Ashes in a breeze. "You mean like you did to us?"

Natan looks so different. Not just the bowl cut he's shaved off, but his eyes, too, which had been gentle, now look icy. When he smiles, though, I see he's still in there. And his voice is just as soft as the morning that chaos landed on his family. "I heard what happened to you during Cast Lead. I'm sorry."

I look down at my empty shirtsleeve and back at him. "That's OK," I say. "I know. We all knew it was you who—I wanted to tell you that . . ."

He brushes me off with a swift gesture that shuts my mouth. The silence that follows tears a hole in my chest. "Sir, we all realized that attack . . . that your brother . . . We were all crushed that we couldn't—you know, we couldn't—"

"That's OK," he says, and that voice brings me back four years, the voice as tender as the first time I heard it. "Please. I know."

OUT OF HAND

December 2011. My soldiers have just completed their march to gain their purple berets. I've led them sixty-two kilometers through the fields down south. They're still full of energy. I've trained some badass dudes. The unique stench of stale uniform and sweat-marinated human hovers in the cold like exhaust from a generator. I've gotten used to that aroma, and come to enjoy it the way some love the odor of gasoline. It's the smell of hard work paying off. I smile at my long-suffering lot, and say, "You've changed me forever, boys. I promise, I'll down a double-shot of Jack for each of you before my flight touches down."

Within twenty-four hours of finishing my service, I'm in Thailand. Three years—and that little rough spot in the middle—necessitate severe and rapid unwinding. I arrive in Bangkok on New Year's Eve. I'm going to meet my friend Snoop on the island of Phuket, then we'll head together to our next destination, Ko Samui.

Snoop and I had met on Givati's training base while I was fighting my uphill battle toward reinstatement. He was still a recruit, one impossible to miss: Towering at 6´4˝, he had a heavy machine gun strapped over his monstrous, square shoulders, and a terrible, terrible American accent when he attempted to speak Hebrew. Like me, he grew up in South Florida. We were fast friends.

I land in Phuket around 11 p.m. As fireworks start yowling and popping through the air, I'm on the back of a motorbike taxi, trying to balance with my heavy backpack. The driver's not too balanced, either, as he holds in his left hand a bottle of rum from which he's taking generous celebratory swigs every few seconds. I look up at the "bombs bursting in air" and howl like a monkey. The driver joins in.

When I meet Snoop, he's already wasted. Together we get so fantastically drunk, we lose each other till New Year's Day.

I'm no stranger to alcohol. There was that month in Miami with Ian. Those dangerous nights trawling the streets of Jerusalem when I was eighteen. And well before that, too. Sometimes, there were significant consequences:

Like that time when I was seventeen. Living in New York City and working for Ian Ash's company. I just had my car shipped up from Florida—a teal Mini Cooper. And I wanted to take a road trip. So Brik and I agree to venture to Wilkes-Barre, Pennsylvania, where we went to high school after Tucson.

Our second night there, we decide to visit one of the King's College frat parties I used to frequent back in the day (the yeshiva was very stupidly abutting the campus). Back then, you have to imagine a religious sixteen-year-old sneaking out of the dorm and pretending to be a traveling businessman, looking for a groovy time while he passes through town. Only an idiot would believe that back-story. But the local frat boys got a kick out of the eccentric kid who stuck to his guns regardless of the scrutiny, and they loved winning his ten bucks at their weekly poker games. In this manner, I saw my fifth, sixth, and seventh up-close boobs in one of those basement frat parties, all on Saint Patrick's Day when the beads were making the rounds. Ah, youth.

So, we revisit my old stomping grounds, but, alas, the party's "kegged-out." We drive straight to a Citgo station to buy beer. I attempt to use the sad excuse for a fake ID I've recently procured in New York. "Nope," declares the butch blonde behind the counter. "Can't sell you with that, hun."

"I can buy it for him," growls a massive dude behind me. Despite his hunched shoulders, he's so big he's casting me in the shadow of the fluorescent light above his head. He's way too close to me. He smells like bananas and motor oil.

"You'll need him to hand me the money, hun," Blondie says to me.

Without a second thought, I hand my knight in shabby armor a crisp $100 bill—one I'd worked hard to earn at my thankless customer-service job—and my $5.97 six-pack of Corona. Transaction complete, we stroll outside, and my new friend, the Incredible Skulk, hands me the beer. But he makes no move to return my $93 of change. "Keepin' it. Commission."

Brik is watching all of this unfold from the safety of the car.

"But—"

"Feenin', too. And packin'. You get me?"

You just don't hustle a Miami Jew. Do I look like a *freier* to you? "Got a cigarette?"

Surprisingly, he hands me one, and puts the other in his mouth. He lights them both. It's my first ever smoke. Kool Mintrigue. I strike up a chat for two or three minutes—God knows about what; I'm busy trying not to cough and also eyeing the bulge in his pocket, which might be a Glock 19, or possibly a tuna sandwich. I propose a deal.

When he rides off on his comically small bike, it's with $40 of my money. I successfully negotiated the return of the rest.

But I'm still pissed. I just lost hard-earned cash out of sheer stupidity. Brik and I head back to campus. Four of the Coronas find their way down my gullet, and Brik consumes the other two. I start asking random students crossing the quad if they have any expendable alcohol. Most laugh. Then along comes a horde of football jocks. "You guys have any booze?"

"Yeah," replies a kid wearing a black JanSport knapsack. "But—"

"Yeah, only if you chug!" shouts the shortest of his buddies, towel around his neck. They have no idea who they're dealing with here.

JanSport slides a fresh party-sized bottle of Smirnoff up out of his pack like it's a gold brick and, with a resounding crack, twists off the cap. "Chug, chug, chug!" they start chanting as I upend the bottle. Their chugs soon taper off and turn to, "Dude. Dude . . . How the . . ?" Meanwhile, their precious alcohol dwindles before their eyes.

JanSport snaps the bottle away, but not until two-thirds of it is already gone. Towel Neck says, "Christ almighty, good luck with *that*." I commence to rip off my shirt off like Hulk Hogan, and fall backward into the grass.

And . . . *scene*.

The events that follow are relayed back to me the following afternoon, when I finally wake up, by one Aaron Brik.

Seems only moments after I passed out, I popped back up and started randomly hugging coed passersby. The campus "police" (geeks in shorts) soon arrive. When I won't vacate the quad, they call the real men in blue. The ones with Tasers and loaded SIG Sauers.

Brik tells how five of them tackle me to the ground, hold me down, and radio for an ambulance. When it arrives, I refuse to comply with their polite requests for me to say good-bye to the good folks of King's College. So they toss me bodily into the back of the rescue truck.

"Are you going to comply, kid?"

"OK, OK, I'm complying . . ."

As soon as they turn away, I jump off the gurney and make a comically drunk, stumbling break for it, a blood pressure cuff dangling from my left arm. A minute later, I'm double handcuffed to the gurney and Brik is cracking up in the jump seat beside me. Before the cops slam the back doors shut, one of them looks earnestly at him and says, "What kind of awful friend laughs at a situation like this? Your friend has a serious problem." Which causes Brik to double over with magnified laughter.

Brik resumes the story: "At the hospital, your hero complex kicked in. Yeah, I guess you wanted to keep me out of trouble or something, so when they asked you if Aaron Brik was your friend, you said, 'I don't know any Aaron Brik. Run, Brik, run!' They pumped your stomach, diluted your blood with, like, a million IV bags of whatever, and I was just stuck in the waiting room, asshole, until they finally agreed to release you."

I wake up the following afternoon, lying face-down on a mattress in our old yeshiva's dorm. How did I get here? I twist my throbbing head to find a rabbi standing over me, shaking his head with disdain. My naked butt and likely some other stuff is sticking out the back of an open hospital gown.

A month later, back in New York, and just when I think the whole debacle is behind me, I get a call from my father. "Hey, Izzy. You all right?"

"Yeah. Why?"

"Well, I'm looking at a bill from a hospital in Pennsylvania. Five thousand dollars."

"Uh. Right. Listen, about that . . ."

Well, here in Thailand, every day is like that. Snoop and I nurse our hangovers with beer all day and then drink all night until we black out. We spend the first week pounding Long Island Iced Teas, then the second week we switch to Costco-sized bottles of wine. So much for daily acts of heroism. At the Kent Bar on the beach, I learn how to play one-handed pool well enough to beat a semi-pro while seventy people are cheering. I get into fights. I streak. I skinny-dip. For the first time in my life, I smoke weed every single night. I'm having a blast.

So I'm twenty-three years old, agnostic, and zip-lining down a mountain in Chiang Mai. Despite the danger, I've discarded my helmet, because "YOLO, bitches!" Surrounding me are ancient temples, drunken backpackers, and little else. I'm pretty sure I know how things will turn out. Maybe . . . Family. Life. Is there an after-life? I'll be in a serious relationship shortly after I turn thirty (possibly thirty-five). My fiancée and I will be well-traveled, well-versed in the ways of the world outside of Orthodoxy. She'll dress to the nines so that heads turn when she enters a room. We'll have two dogs—male, female, whatever—that curl up at the foot of our bed. Having canines instead of children, well, that'll make life just a little bit easier.

When Snoop meets his future wife on the beach, I respond to my new position as third wheel by pushing human limits of alcohol consumption. One night, while walking back to the hostel, I hurl my body into the bed of someone's pickup (no idea why) and land hard enough to bend two golf clubs. He comes after me with one of them. I throw our room key over a seven-foot wall and subsequently scale it to retrieve said keys, leaving bloody slug-trails down the concrete from both my shins. I land on my head, and when I come up, I'm face-to-face with a pissed-off, gnarly dog. He starts barking maniacally, slobber swinging from his lips. I snarl back, viciously, then start barking as I slam my fist into my chest. He backs off, whimpering.

Don't you think this is getting out of hand?

You know you're in trouble when Phantom starts questioning your life decisions.

I've got problems. Yeah, I'm really messed up. But I have no intention of dealing with anything, not now. Not until I've finished wreaking havoc on what's left of my body. I may have lost my mind.

In the morning, Snoop and his new girlfriend stage a mini, ad hoc intervention. "You're getting out of control. You know, all you went through—"

"All I went through *what?*"

The next day I leave them there in their love nest and fly to Laos.

LAST LEGS

February 2012. I'm convinced that what I need right now is a place to live wild without repercussions. Why not one of the last remaining Marxist-Leninist bastions in the world? When I arrive in the capital, Vientiane, I can tell I'm not exactly in the best headspace. I haven't gone more than six hours without a drink in the whole month prior, when I was in Thailand. There's a name for that. And maybe I was a little more tightly wound from the constant state of pressure I was living in for nearly four years—one war or another. Maybe I'm not entirely unwound yet.

So I "show up" to get "messed up." Which is pretty easy in Laos. I go straight to Vang Vieng, which is known as "the world's most unlikely party town." The first few days are like living in a stack of still frames, going from one surreal image to the next without remembering what happened in between: Dancing on the bar. Launching out over the Nam Song River from stupidly dangerous swings and slides where scores of even stupider tourists have smashed their skulls and killed themselves. Twirling fire *poi* (ropes with weighted-end wicks soaked in fuel, lit on fire, then spun for dramatic effect). Scalding my leg. Vomiting in the street. Vomiting in the jungle. Vomiting in the sacred Nam Song. Vomiting on snakes curled up in the world's most disgusting urinal trough. Kissing a blond girl, possibly from Canada. Kissing a Latina girl, possibly from Spain. Kissing a tall British girl with spectacular teeth. Vomiting on the tall British girl's flip-flop. Sucking nitrous oxide from the cheap balloons they sell at every bar. Everyone sounds like Charlie Brown's parents, and everything is hilarious.

A Boston chick in my room, so out of it I have to wake her up and walk her to her hostel, delivering a stern lecture about not going home with random boys in bars because some boys are not so good, and won't do what's right. "I've got three sisters," I say, "and I pray . . ." But the girl's already passed out. I never see her again.

Tubing down the Nam Song with hundreds of twenty-some-things from Australia, Germany, and South Korea, every one of them bombed off their asses. Small boys, nearly naked, fling out ropes for us to grab, and pull us in to shore at every raucous bar, all their stacked speakers competing and colliding over the swift-flowing water. Scraggly dogs trying to snatch my stick of spicy chicken. Chickens on the *tuk-tuks*. "Ladyboys" in all the bars, eyeing me with sultry looks. Kissing a freckled Dutch girl so they don't get the wrong idea.

Suddenly, while lying on my back atop a picnic table, spinning on nitrous oxide, people playing beer pong on either side of me, I realize Phantom's gone. Vanished. As though I've just remembered I've left him on the baggage carousel. A certain pang. I can't possibly *miss* him. Can I? A French girl, buxom, hands me another balloon, pinched at the sphincter between her fingers. Kissing the balloon. Kissing her, too.

On day four, give or take a few, I find myself standing behind a noisy, crowded indoor bar that smells of cheap beer and frat boys. The floors are made of pallets, some of them broken and splintered. I'm pouring drinks. I must have a job. It feels good to be on this side of the bar, even if my only pay is "room" (shack) and "board" (booze). I could stay here forever. The DJ and his girlfriend, both tattooed South Africans, become fast friends. The other bartenders, mostly Brits and Canadians, every one with a sad story rendered temporarily happier by chemistry, become my unit. The Lost Boys. We all get wasted together. And otherwise live as though there are no costs or aftermaths to this behavior.

Very soon, Israelis whom I've never met begin ordering their drinks in Hebrew, high-fiving me. News has traveled on the Southeast Asian backpacker trail that Vang Vieng has spawned some crazy mutant bartender, you gotta meet this guy. Soon after, New Zealanders who heard about the one-armed barman from French Canadians on Philippine beaches are stopping by for a drink; Londoners coming from Cambodia and on their way to trace the Ho Chi Minh trail; Bulgarians who met Greeks at crappy hostels in Bali who told of the mythical one-armed loon behind the bar—he's real. I'm known. A destination. And it feels good.

The owner of the bar, Mrs. Thong, owns another on the river circuit. So my friends and I unpeel ourselves from our various heaps every afternoon, and chip in for a *tuk-tuk* down to the river, so we can work behind the bar, serving drunk young tourists with their passports and their cell phones in overpriced plastic protectors around their necks, which we behind the bar all know will never keep the water out.

If there were ever a movie made of my life, I would want it to start right here, with me juggling bottles of Laotian vodka, the awesome one-armed bartender on a ridiculous river, deep in the limestone karsts of Laos. I'm sandwiched between two Swedish girls covered in tattoos that I drew all over their bodies in Sharpie: "I love one-armed men!"

One day I wake up to find that all the male bartenders are putting on dresses and makeup. We all lose our boxers and head to work free-balling, nitrous-balloons crammed into our bras. I spend the whole day that way, pouring drinks on the river, not caring that I can feel a breeze on my biscuits for the first time ever, or that all five of my nails sport shiny red nail polish. Girls keep manhandling my balloons, and they don't seem to mind when I man their handles in return.

Two weeks in, I do mushrooms for the first time. It's a happy accident. Still drunk between the day and night shifts, I flip-flop to the restaurant across the street and order a pizza with mushroom topping. I down the entire pie without thinking twice, and run to the nightclub to get to work. Twenty minutes later, beer bottles start asking me for directions to the nearest ATM. Stools are dancing techno with the ladyboys. My Tasmanian coworker takes one look at me and proclaims, "You're mushed out of your mind, mate." So he buys some shrooms, too, and we spend the night hallucinating together. Some guy from another bar turns into a flying, horned purple imp and freaks me the hell out, but my mate is able to talk me down before he goes off to start a long conversation with a giant fishtail palm. He might have proposed.

It's difficult to explain why all of this feels so liberating. Or maybe it isn't so difficult. There's just something very freeing about being so far from people who know me—I mean the "heroic" me. Here, I don't have to behave in a way that fits the image people expect me to uphold.

When I call my mother from the airport, right before my flight back to Israel, I'm still drunk. They're boarding, and I'm still drunk.

I tell my mother I'm going to stay longer, that I'm not ready to go home. She begs me to board the plane. So I do.

How do I get back to doing the right thing—even when nobody's watching? I probably need therapy. But I've got reserve duty coming up. And if I stay in Laos it will kill my mother.

NO LEG TO STAND ON

2011–2012. Why can't I meet a girl when I'm sober? I have this recurring dream: A Number 12-*alef* bus pulls up to the stop in front of Sheba rehab. The doors unfold. "I have to go," says Katya, but her eyes tell me a different story. What started as med-student/patient is clearly evolving—in this very moment—into full-on love. What a day. My God, her eyes are so . . . radiant.

Behind her, the hydraulic sigh of the green giant sings its impatience. It sounds oddly human. The sun is reflecting off the row of tinted windows, and it streams over her translucent skin.

Why is my married therapist suddenly so into me? What's my move?

Now the bus engine growls. I raise my hand to silence it, and instantly it settles down to a puppy's whimper. Katya cocks her head quizzically—yes, with this hand, I can do magic, Katya.

A lock of raven hair slips down her forehead, begging me to brush it back. My hand is getting closer. I tuck the strands back in place behind her ear. I touch her arm. Goose bumps erupt beneath my fingers. I lean in for the kiss. I go precisely 80 percent of the way, and she moves the rest. Our lips touch, and the bus stop rockets upward, thirty feet into the air, then explodes like fireworks. Her eyes reflect the explosion.

"You're about to miss your bus," I say. I kiss her again. "You have to go now."

DISARMED

I watch her force herself up the steps and into the first vacant seat. She peers through the glass. She's searching for me, but I'm completely unrecognizable. A thick beard is sprouting from my chin, handlebars from my upper lip. I'm a man.

But now my beard begins to stink. I can taste it. Like someone's insides. I shake and shake my head, but I can't escape the rancid funk. I shake so much I always shake myself awake. The first time, it was the night Benny shat himself in the next bed. Tonight the stench is coming from my own dry, liquored breath.

Here's my take on the dream: There's something inside me that's repugnant, and eventually it'll find its way out. It's obvious why, even in my dreams, I don't get the girl. If I can't see my own self-worth, how can I expect her to see it? I thought I'd be married by eighteen. Now I'm not sure it'll happen at all. What scares me most is that the idea of staying single forever is starting to scare me less and less. Maybe I'm just not meant to share my life with anyone. Maybe I should get a dog.

Maybe I'm too picky. Maybe I'm aiming too high up the chain for a one-armed nerd with ears that can pick up DirecTV. When does the zombie in the movie ever get the girl? Well, there was that one movie. But I'd rather rot alone than settle for second best. That's an expression, right?

HANDS AND KNEES

In 2012, a year or so after I finish my active service, Ziv Shilon, the officer who saved me from the infinite pull of my own black hole on my first, failed, day back in service, is on a foot patrol on the Gaza Strip near Kibbutz Kissufim. He's been promoted to captain of his unit. Snipers have been picking off Israelis from the windows and rooftops of Gazan buildings on the border. Instead of attacking these targets from the air, the IDF employs squads of foot soldiers to isolate the firing locations and take down the terrorists at close range. It's the company's final mission of operational training. Soon they'll all head by bus to their combat qualification ceremony. But first they have to pass through one last gate along the border.

Ziv orders his men to wait one hundred fifty meters behind him—he knows the risks. He says, "I'll be right back." Then he advances slowly toward the gate. That's when an IED explodes in his face.

The blast obliterates one of his arms and horribly mangles the other. He scoops up his limbs and heads back toward his men, who are mostly frozen in shock. He head-butts one of them to get him back in the game, then orders the guy to apply tourniquets and start an IV.

In the following months, he'll have dozens of operations. He'll take that nightmare ride though the long, dark night of the soul. And then he'll make it over his first proverbial wall, tentatively at first. And up his first rope. But far sooner than I, he'll kick ass and take names again. Run marathons. Get married, have a kid. I still don't feel comfortable placing myself in league with guys like Ziv (or Yakir or Zvika). But I like to think that maybe I played a tiny role in his recovery. He knows it can be done, he can recover—because I did it while under his charge. I hope whenever he suffers a setback, someone pats him on the back and says, "You rocked today. I was watching you. Don't sweat it, guy, you'll be back in form tomorrow."

A HEART THAT BEATS FOR TWENTY

In 2015, I see Ido Dan after my reserve duty. We meet for dinner before my flight back to New York, where I've been living. He doesn't look anything like the boy who volunteered to surrender his bedroom to a recovering stranger. His eyes, now sunken and worn, seem to scan our surroundings without pause, searching for signs of danger—he's been posted in Chevron. He wears the same purple beret his father, David, wore as a commander in Givati, at the same age. The same one I wore. But he's achieved so much more than I did. At eighteen, he was drafted, along with most Israeli kids, into the IDF. Within a year and half, he earned the rank of lieutenant. He and his twenty troops have been attacked by Molotov cocktails; they've been ambushed with blades, bombs, and gunfire. He hasn't lost one yet, but he still has a few recovering men in the same rehab where his mother met and adopted me into the Dan family.

My flight time is approaching all too fast. He's hardly touched his food. "Are you doing OK? I mean, really OK?"

Ido smiles tiredly, and around the eyes he looks like his mother, Shachar, at her most fretful. "Just need a good night's rest."

"Good thing you don't have some random schmuck entrenched in your bedroom."

We embrace farewell. And there, beneath his uniform, beneath the rifle he holds in a vise grip, I can feel his heart beating. It still feels like a child's heart. Once it beat for me. Now it beats for twenty.

A SLAP ON THE WRIST

December 2015. Brutal week and a half of reserve duty training. Even the Spartan-like reservists are falling like Confederates at Appomattox. Epic trek, freezing rain, harsh wind. I just want to lighten the mood. So when we get back to camp, I walk around, borrowing officers' rifles, never telling them why. I take off the straps and shove eight M16s in a neat row on their butts into the whitewashed pebbles, barrels facing the night sky. Then I stick a candle in each, light the four on the right. I pose and have someone take a picture. I post it on Facebook: "Happy Hanukkah from the IDF Reserves."

"Machine Gun Menorah" goes viral in a matter of hours. It reaches Russia, Europe, and America. And then bounces back to the desk of the head safety officer of the IDF. I get a call the next day from the commander of my unit asking if I was the simpleton who posted the picture. I confess. He orders me to report to him immediately so he can attempt to save me from the whoop-ass about to come down on me from top brass. "Here's what we're gonna do," he says. "The rules are, if a soldier is tried within his unit for a crime, he can't be retried by higher military court. So consider this your 'trial.' My finding is you're an idiot. My sentence is don't be an idiot again. A menorah made out of guns. What's next?"

I tell my squad mates that the only reason I didn't get arrested by the MPs is because I cannot be handcuffed. I'm here all day; try the veal.

SHAKE A LEG

I'm twenty-seven years old as I put the finishing touches on the manuscript of this book. I've chronicled a slow start, a protracted rise, a tragedy, a stagnation, a miasma, a resurrection, and my present plateau. But I feel that my journey is yet to begin. I'm still confused, often lonely, relatively self-loathing. I still whine at paper cuts. I'm living in New York City with my dog, Punch, a sweet and rowdy Shiba Inu. No mountains here. No ancient temples. And my mother, she keeps asking me over the phone, "Izzy, when are you going to meet a nice Jewish girl already?" Surrounded by hollowed-out hipsters and discarded coffee cups, I don't have an answer.

I wake up many a morning truly believing that I'll croak before finding a suitable match. There are months when I completely give up, drawing myself ever inward, building an antisocial bubble of self-pity. Carting my lonely bones around in a perpetual state of emergency. Maybe my problem is that I think of this process as "finding a suitable match." Doesn't allow for much spontaneity, does it? Nothing to do with falling in love. It's becoming increasingly obvious how this simply isn't working.

Thank God for Punch. He's my best friend. He's got no choice. I'm the guy who feeds him.

I say I feel lonely. Yet, somehow, I sense I'm not alone anymore. Whenever I return to Israel, and when I find myself with an open palm against the warm stone of the Western Wall, I allow my brain to entertain a train of thought I once considered the ultimate weakness—the likelihood of Rabbi's Higher Power—some version of it—watching over me. And, while I still can't bring myself to actually ask anything of this entity, this possible drunk wizard in the sky, or to recite any of the prayers pounded into me when I was young, I've found a measure of peace in thanking Him—Whoever and wherever He is—for all the good I've received, for all the amazing gifts I've been blessed with, and which I did not in any way deserve.

I doubt that today's therapists would label the atmosphere of the chilling, bloody place where I first committed to my mission as conducive to healthy psycho-spiritual growth. But whatever their years of research may tell them, I have found that I needed that calamitous event, that long, dark night, and then that wall, and then the rope, and the boots, and all the milestones on my expedition here. We need hurricane winds to blow away layers of nonsense, to uncover our core, the true heart hidden underneath all of our insecurity and guilt and shame that took years to accrete. Moments like the Big Bang that nearly took my life, and yet, without my knowing at the time, also rebirthed me. Assuming we survive such storms and explosions, they allow us to choose how we plan to navigate life's testing tide. Never whether we will sink or swim, but rather which stroke will bring us to the finish line.

Even if we strive only to endure another day, to not completely give up, we'll find our backbones grow out of our despair, out of the wreckage of our lives. Even if we have to crawl to the call, we ought to crawl. That said, I find it difficult to offer anyone advice. Who am I to tell you how to live your life? I can't be a model for anyone. I'm not a happy person now. But I'm a whole person, probably for the first time in my life. It's hard to put my finger on my problem. If I'm honest, I think it's that I'm terrified that I will never accomplish anything as amazing and improbable as I did when I was twenty-one. I've peaked. That's seriously scary. I don't want to be like one of those fat, bald guys who played football in high school and still gets drunk with his buddies while they reminisce about that one Big Game, that perfect touchdown.

Yes. I hear you. I need to go easier on myself, I know. I need to talk to Izzy nicely, to say, "Hey, buddy, you're doing OK. Stop beating yourself up all the time." If a friend talked to me the way I talk to myself most of the time, I'd feed him to my ever-present Phantom. Yet, for some unaccountable reason, I constantly put myself down, and this habit is harder to curb than pasting that patch on my back for sweet relief. It's the part of me maybe most responsible for my recovery, for accomplishing my mission. But it's a two-headed monster that can just as easily dissuade me from getting out of bed.

There's hope. One day of late I woke up, Punch licking my ear, and I felt as though I were emerging from a longtime foggy haze. As if I never experienced a clear thought until now, not once in my entire life before this moment. And when this mist lifted, I saw that there are no superheroes in the universe. Those are just fictional, aspirational figures, extensions of our wish to conquer the demons of our lives. My father isn't Spider-Man. He's a real man, and real men are fallible. Someday they die. True heroism is being a great father every day. I'm not Superman. But I am Izzy, and that's got to be good enough. There are days I almost believe that's true.

Sure, I'd still love to look out my window one day and see a billboard, a giant advertisement for the soon-to-be-released action flick, *Single-Handed* a (CGI-) one-armed Joseph Gordon-Levitt with a machine gun and a steely look, each of his eyes the size of a Smart Car. The cheesy tagline: "You don't need two hands to grab your destiny by the balls." Is that going to happen? Who knows. Stranger and more amazing things have happened in my life.

In the meantime, it's enough to run the streets of Brooklyn with my quadruped partner. It's enough to let myself be happily used to raise millions of dollars for charities, and still eat ramen some weeks. It's enough to speak in front of other amputees, and simply listen to their troubles. To walk silently through a Laotian museum dedicated to the thousands of children who've lost limbs from unexploded ordnance, many the exact same mortar that fell on top of me, holding a little boy's only hand. It's enough to return regularly for my reserve duty in the little land where I left my arm, and where I keep my heart.

THE FICKLE FINGER OF FATE

t's dusk as I sit alone on this beach in Miami, between speaking engagements. So close to my past life. And I'm wondering . . . *Am I a better man for all that I've gone through? For my sacrifice? Why do I feel like that drowning girl? Ready to give up and sink, my only hope of survival that someone will see my hair undulating like waterweeds, dive in, and descend to my depth. Am I good, honorable, just? Or am I still what Amir used to call me during training? Was it just a random accident of chance that saved me that day on the border of Gaza? Or did some benevolent overseer save me for a reason? Will I ever be truly happy?*

The lifeguard, just a kid, comes up. Ray-Bans. Peeling nose. "You can't be here, bud. Beach is off-limits after sundown."

AUTHOR'S NOTE

Out of respect for their privacy, I have used pseudonyms for some individuals. I have also quoted from a few published works:

Applegate, K. A. *Animorphs: The Invasion*. New York: Scholastic, 1996.

Francis, Alan. *Everything Men Know about Women: 25th Anniversary Edition*. Kansas City, MO: Andrews McMeel Publishing, 1995.

Frost, Robert. "Out, Out—" *Mountain Interval*. New York: Henry Holt, 1916.

Leshem, Ron. *Beaufort*. New York: Delta Trade Paperbacks, 2009. Originally published in Hebrew as *Im Yesh Gan Eden* in 2005.

Steinbeck, John. *East of Eden*. London: Penguin, 2017. Originally published 1952.

Vonnegut, Kurt. *Mother Night*. London: Vintage Books, 2015. Originally published 1961.

White, E. B. *Charlotte's Web*. Classic ed. New York: Harper, 2017. Originally published 1952.

Williams, Margery. *The Velveteen Rabbit*. London: Egmont UK, 2017. Originally published 1922.

ACKNOWLEDGMENTS

Even a memoir requires the effort of a crack squad. First and foremost, I want to thank Erica Meyer Rauzin for sticking with me from "*Tzeh*" to the finish line, for your unwavering support on and off the page, for being far kinder to me than I'll ever be to myself.

I owe thanks to Ian Blake Newhem for clobbering me in the teeth until the right words came tumbling out my behemoth ears, for trekking to Southeast Asia just to meet up for drinks. Crazy bastard. Without you, this book wouldn't be.

To all the men and women I served with and commanded in Kfir and Givati. What can I say, I'd still die for you if I had to.

To Leon, Simon, and Jerome for assuring me that life would work out OK, and for showing me what to strive for in a family and its values.

To the Michael and Andrea Leven Family Foundation for arming the disarmed with the necessary tools to publish this book.

To Ian Ash for "rushin'" headlong into stripping me of all angst after the injury, and promptly returning that angst in the form of Russian strippers.

To Aaron Brik for teaching a young, awkward Izzy how to interact with normal human boys. I continue to fool most of them, *beep boop*.

To General Yoav Galant, of late Israeli Minister of Construction, for believing in me, and for your laudable leadership, which honored thousands of soldiers, including the parts of this soldier that remain.

To the Dans: Shachar for pouncing on me in rehab; David for patiently panning through my muddy mind until uncovering the shiny scraps; and Ido, simply for being who you are. Stay safe, *achi*.

ACKNOWLEDGMENTS

Thanks to everyone at Prometheus Books, and Maryann Karinch at the Rudy Agency. Also, to Jason Schwartz and Eva Synalovski, to Kira and Francesca at the Bean.

I owe a huge debt of gratitude to my sisters, Jaz, Shoshi, and Emu, for loving their older brother despite his innumerable imperfections. I appreciate your choosing to see the subtle strands of good in me. And to Ma for inspiring faith in all you touch, for sticking by me despite our conflicting views on the Omnipresent. And Ta for showing me, firsthand, what it means to sacrifice for others, for keeping your chin up when the chips were down, and for still giving, even though it continues to pain you. You are my hero and always will be.

Punch, for being my left arm, for never letting your size be a minus when it comes to fighting bullies, and for licking my face even when it's not covered in peanut butter.

Thank you to my left arm for those two straight decades of handling my antics. You may have split, but I don't hold it against you.

Drunk Wizard in the Sky, I acknowledge You for creating Heaven and Earth. Also beer and doughnuts.

Girl on the Beach for reminding me of my own value. Our love was like a winged turtle: purely mythic, fun to imagine, not at all aerodynamic.

To the girl of my dreams: I must believe you exist somewhere. I don't enjoy this game, not hide nor seek. Neither of us is getting any younger, dear.

Finally, I have to thank Phantom. I know now that we're brothers, come what may, for life, and I recognize the vital role you play. It's OK that you're an asshole; I can understand why, and I forgive you.